THE NURSE'S GUIDE
TO THE LAW

THE NURSE'S GUIDE
TO THE LAW

SIDNEY H. WILLIG, A.B., B.S.PH., J.D.

Professor of Law and the Health Sciences,
Health Sciences Center, Temple University
and Unit Director,
Institute for Law and the Health Sciences,
Temple University

McGRAW-HILL BOOK COMPANY
A BLAKISTON PUBLICATION
New York St. Louis San Francisco Düsseldorf London Mexico
Panama Sydney Toronto

This book was set in Optima by Brown Bros. Linotypers, Inc., and printed on permanent paper and bound by The Maple Press Company. The drawings were done by John Cordes, J. & R. Technical Services, Inc. The editors were Joseph J. Brehm, Bernice Heller, and Stuart D. Boynton. William P. Weiss supervised the production.

THE NURSE'S GUIDE TO THE LAW

Library of Congress Catalog Card Number 79–76826

70580

1234567890 MAMM 79876543210

This book is dedicated with love and gratitude to my parents, Jennie and Wolf Willig, who taught me to love everyone; to my dear in-laws, Belle and Jacob Huss, who taught me to appreciate nurses as a special kind of people; to my wife, Eleanor, who has brought love and nursing into my own life.

PREFACE

Beyond the natural interest most nurses have in the responsibilities that they are held accountable for, and the time and circumstances of such accountability, there are other objectives in teaching legal principles to the nursing team.

In view of the dynamic nature of curricula and nursing practice in all categories, nursing educators have shown a preference for flexible syllabi that lend themselves to updating, yet codify both the spirit and the letter of the law. They must be capable of change with the upward expansion of nursing responsibility in every category and the resultant differentiation of function and downward delegation of tasks.

Using this concept of nonrigidity, coupled with an overview of general needs of teacher and student, we recommend that a syllabus consider at least these general objectives, which are discussed in detail in the text:

1. Understanding of the historic development of the governmental and legal systems resulting in the force of law in contemporary society.

2. Appreciation of the balance and relationship in purpose, in status, and sometimes in licensure among the various levels of nursing care.

3. Interest in further study and information as to sociolegal problems and economic and political factors that influence the nurse's working environment.

4. Understanding the purpose and the spirit of nursing practice acts and their equivalents for other members

of the health care team, as well as their actual language and construction.

5. Critical thinking about legal implications surrounding interrelationships of all members of the health service staff, professional and nonprofessional, in the home, in the office, and in the hospital.

6. Information leading to basic comprehension of the relationship and extent of mandatory licensure, to the fulfillment of its purpose and justification of its prerogatives.

7. Understanding the role of nursing associations, of general or special purpose and constituency, and their values to the public at large as well as to their membership.

8. Investigating in sufficient detail the principles and mechanics of the legislative system so that the nurse may fulfill her responsibilities as a citizen.

9. Examining the key position of members of the nursing team in legal situations involving them as employers or employees, by direction or indirection.

10. Describing in a comprehensive manner the importance of nursing practice and functions in terms of litigation involving patients bringing suit against nurses, physicians, and hospitals.

11. Developing an appreciation of those legal safeguards which may be taken, in addition to unswerving truth and loyalty to all that personal and professional ethics demands.

12. Developing some acquaintance with legal terminology, legal instruments, and both civil and criminal responsibilities that have particular significance for those carrying out nursing functions.

These objectives should enable nursing educators, as well as those in nursing service, to search out the patterns of predictability and of behavioral outcome as they relate to the student or practitioner with respect to their prior educational training, their capacity for comprehension, and the projection of their potentials of practice. Most of all, perhaps, they will allow for the broad appreciation of the balance of privilege and obligation possessed as individuals, as members of skilled and professional groups, and as citizen participants.

In the text we have sought to emphasize the direct application and meaningfulness of both objectives and substance to professional, technical, and ancillary staff who are equally and jointly concerned about ethical and legal responsibilities in practice as well as cases cited in this text.

No matter what the basis for legal responsibility, some individual will have primary liability in the estimation of the general public, a governmental agency, and a court of law. This will be true notwithstanding that someone else, by prearrangement, by accident, or by legal design, may answer for her and with her. Obviously, even in these latter circumstances, the onus of civil or criminal wrongdoing remains with the individual, as does the likelihood of all or a portion of the penalty assessed. Nurses are, however, seeking new definition in general public understanding, in private and institutional status, and in nursing practice acts. Such new definition should take cognizance of the escalation of function and responsibility that is taking place throughout the different categories of the nursing team and generally up the ladder as well.

Society expects and law details that the philosophical and practical framework of agreements will be carried out to good purpose, that all persons will respect the rights of others to health, safety, comfort, and freedom from physical or mental harassment, or be penalized for the disrespect. Therefore, we hope to aid in the development of personal and general guidelines that will give a feeling of safety and fulfillment to the practicing nurse, or a warning feeling of discomfort that will make her stop and question, when she senses some irregularity in the prospective action. This is true for other members of the health team as well. Whether a professional or a nonprofessional, society expects its members who have undertaken care of the sick, diseased, or infirm to assume carefully measured responsibilities in conjunction with the position of public trust that is their employment environment. The nurse, too, is held responsible for applying the degree of skill, judgment, and prudence that is generally and ordinarily available from others in the community with similar training, licensure, experience, and status. Therefore, North American nursing educators in both collegiate and hospital programs deem it important to advise all members of the nursing team concerning the elementary principles of pertinent law.

The nursing staff should also be familiar with the legal requirements attaching to specific practical activities, such as buying or caring for medical supplies, equipment, drugs, and narcotics and the significance of civil rights, and public care legislation to employers and employees. They must gain some indication of when their activities need legal review as regards gifts, wills, collection of debts, court appearance in general, and even the danger areas of criminality. To some extent legal principles that outline the prerogatives and responsibilities inherent in the total area of nursing functions are expressed in statutes, local nursing practice acts, and diverse regulations. Study must also be made of court decisions involving all members of the health team. Frequently these indicate with reasonable probability the results to be anticipated in individual nursing experiences that arise from contractual difficulties or tortious conduct, such as negligence, invasion of privacy, false imprisonment, assault and battery, and defamation. Therefore, in illustration, we have used many decided cases of the law in both the United States and Canada. These have been selected with emphasis on nursing and medical situations and will demonstrate that the facts modify the application of the rules of law in many instances. However, since they are readily translated into the daily activities of our readers, they should further serve as beacons to a path of safety.

Our ultimate goal, therefore, is not to provide a text for nurse lawyers, or lawyer nurses, but to point out that the nurse who requires legal assistance cannot use this book as a "do-it-yourself" instrument. She will require the services of a lawyer acquainted with the legal doctrine, court system, and tradition of her particular geographic area. This is true to the same measure that a lawyer who read a text on nursing practice and theory would not be a competent nurse on that basis. We have tried to do this in a brief, nontechnical, yet factual manner which will help alert nurses to their rights and duties within the context of their usual dependent or independent functions.

While we have set brevity as a goal, with the growth of nursing stature there has developed a considerable body of law concerning nursing, of groups and associations with progressive ideas and organizational advice, and of good counsel on many aspects of nursing practice. For that reason we have provided material of this type in an Appendix to which we hope the reader will refer. Here also in our choice we intended to be exemplary rather than arbitrary, and just as our text has considered nursing law requirements within a North American context, our Appendix too contains Canadian references.

Sidney H. Willig

ACKNOWLEDGMENTS

I acknowledge the substantial assistance in researching and reporting of pertinent case law supplied by Kenneth C. Willig and Steven E. Willig, organizational assistance by Randi D. Willig, and frequent emergency typing help by Patricia Anzelone. Among the many members of the profession who tendered encouragement, suggestions, commentary on nursing episodes, codes, and organizations, I recognize especially the following: Sr. Bernadette Armiger, R.N., Edythe Harris, R.N., Ann d'Este, R.N., Ethel Streuben, R.N., Madolen M. Dickenson, R.N., Mary E. Reap, R.N., William Patterson, R.N., Charles Heroy, R.N., Carol Larson, R.N., K. Mary Straub, R.N., Ed.D., Marion R. Fleck, R.N., Mary E. MacDonald, R.N., Lucille Notter, R.N., Dorothea Orem, R.N., Ed.D., Barbara G. Schutt, R.N., James L. Hudson, R.N., Janice M. Gray, R.N., W. M. Coghlin, Esq., Audrey Logsdon, R.N., Ruth W. Harper, R.N., and Lydia E. Hall, R.N.

Sidney H. Willig

CONTENTS

Preface   vii

Acknowledgments   xi

**1. EVOLUTION OF LAW AND EXISTING LEGAL
    SYSTEMS**   1

   Roman Law
   Common Law
   Constitutional Law
   Public or Statutory Law
   Private Law
   Decisional Law
   Administrative (Agency) Law
   Law and the Health Sciences
   Civil Law and Criminal Law
   Unique Nature of American Law
   Canadian Legal Development

**2. LEGAL, PROFESSIONAL, AND PUBLIC STATUS
    OF THE NURSE**   20

   The Nurse's Role
   Licensure (General)
   Licensure (Nursing)
   Police Power
   Professional Discipline

Definition of the Professional Nurse
Statutory Limits on Professional Nursing
Definition of the Practical Nurse
Statutory Limits on Practical Nursing
Upgrading the Status of the Practical Nurse
Nursing Code of Ethics
Auxiliary Personnel
Nursing Associations

3. **THE NURSE AS AN AGENT, AN INDEPENDENT CONTRACTOR, AND AN EMPLOYEE**   39

Independent Contractor
Employee
Employer's Duties to Employees
Civil Rights of Employees
Personal and Statutory Rights of Employees
Assumption of Risks by Employees
Responsibilities of Visitors, Patients, and Employees
Workmen's Compensation Laws
Doctrines Governing Nursing Practice
Application of the Foregoing Theories

4. **DELEGATION**   65

Problems Involved in Delegation
Importance of Proper Delegation within the Nursing Team
Formalizing Delegation
Laboratory Tests
Nursing Practice Acts
Successful Delegation of Medical Functions
Litigation
Immunities

5. **TORT LAW: UNINTENTIONAL TORT**   102

What Is a Tort?
Tort Contrasted with Crime

Responsibility for Tort
Malpractice and Negligence
Damages

6. TORT LAW: INTENTIONAL TORTS 136

Fraud and Deceit
Assault and Battery
False Imprisonment
False Arrest
Malicious Prosecution
Conversion

7. THE DEFAMATORY TORTS: LIBEL AND SLANDER 151

Libel and Slander
Invasion of Privacy
Privileged Communication

8. CONTRACTS 162

Contractual Responsibility
Elements of the Contract
Types of Contracts
Invalid and Unenforceable Contracts
Problems in Contracts
Abandonment

**9. AGREEMENTS OF GUARANTY, WARRANTY, AND SPECIAL
   PERFORMANCE** 174

Rights and Obligations of Buyer and Seller
Guaranty and Warranty
Breach of Warranty: Summation
Supplying Blood: Sale or Service?
Warranty Liability of Physicians and Dentists
Labeling of Medical Products and Equipment

10. THE NURSE AND CRIMINAL LAW 180

Definition of Crime
Felonies and Misdemeanors
Specific Crimes
Criminal Law
Detention and Search
Arrest and Pretrial Proceedings

11. DRUGS AND NARCOTICS VIOLATIONS 197

Stimulant and Depressant Drugs: The Federal Law
Stimulant and Depressant Drugs: The State Laws

12. STATUTES OF LIMITATIONS 204

13. FIDUCIARY RESPONSIBILITY OF THE NURSE 209

Importance of a Will
The Nurse's Responsibility
The Physical Form of the Will
Terminal-care Patients

14. THE TRIAL 214

Summons and Complaint
Conduct as a Witness
The Medical Record and the Nurse's Chart
The Nurse and Physician as Expert Witnesses
Admissions against Interest
Summary Judgment
Instructing the Jury
Litigation Expenditures

Index 251

THE NURSE'S GUIDE
TO THE LAW

CHAPTER 1

EVOLUTION OF LAW AND EXISTING LEGAL SYSTEMS

The history of law is in many respects the history of civilization. Therefore, although our own system of law seems old and is based on the "old" English common-law system, it has a relatively recent place in the histories of both law and civilization. While the definitions of law place it close to custom, ethics, tradition, and morality, it is either more or less than any of these; it is never synonymous.

We know from our study of the ancients and the Bible that men grew to respect the need to define their relationships with their neighbors first, with their tribal groups next, then with their nations, and finally with other nations. As man developed politically and the nomads gathered together for mutual protection and then for economic and social objectives, individuals voluntarily gave up some of their autonomy, and law replaced anarchy. Chosen leaders laid down rules, some out of a sense of equity, some out of a position of power —but whatever the origin, law was fashioned. As unjust rulers and their sycophants gave way to change, a gradual weeding-out process (to be described later) left legal principles upon which people and their rulers could rely and under which some form of justice could be dispensed. These principles were a hallmark of the Judeo-Christian heritage, which has been parent to the legal systems of Western nations. While many of the same principles evolved from other civilizations, their character, evolution, and forms were different. Even in the more modern context of our Western civilization, two variant systems of law have developed.

ROMAN LAW

One system developed from the Roman civilization and hence bears the name Roman law. As Roman law underwent further development, it became known as civil law and, in later centuries, as the Napoleonic code. Roman law antedates the other system, common law, and is more authoritarian and inflexible. However, the years have refined it, and it serves modern nations and states satisfactorily.

The source of Roman law was the concept of the almighty power of the monarch, whether chosen by God or by circumstances of personal strength or collective power. The prototype was the decree of the all-powerful Roman emperor, who determined the rights of all under his domain. Whatever the aura surrounding him, however, the so-called "divine" Roman monarch had very human frailties and whims. Thus laws fluctuated from ruler to ruler, from year to year, and the people were victimized by their current ruler's caprices. To satisfy their need for stability, men began to record their laws, that they might span generations and provide some measure of protection. The first set of recorded laws, the Digests, was published in A.D. 553. The impetus behind this work came from the Emperor Justinian, who twenty years earlier had commissioned a group of legal experts to collect and codify Roman law. The Digests constitute a milestone in the history of civilization. They form an immediate base for the law of Europe and South America, and indirectly, through English common law, influence the legal structure of the United States.*

The Digests, and all subsequent compilations of Roman law, were issued in the form of codes to guide people in their interrelationships. These codes detailed rights and prohibitions as well as liabilities or punishments for failure to comply. Although the codes were based on legal principles that had gradually evolved, only one interpretation, that of the central authority, was permissible. Courts, therefore, were not courts in the modern sense, but rather tribunals composed of one or more appointees of the central power who dispensed justice in strict accordance with a code that had been elaborated for such circumstances.

* The Bill of Rights was conceived from the same motive as the Digests: to clarify for the people, once and for all, what their rights were and to prevent these rights from being later distorted or taken away.

The codes were many, and classification grew. As new situations arose, those who dispensed justice had no latitude of interpretation but instead appealed to the central authority for advice and decision. Thereby, either the codes were supplemented or a new code was created. Although in relatively modern times a jury was grafted to this structure, it never attained the vitality or importance of a jury in the common-law system. The codes, however, apparently served their purpose well. Their uniformity aided in maintaining order in business, in society, and even in the health needs of all the people of the widespread empire.

Roman, or civil, law uses the same codification that governs commercial and political relationships to detail crime and punishment. The inflexibility of these codes and the importance of maintaining the central authority by quick and severe punishment have given rise to principles and exercises of judgment that are considerably at variance with the present common-law system. For example, military and police powers were established which were far greater than those of the citizenry, and there was a presumption of guilt rather than innocence. Justice might be somewhat summary, even though it might be the same for all. The rigid requirements of the Roman legal system might see an innocent punished to maintain the power and dignity of the code, whereas under the common law the system might be punished to maintain the dignity of the individual. The culprit might go unfettered because the court would not chance the conviction of an innocent through inflexibility of rule which would conflict with democratic principles and privileges.

COMMON LAW

The common-law system (Fig. 1), like the Roman system, had its roots in monarchial power; and here again, the ruler delegated judicial powers to specially chosen members of royalty. The feudal lords, who were autonomous within their own fiefdoms, each appointed men whose duty it was to travel from place to place, hearing and settling civil and criminal cases. The king later placed this judicial function under his own control. As communications improved and the central government began to circumscribe the barons' authority, the machinery of justice later imported to the English Colonies was established. This included permanent courts, judges, rights of appeal to higher authority (ultimately to the Crown), and written records and decisions.

The last-mentioned item embraces the concept which most immediately characterizes English common law: the validity of prece-

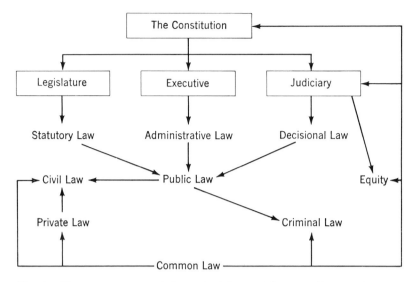

Fig. 1. *The court systems of the United States. Schematic diagram. Arrows indicate the path of cases going from lowest to highest courts.*

dent. Indeed, the concept of precedent reaches back in time to the arbitrary decisions of the king and his barons. It provided some protection to their subjects in this way: While they could display favoritism, the saving feature was that common law depended on precedent, and there was danger in establishing a prejudicial or unwise precedent.

This most important principle of common law is called *stare decisis,* literally, "the previous decision stands." When a question of law has once been settled by a judicial decision, it forms a precedent which is not afterward to be departed from or lightly overruled, even though it may seem archaic. And today, centuries later, courts will respect the decision of another court if the issues are similarly drawn. In our present application of the common-law system, an inferior (lower) court is generally bound to recognize a prior decision rendered in a superior (higher) court. On the other hand, higher courts frequently will not apply stare decisis if the precedent has become unsound. Our discussion of the doctrine of charitable immunity later in this book will be a good example of this.

Common law, unlike civil law, is flexible because the courts can consider situations that are at variance with precedent and fact patterns which have never before existed, and yet make a judgment in keeping with the constitutional and social philosophy of the system by recourse to analogy and principles. At the same time, once a matter has gone through a proper court hearing and is terminated, it becomes *res judicata,* an adjudicated thing that will stand, so that the same plaintiff and defendant cannot come back to the same court in lengthy squabbles on the same issue.

Common law growth was largely responsible for the Magna Carta (1215), the foundation of constitutional liberty as opposed to absolutism and unrestricted exercise of governmental power under the divine-right concept of monarchy. When King John of England signed the Magna Carta at Runnymede, however, he not only delegated rights to the barons and ruling classes, but he gave certain guarantees to all men who try their rights. Many of these same rights are in latter-day constitutions.

Again, the evolution of law was closely allied to political development. As divine right and absolute power gave way to limited monarchy and legislative concepts, the contracts that stated these reformations, or constitutions, formed a source for the law. Embracing as they did the legal principles that served the majority, they created the primary basis of legal consideration.

This basis was the prelude to our modern use of the law for two purposes. These are:

1. To provide a framework of government together with its powers and to restrict the exercise of those powers.
2. To confirm certain rights and privileges of the individual and to provide means for their enforcement.

Both of these purposes established in our law standards of human conduct and enforced those standards by the authority of organized society through its government. As specific rights were enunciated in general terms, the jurists and jurors began to exercise latitude in interpretation.

CONSTITUTIONAL LAW

The American Constitution describes the proper legal relationship between the citizen and the government and outlines the procedure for making national laws. It also sets out the rights, duties, and limitations for a three-part system of government composed of legislative, executive, and judicial branches.

Federal Government: Separation of Powers

One of the significant things to note in the American form of government is that constituent units are separate and, to a considerable extent, independant political powers; the doctrine of separation of powers actually exists. The legislative branch is composed of the two houses of Congress. The executive branch consists of the President and the various departments and agencies that he directs. The judiciary branch embraces the total federal court system from the district court to the Supreme Court of the United States. The operation of these three branches provides a number of checks and balances: the legislature may create new laws, the executive (President) may veto them, and the judiciary may review them. Also, through its power over the pursestrings and its right to legislate, Congress can affect both the executive and judicial branches.

Federal and State Governments: Division of Powers

The Constitution also divides total responsibilities between the federal and state governments. Under the U.S. Constitution, the states retain all powers not specifically conferred on the federal government. Some powers may be exercised by both federal and state governments concurrently. Moreover, since this system creates two sovereigns (the federal and state governments), a conviction under the laws of one does not preclude a conviction under the laws of the other for the same offense. Nonetheless, the Constitution grants greater power to the federal government than to the state governments in certain areas of conduct.

Actually, there are three levels of government in the United States: federal, state and/or county, and local and/or municipal. The two lower levels are also organized under a three-part separation of powers. Inevitably there is duplication of laws and conflict of laws in some areas. However, the Constitution of the United States is the organic law of the land—that is, it defines or establishes the very organization of the government and the separation of the federal government into the legislative, executive, and judicial branches.

Only the states have been delegated police powers by the Constitution to oversee the conduct of professional and paramedical persons and the industries and utilities that serve the public needs for safety and health. These police powers can be passed along as need be to the smaller local units of the states. The federal government, on the other hand, having seen these powers expressly delegated to the states, seeks some similar authority in the Constitution through indirect means. So we see narcotics acts stemming from the right to tax, food and drug acts derived from the right to regulate interstate and foreign commerce, and other laws which seek to regulate the activities of man as an individual, a corporate entity, and a member of society. These acts and laws are derived from the varied and indirect congressional powers to spend money, make treaties, and conduct investigations.

The right of Congress to use these powers to promote the general welfare has often been upheld in the face of specific challenges. However, Congress does suffer constitutional limitations of various kinds, such as the due process of law provision of the Fifth Amendment.

PUBLIC OR STATUTORY LAW

When Congress exercises the legislative powers granted it in the Constitution, its enactments are known as statutory laws. The same is true for state legislative bodies. When statutes are published in a cumulative manner, they are called codes—thus the federal statutes appear in the United States Code. City council laws are ordinances. Statutory law is for the most part synonymous with public law. When business, political, or social changes show the need for an expansion of legal principles, these are legislatively enacted. Such statutes then become a second pillar of the legal edifice. Many of these statutes describe public response to needs and determine the basis for man's relationship with his government and its institutions; thus, they are called public laws. For example, these laws might have to do with taxation, business formation, conscription, and the like.

PRIVATE LAW

By contrast there is a body of private law. Much of this originates from common law. It is generally concerned with maintaining rights, duties, and other legal relations involving private individuals. These relations include the law of contracts, negligence, and agent-principal dealings. Other private laws are passed to answer the needs of private individuals or organizations in their dealings with other private individuals or organizations or with the state. These laws are frequently based on *decisional law* (law determined by reference to previous court decisions) which remains the major source of the private laws and principles which regulate relationships between two or more persons.

DECISIONAL LAW

The third portion of law as we know it is decisional law. While case law, as it is sometimes called, must observe the law of the Constitution and of the statutes, it is the individual arbiter where these have no application or solution. We have noted that the unique characteristic of a so-called "common-law system," such as our own, is that it builds its rules and sanctions by the accumulation of individual case decisions. This is much the same as when it first began to evolve. The system has been modified to some extent by newer social and economic concepts, and can be altered by a new type of judge or by changed advocacy.

While we have separated the Constitution as a source of law from statutory enactments which are a secondary source of law, the constitution has an influence which pervades both statutory and decisional law, both public and private law.

ADMINISTRATIVE (AGENCY) LAW

For some time now, especially in the field of commodities and services that are provided to the public as a matter of national as well as individual necessity, another branch of public law has grown in importance. This is called administrative or agency law. To some extent, federal actions in this area of law have been duplicated in structure, purpose, and action on the state level. This type of law directly affects the health science practitioner in that it determines the basis for receiving and continuing his right to practice. While administrative law is derived from the executive's right to use efficient means to carry out his duties, there are generally legislative provisions for this branch of law.

Agency law is very much like Roman law or the Napoleonic code in many respects. Their similarities include hearing procedures where agency officials prepare the evidence and hear it, make the decision, and implement it on the basis of promulgated regulations that define punishments for various offenses.

In discussing the growth of common law through decisional law, we noted the importance of previous decisions on similar facts and circumstances (stare decisis). However, common law is dynamic, and while stare decisis will aid a court's finding or be the basis of an appeal from a court's decision, if the precedent is out of date or inapplicable, the court will announce a new rule. Agencies are bound to this principle only in the sense that when they do not treat parties similarly, they are open to a charge of discriminatory conduct.

Administrative law is elaborated to regulate not only agencies such as those dealing with foods, drugs, and utilities, but many other specific areas of commerce, communication, and transportation as well. The legislature provides for this regulatory power by establishing the agency, cloaking it with power to make rules or regulations

which have the force of law, and often giving it the right to pro-
pound orders which have the effect of court orders. This is true despite the fact that many ordinary judicial procedures and requirements do not exist in this process. Further enforcement is often at
the option of the agency, whether the case is civil or criminal in
nature. The agency's actions, however, may be appealed in an appropriate court depending on the citizenship of the appellant and
the national or state origin of the agency. Appeals may be made when
circumstances demonstrate discriminatory handling of a right, license,
franchise, etc. Discrimination is equatable with arbitrary and capricious behavior—and this is grounds for appeal to the courts on any
level of government.

In a judicial review of an administrative decision, new evidence is
admissible only upon a showing that it could not, with reasonable
diligence, have been presented earlier to the agency. Therefore, a
trial court is well within its rights in refusing to admit additional
evidence in litigation if the party charged had a full opportunity to
present such evidence at the administrative hearing.[1] This has damaging application for one who is led by off-the-record promises or
discussions to first tell his story in brief at the hearing without challenge or lengthy testimony from witnesses, etc., on the understanding
that he will be shown leniency or consideration.

An administrative agency's adoption of regulations subject to
judicial review allows the court on such review to determine whether
the agency exceeded its statutory powers. The relationship between
policy and regulations to carry out that policy is peculiarly a matter
for administrative determination. It can be set aside if arbitrary,
capricious, or irrational.[2]

We have devoted some time to discussing the varying legal systems and the sources of law. Another important differentiation is
made in everyday language between civil law and criminal law.

CIVIL LAW AND CRIMINAL LAW

Some acts are in a sense private or personal wrongs. These are punishable in terms of monetary remedies and therefore come under
the general heading of civil law. Other offenses by nature represent
not only a wrong to an individual member of society but a danger
to all of society if not adequately exposed and the offender punished.
These offenses are called crimes, and while we shall discuss civil law
in some detail in reference to contracts and torts, we shall also examine criminal law as it applies to our overall objectives.

While American civil law has developed from common law and

has retained not only its principle but its format, criminal law, because of its nature, has had a somewhat different development. It is also derived from common-law precedents and principles. However, certain statutes based on these and modified by the stated constitutional rights have been collected into penal codes by state and federal governing bodies.

Since the offender is punished more severely under criminal law than under civil law—by fine, imprisonment, or death—the quality and quantity of evidence required to convict him are greater than those required to win a judgment against a defendant in a civil action. Therefore, it is fitting that the government itself initiate and maintain an action against an alleged criminal, even though the first inkling of the crime or the complaint may come from an individual source. Civil proceedings, on the other hand, are brought and maintained by the individual who wants a situation righted or repayment for a wrong done him or those to whom he has a responsible relationship.

In certain instances, the same act can provide evidence of violation of both civil and criminal law, and the defendant can be prosecuted separately on the two counts. Most states recognize gross dereliction from duty and willful acts of harm in treatment or care of patients as criminal acts. At the same time, the patient or his legal representatives can sue for damages in a civil suit. Or, following a criminal attack for which the state prosecutes, successfully or not, the victim can seek a judgment from the attacker to repay him for pain, suffering, hospital expenses, loss of employment, and the like.

LAW AND THE HEALTH SCIENCES

Law seems to affect members of the health team more than ever before. Whether the responsibilities and liabilities are individual or shared, whether they apply to a registered professional or a nonprofessional, a student or a technician, the public demands and requires protection. It is interesting to note that in ancient times, the laws governing those who practiced the medical, surgical, and pharmaceutical skills were most severe. Some of the earliest writings, such as the Code of Hammurabi and the words of Hippocrates, deal with medicine. These early practitioners held a unique place in their community and nation, and they were surrounded with a certain mystique. Therefore, their failures became evil things, and mishaps that arose through lack of basic scientific knowledge seemed incidents of willful criminal action or intrigue. Legal actions taken against them, therefore, were often criminal in nature.

Over the centuries, the practice of medicine and nursing has come to be bound by many different types of law. In the United States, police power, derived from constitutional law, provides for the establishment of nursing practice acts (see Chapter 2). These acts constitute the organic law of nursing practice, just as the Constitution is the organic law of the United States. Administrative law, as we have seen, most immediately affects the health sciences through practice acts, workmen's compensation, and other board activities. The laws of torts and crimes are used to determine negligence and culpability (see Chapter 5). Contract law is involved in day-to-day activities within and without the nursing function. Most areas of nursing concern and litigation fall under the general category of civil law. The nursing practice acts are a mixture of civil law and criminal law. Any person who calls herself a licensed nurse, professional or practical, when she is not in fact licensed, may be prosecuted under criminal law. In fact, all punishments under practice acts are misdemeanors or felonies, and this is their criminal aspect.

Today our society expects any member of the health service professions and his assistants who undertake any aspect of the diagnosis, treatment, or care of the sick, diseased, or infirm to satisfy their responsibilities according to expected standards of competence and conscience. In turn, society endows them with respect and a position of public trust. In decisions as well as procedures, courts reflect this public respect by requiring the person who accuses a member of the health service professions of harm arising from neglect or lack of skill to bear the burden of proving this by the greater weight of the evidence.

UNIQUE NATURE OF AMERICAN LAW

We have briefly reviewed some of the categories of law, their development, and their definitions. The reader cannot have failed to sense that U.S. law is different from that in other countries. It has been developed to coincide with a political, social, and economic philosophy that, while recognizing the need for law and order, acknowledges at the same time that the will of the majority of the people shall define and implement these aims. This may be called the democratic process. This same root philosophy pervades the application of our laws. In order for our local or national community to benefit from the system and the substance of our laws, there must be a means to invite their use, to enjoy their benefits, and to enforce them. Lawyers and courts, including the judge and jury, serve this purpose.

The Role of the Lawyer

A lawyer practices an ancient profession known by many names both in past centuries and now. Sometimes the names have the special effect of defining his major concerns, much as a title does. He has been called, therefore, squire, solicitor, barrister, counselor, advocate, but, more often, attorney. He has completed certain requirements of study on a graduate level and has acquired the experience that qualifies him to prepare and try cases before courts. Just as important, however, he is qualified to advise the public about their rights and liabilities under all forms of law and within given circumstances and situations. A lawyer is trained to prevent litigation as well as to propose, execute, or defend, just as members of the health professions are trained to prevent illness as well as to treat it. Also, in all his activities, a lawyer is subject to the same general principles of professional negligence and malpractice that affect health professionals. However, since he is a sworn officer of the court and in a position of great trust, these principles apply to him with even greater stringency.

He has many prerogatives that we might mention now, but they will become apparent in greater detail as we study actual cases. He may issue subpoenas and written orders to appear in court. He can choose and challenge jurors and request the court to take certain procedural steps or make certain charges to benefit his client's case. He can examine the plaintiff and defendant before trial, as well as their supporters and their records. In particular instances he can appeal the decision of the court if he feels that it is unjust. However, there are some limits on the lawyer's authority. He may not abuse process or call witnesses "witty-nilly." For example, the plaintiff's attorney would most likely be halted if he sought to take the testimony of an inordinate number of the defendant's employees or colleagues, since such an action would be highly disruptive of their duties and not in the public's welfare. The court may modify the order to include one or more officers or employees of a hospital, for instance, who have knowledge of the facts.[3]

While most independent professional practitioners have the right to select their patients or clients, the lawyer is held to a high ethical duty which demands that he defend the unpopular cause and even the heinous criminal.

A man's rights are to be determined by the court, and not by his attorney or counsel. It is for want of remembering this that foolish people object to lawyers that they will advocate a case against their own opinion. A client is entitled to say to his counsel, "I want your advocacy and not your judgment. I prefer the judgment of the court." [4]

Courts

The forum for lawyers and their clients is generally a courtroom, the basic unit for the administration of justice according to the law. We have discussed the growth of law and our trifurcated system of government which separates authority and responsibility among the legislative, executive, and judicial branches. Courts are the instruments of the judiciary departments established by government units, federal, state, or local, to decide disputes resulting in litigation.

JURISDICTION

Jurisdiction, that is, the right of a particular court to try a lawsuit, is based on two principles. First, the kind of court in which a case is brought depends upon the offense or complaint involved; e.g., if the charge is a traffic violation or manslaughter, suit would be filed in a criminal court. If a claim for damages grows out of relationships, of rights and duties of individuals to each other as imposed by law or agreed upon by contract, it is a civil controversy and goes into the particular type of civil court with jurisdiction over it. This has been made necessary by the increasing specialization of modern life. Therefore, various kinds of courts have been established to handle lawsuits whose nature may vary according to the subject matter of the litigation, its value, the kind of contracts or documents at issue, the citizenship of the parties, and so forth.

Second, jurisdiction is established in terms of the court's province over the person, the geographical location of the property involved, the amount of the claim, and the nature of the subject. If the litigation concerns wills or estates of decedents, as in probate proceedings, it will be heard in courts of general jurisdiction, or, in some states, in surrogates' or orphans' courts.

Before the courts and trials are more fully discussed, some brief definitions of basic terms may prove helpful. A *lawsuit* is an action or case in court where one party has challenged another to a trial on the issue between them. Either party can be called a *litigant,* but the person who initiates the lawsuit, the challenger, is called the *plaintiff.* Sometimes he is referred to as a *complainant,* since his attorney files a complaint with the court on his behalf. Most writers feel, however, that the term *complainant* should be reserved for one who brings a criminal action, such as the state, on behalf of the alleged victim. In either civil or criminal proceedings, however, the person against whom the suit is brought is the *defendant.*

When the decision of one court is appealed to a higher court, the person bringing the appeal is the *appellant.* His adversary, who claims that the initial decision should stand, can be termed the *appellee* or *respondent.* When a case is cited, the plaintiff's name is presented first. This order is sometimes reversed on appeal.

The period of time during which a suit may be filed is governed by a *statute of limitations* in each state and federally. We shall discuss this in greater detail in Chapter 12, but the time limit depends on the kind of action, civil or criminal, and subdivisions of these. As a general rule, a minor is allowed at least to come of age before losing the right to open a suit.

FEDERAL COURT SYSTEM

In the United States, there are three main court systems in which actions may be brought and defended. The first of these is the federal court system (Fig. 2), which has the Supreme Court of the United States at its summit. It is the highest court in the nation, regardless of system, and its rights and responsibilities are established by the Constitution. The federal system is primarily used as a forum for lawsuits between citizens of different states and between citizens and governmental units for cases that violate a federal law, for cases which may pose a federal problem because of their economic, political, or social implications. Today many negligence suits are tried in federal courts because patients are treated away from home with greater frequency.

The federal court system offers the plaintiff a solution to some of the usual difficulties that arise when the parties to the suit reside in different geographical locations. For example, a vacationer from Texas is taken ill while in Palm Beach, Florida.[5] He receives treatment and is enabled to return to Texas. There his own physician finds that the diagnosis and treatment given by the Florida physician were erroneous and unnecessarily painful, and that the care given by the nurse and the hospital was deficient. Since there is a diversity of citizenship, the plaintiff brings the action against all three in his federal district court in Texas. Should he have difficulty serving a summons on those named defendants because they are nonresidents, he can apply to the Texas federal court to transfer the case to a federal court in Florida. Any party can file for such a removal so long as the diversity of citizenship and the damages required for federal jurisdiction are satisfied.[6]

The federal court, however, will apply the law of the state that

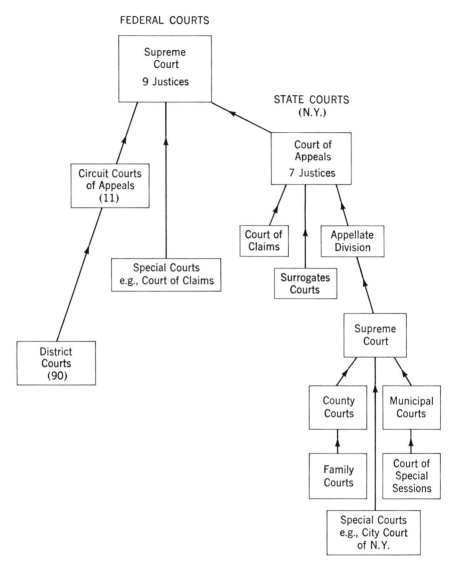

Fig. 2. *Derivation and influence of legal growth in the United States. Schematic diagram. This structure lasts and is self-modernizing because it is dynamic and the direction of every arrow can be changed.*

relates to the substance of the suit.[7] This was shown in a case where representatives of a deceased patient brought suit against a hospital and the three physicians who had attended the decedent. The patient had died in June, 1964, and one of the physicians was not served until

September, 1966. The physician's attorney moved that the federal court apply the New York Wrongful Death Act, which states that there is a two-year statute of limitations for bringing such an action. This New York statute differs from the rules of federal procedure substantially in the manner in which the time is measured. New York measures it from the time a defendant is actually served or the summons is delivered for serving. The Federal Rules of Civil Practice provide that an action is commenced by filing a complaint with the court. The other physicians and the hospital failed to assert this type of defense, and they were not barred from the action.[8]

STATE COURT SYSTEM

A second system is set up within the framework of the state (Fig. 2). Like the federal system, it is established by constitutional fiat. The highest state court, the state supreme court, has final appellate jurisdiction for all cases within the state system except those few that qualify for a hearing in the Supreme Court of the United States. There are generally lower appellate courts in the state as well as courts that have divided and specialized response to urbanization and special needs of society. For example, courts may specialize in handling cases involving wills, contracts, torts, domestic relations, and criminal offenses.

Under the law of most states, a suit is begun by actual service of process, summons, and/or complaint on the defendant named in the papers. In other states, the suit begins when the complaint is filed in the manner required by the civil practice rules of the particular jurisdiction. In this latter instance, however, the potential plaintiff must be reasonably diligent in serving the process.

LOCAL COURT SYSTEM

There is a third system, of local courts (Fig. 2), that sometimes dovetails with the other two and sometimes is merely duplicative. Its structure depends on the custom or political subdivisions of the state and on the community's needs. Therefore, it may be either archaic or very modern. This system may start with justices of the peace and local squires who hear traffic offenses and other petty suits and rise to county or city courts with substantial jurisdiction. For example, the City Court of New York has great jurisdiction in admiralty law or maritime controversies, since it is located in a city with a world-famous harbor. Whatever the court, however, its jurisdiction is based on either the party or the *res,* the subject matter of the suit. Therefore, a court in a particular community seeks to exert jurisdiction over all matters pertaining to the safety and welfare of persons who live in that area.

RELATIONSHIP BETWEEN TRIAL AND APPELLATE COURTS

The first court to hear the parties to the controversy is known by various names in state judicial systems. In the federal system it is the district court. In common parlance, however, this court of first instance is termed the *trial court*. The chief judicial officer of such a court is generally called a judge or magistrate.

Trial courts are given considerable latitude, and in general their findings of fact are not reviewable unless clearly erroneous. After all, someone must reconcile conflicting testimony from persons whose interests are antagonistic. Since trial courts have a chance to see all evidence, admissible and otherwise, to observe the demeanor of the parties and the witnesses, and to hear and see the way in which questions are put and answers given, appellate courts respect their decisions as to the facts.[9]

A jury trial must be requested in a timely manner. Where one party makes such a demand belatedly and the trial court in its discretion rejects it, the appellant must prove that the request was timely made, or the appellate court will not act in his behalf.[10]

Questions of law are, of course, within appellate jurisdiction. Thus, an appellate court will undertake a trial *de novo* (as new) on the premise that determining the presence or absence of the offense charged is essentially a question of law as well as a question of fact. The trial court's conclusion on a question of law is freely reviewable on appeal. After hearing the case, the jurors make a finding concerning the facts submitted by each side. They announce their verdict or conclusion in accordance with agreement among themselves on what it should be. It is then that the judge applies his knowledge of the legal principles and precedents to determine the measure of relief that will be accorded. This is the *judgment,* or final order, of the court, based on the verdict. This judgment, of course, may later be appealed for reduction or reversal on certain established grounds and by adherence to certain rules of procedure.

In the case of a civil law trial, should the judgment stand or be uncontested, it has an immediate first life of twenty years. The money may be collected at any time that a person's assets are available to the jurisdiction of that court. The judgment may be satisfied from a bank account, real estate, personal property, wages, etc. If the defendant's assets are beyond the state's jurisdiction, the plaintiff may use the constitutional tenet of "full faith and credit" and get a judgment in the foreign jurisdiction enabling him to press his claim there.

In our discussion of tort liability (Chapter 5), we shall consider further details of the trial procedure as they affect the nurse as witness or defendant, as well as other actors in the lawsuit.

The Judge and Jury

The chief minister of justice in each particular court is called a *judge*, although an alternate title of magistrate or justice may be used to betoken his status within a particular legal system. In past centuries, kings and other members of the royal family or constituency were the judges. The priorities of cases on their calendars were based on the urgency or importance of the case or on the relative importance of the adverse parties. Today, priority is determined by the date of filing for the particular court.

At trials, only one judge sits. In courts of appeal, three, five, seven, or nine judges may hear the appeal. Whatever the number, the duties of the judge are the same. He examines the legal process that precedes the actual trial—the complaints, the answers, and the counterclaims. He may decide that certain preliminary privileges can be exerted by the attorneys on behalf of their clients, or he may limit or revoke these as a matter of his judgment and discretion. As we shall see, he can make preliminary judgments about whether a jury is selected. He can rule that either the plaintiff's or the defendant's case has technical and evidentiary shortcomings and can therefore dispense summary judgment.

During the trial, the judge conducts the proceedings as master of the courtroom. He decides which rules governing procedure and evidence should be followed and determines the law that applies. He guides the jurors in understanding their responsibilities as triers of the *facts* of the case, while he is trier of the *law*. By preliminary agreement between the litigants, a nonjury trial may be held, in which case the judge serves as trier of both the facts and the law.

CANADIAN LEGAL DEVELOPMENT

Canadian law is derived from two sources: (1) judgments of courts and (2) statutes. The collected judgments of courts, derived from centuries of practice, make up the common law. Originating in England, these legal precedents have been observed in all the common-law countries, including Canada and the United States. In deciding a case in a Canadian court today, a judge may refer back to a principle enunciated in an English court in the distant past. The other source of law is the statutes, which are enacted by the Parliament of Canada or the legislatures of the ten provinces. Parliament and the legislatures have the power to legislate upon any subject and to modify the common law. It follows that any attempt to change the law will be through persuasion of the appropriate legislative body.

In order to ascertain what is the appropriate legislative body, one must consult the distribution of legislative powers contained in the British North America Act. At the time of federation in 1867, this act laid down the division of legislative powers between the federal government, on the one hand, and provincial governments on the other, much as did the United States Constitution. Legislative authority over a number of stated subjects, such as property and civil rights, is vested in the legislatures, whereas legislative authority over the remaining subjects, such as crime, is vested in Parliament. Most of the matters which pertain to nursing, such as licensing, registration, and control of hospitals, are within the exclusive jurisdiction of the provinces.[11] This is then equivalent to the United States system.

CASE CITATIONS

1. *Schoenen v. Board,* 54 Cal. Rptr. 364 (1967).
2. *Mulry v. Driver,* 366 Fed. 2d 544 (1966).
3. *Curry v. Corn,* 277 N.Y.S. 2d 470 (1966).
4. *Baron, Bramwell, Johnson v. Emerson and Sparrow,* Court of Exchequer (1871).
5. *Rozell v. Kaye,* 276 F. Supp. 392 (1967).
6. *Pitman v. Rompton,* 277 F. Supp. 772 (1968).
7. *Kaiser v. Mayo Clinic,* 260 F. Supp. 900 (1966).
8. *Hendriksen v. Roosevelt Hospital,* 276 F. Supp. 731 (1967).
9. *Gailitis v. Bassett,* 146 N.W. 2d 708 (1966).
10. *Hicks v. United States,* 368 F. 2d 626 (1966).
11. K. G. Gray, "Law and Nursing," *The Canadian Nurse,* **60**(6):545 (1969).

CHAPTER 2

LEGAL, PROFESSIONAL, AND PUBLIC STATUS OF THE NURSE

THE NURSE'S ROLE

Essentially, the public and the courts regard nurses as skilled persons who exercise their calling on behalf of a patient both on their own responsibility (independent nursing function) and under the general or specific direction of other professionals or qualified institutions (dependent nursing function). These concepts are further qualified by education, training, and other circumstances that modify the level at which each function is performed. *Any form of nursing,* professional or practical, involves care of the ill, injured, or infirm for compensation.

As long as the nurse is remunerated in some manner, whether by a third person or by the patient himself, her nursing responsibility is not negated. Even a gratuitous service must be performed in a responsible manner.

A nurse must discharge her responsibility to the public according to the standards of skill, knowledge, and procedure established at the time and place she is practicing. This responsibility is further determined by the nurse's training, experience, and licensure, all of which are reflected in the title accorded her and the status she achieves in practice.

LICENSURE (GENERAL)

A person's right to exercise a skill to earn an honest livelihood is a property within our constitutional protection. It is assured by the right of liberty and the pursuit of happiness and may not be taken away or denied without due process of law. However, it is also recognized that a state may, under the *police power* clause of the Constitution, regulate an occupation, a profession, or a business when it affects the public health, morals, and welfare. Therefore, the state legislature may regulate the practice and conduct of nursing, may reasonably establish detailed requirements for licensure, and may reserve the right to suspend or revoke a license for offenses. In exercising these powers, the state may set new standards, or it may simply affirm legislatively those which exist by practice, custom, and tradition.

LICENSURE (NURSING)

In nursing the present trend is to mandatory licensure. In general, a *license* is a legal document that permits a person to offer the public skills and knowledge whose practice would otherwise be unlawful. A nursing license is granted by the appropriate authority to applicants who have fulfilled certain established requirements of education, experience, and character consonant with their degree of practice.

State Boards of Nursing

The government agency that grants nursing licenses and carries out nursing practice acts is generally called a *board of nursing*. This board consists of nurses and nursing educators, members who are licensed as professional and practical nurses, and various administrative employees. In addition to the board, there may be an *advisory council* as in New York, which selects its members from among nurses, physicians, and hospital administrators. They meet with the board on all matters that come within the scope of the nursing practice act and its enforcement. The legislature endows the board with general rule-making powers enabling it to establish educational and training requirements, to give examinations, and to regulate the particular professional practice involved. Thus, the board shares many of the characteristics of the other federal or state agencies that we discussed under "Administrative Law" in Chapter 1. The state board may therefore promulgate regulations that serve as a basis for establishing prerogatives and prohibitions that are matters of policy and interpretation. When new laws or amendments are required, the board may seek legislative assistance.

Nursing Practice Acts

The *nursing practice acts,* as mentioned in Chapter 1, constitute the organic law, or basis, on which nursing legislation rests. Though they may differ in minor details from state to state, the typical nursing practice act contains the following:

1. Definition of professional and practical nursing
2. Requirements for licensure as a professional or practical nurse
3. Exemptions from licensure
4. Grounds for revocation of licensure
5. Provisions for reciprocity for persons licensed in other states
6. Creation of a board of nursing examiners
7. Responsibilities of the board of nursing examiners
8. Penalties for practicing without a license

The last is particularly important. The one feature common to all nursing practice acts is that they protect the public against persons who practice without a license.

Status of the Nurse

In the United States there is some variance in the manner in which protection of the registered nurse or licensed practical nurse is accorded. In general, one who uses either the title or its equivalent in a particular jurisdiction without meeting statutory requirements and enjoying actual authority to do so is liable to a substantial fine and/or imprisonment.

In Canada also this protection is determined by the individual province, but at the present time false and fraudulent assumption of nursing titles is not treated quite as harshly. For example, the Alberta Registered Nurse Act permits only members in good standing of the Alberta Nurses' Register to use the title "registered nurse" and the letters "RN" after the person's name. However, one who poses as an RN may be punished by being fined or by being imprisoned no more than 30 days. Action taken against her is subject to a one-year statute of limitations.

Local Regulation of Nursing Practice

The nurse who practices in large urban areas must generally be aware of requirements that are established by county and municipal governmental bodies in addition to those of the federal and state governments. Failure to observe local regulations may readily affect her state licensure, since in most instances such regulations, which are usually more stringent or more detailed, are considered binding and not in conflict with the overall purpose of the state or federal regulation. For example, nursing services in New York City hospitals are governed by the Hospital Code and Regulations of the Board of Directors of Hospitals of the City of New York. Some salient points that follow from these are:

1.   There must be a registered nurse on duty at all times on each floor in addition to other nursing personnel.

2.   A Director of Nursing is mandatory.

3.   There must be an experienced registered nurse in the operating room and recovery room when a patient is there.

4.   All drugs, poisons, stimulants, and medicines shall be plainly labeled and securely locked in a cabinet, closet, or separate room accessible only to the charge nurse.

5.   The cabinet or room for drugs shall be well illuminated.

6.   The provisions of the Sanitary Code of the City of New York concerning the separation and storage of nontoxic solutions which may be used intravenously or for infusion or hypodermoclysis shall be observed.

7.   The nursing service shall have available the following supplies [listed]. Hot water bottles and ice bags shall be covered before being used.

8.   Anesthesia shall be given by a qualified anesthesiologist, or a physician or nurse anesthetist under the supervision of such qualified anesthesiologist.

Detailed instructions like these that govern intrahospital procedures are not considered to conflict with state, or even federal, regulations which might be less strict or not as specific. They must also be obeyed by the nurse and her subordinates, as well as her superiors. When a nurse violates this type of code, she not only endangers her license, but, as we shall see later, such a violation may go far to help prove the nurse's individual liability or the institution's responsibility.

POLICE POWER

Police power, as mentioned before, is the inherent sovereignty exercised by the state government whenever regulations are demanded by public policy to guard society's safety, morals, health, and order within the framework of our social, economic, and political structure. Thus, the regulation of a profession or a health care skill, such as nursing, is a vaild exercise of the state police power, if the purpose of such regulation is to benefit and protect the public. It cannot be intended as economic protection for a particular profession or group from prospective competitors. For this reason, courts have sometimes declared unconstitutional residence qualifications that prevent a non-resident from gaining licensure.[1]

Exemptions

This same police power may be exercised to provide for exemption from the need to be licensed in special circumstances. Examples of such exemptions include free care by members of family or friends, including domestic administration of family remedies; emergency care in the form of nursing assistance; care given by religious organizations in their work; incidental care by a servant; care given by student nurses and orderlies; care by nurses who have not, as yet, received licensure in the particular state; care by those who do not represent themselves to be professional registered nurses or licensed practical nurses; and care by Red Cross personnel in emergencies or by federal personnel in federal institutions.

FEDERAL EXEMPTIONS

It is a well-established principle that activities of the federal government are not subject to state inspection laws or licensure requirements.[2] Therefore, employees of governmental installations carrying out their assignments and functions need not comply with state licensure requirements. However, if they are engaged in nongovernmental duties that require licensure, they are responsible under the law, as is any other unlicensed person.

PROFESSIONAL DISCIPLINE

In general, any professional license may be revoked on such grounds as fraud, moral turpitude, or conviction for a criminal offense. Professional boards, however, may generally revoke a license when only the attempt to commit such offenses can be shown. Some boards will also revoke or suspend a license when the defendant elects not to contend against the charge made against her.[3]

The purpose of disciplinary action against a professional is not solely to punish the offender, but also to deter others in the profession and to demonstrate to the public that the ethics of that profession will be maintained.

Using an actual recent case to outline the course of a professional's violation of the state act covering his profession, we shall consider *Arkansas State Board of Pharmacy v. S. W. Patrick.*[4] The same facts and conclusions stated in this case could sustain a similar action with respect to a nurse, technician, or physician licensee.

The state board had received complaints that people were either buying prescription drugs initially or having them refilled without a physician's authority. This was in violation of a state law, and it would provide grounds for suspension or revocation of license. The state board sent a male investigator to the defendant's pharmacy with a prescription bottle bearing a fictitious label for a Mrs. Nancy Henry and indicating that it was originally issued by a Walgreen drugstore. The bottle still contained one Enovid tablet.

The inspector purchased another twenty-tablet bottle of Enovid simply by saying that he needed a refill. Both in federal and state laws most prescription drugs (excluding certain more dangerous types) can be filled or refilled only by a written or oral prescription or by a written or oral order to refill.

In this case, to substantiate the refill for state record-keeping requirements, a nonpharmacist auxiliary person employed in the store wrote out a prescription and forged the doctor's name to it. The defendant, who was the supervisor and the licensed practitioner, was held jointly responsible; since he had been licensed by the state, he was vulnerable to the board's action. In addition, the defendant had signed his name as dispensing pharmacist in compliance with a regulation of the board that requires a pharmacist who fills a prescription to attest that he has filled it personally. This regulation was promulgated by the board to carry out the state act effectively.

About a month after the Enovid prescription had been refilled, the investigator returned to Patrick's drugstore, once again carrying his empty prescription bottle. The same nonpharmacist auxiliary person accepted it, refilled it, and reissued it to him without any hesitation or consultation with the pharmacist or the physician. Patrick's signature was again shown, however, on the dispensing record and on the face of the forged prescription.

The board ordered Patrick to report for a hearing at which he had the right to an attorney. The board found sufficient evidence to show violation of the state laws and to justify revocation of Patrick's license to practice. Everything was in accordance with proper administrative procedures.

Patrick then exercised his right to appeal the board's decision to the circuit court, which felt that because of the element of entrapment, as they viewed it, the evidence could not sustain the board's findings or action. The circuit court further held that the action of the nonpharmacist in typing a label and putting it on a bottle containing Enovid pills that she had not manufactured did not constitute the practice of pharmacy. Since one of the grounds for revocation of a professional's license is aiding and abetting unlicensed practice of that profession, Patrick was found innocent of that charge by the circuit court. Thus, the circuit court nullified the board's order. The board, in turn, appealed to the state supreme court, where the circuit court's verdict was reversed.

The supreme court held that putting the label on the container within the meaning and purpose of the law did constitute the practice of pharmacy, and that many cases have upheld the right of board agents to "afford opportunities or facilities for the commission of the offense" without this constituting *entrapment*. "Entrapment occurs only when the criminal conduct was the product of the creative activity of law enforcement officials." [5] For example, to gain evidence, police and other agents of governmental units commonly seek to make "buys" of narcotics and other dangerous drugs from suspected physicians, nurses, and others.

The court pointed out, in a statement applicable to all professions, that where duties or prerogatives are spelled out statutorily for a particular profession, any portion of those activities done by one unlicensed, if it can be shown to endanger the public welfare or impair a specific patient's health, is punishable. In a final commentary on a court's right to modify a board decision that is found to be capricious or arbitrary, the court said that the revocation of license should be modified to a one-year suspension of license, in view of the pharmacist's prior twenty-eight-year unblemished record.

In conjunction with this decision, the supreme court adopted the principle that violating "the pharmacy laws of Arkansas included both the state and federal auxiliary statutes dealing with foods and drugs in general, in addition to the state pharmacy act." In regard to analogous professional violations in nursing, medicine, dentistry, etc., this court's decision has set a precedent that may influence the opinions of other high courts, i.e., that a violation of the state practice act of a named profession may look to a consideration of any other federal or state laws that affect the legal practice of that profession. Thus, a nurse or physician who violates a state or federal narcotics law, quarantine law, or mental health act may be charged with violating the nursing or medical practice acts.

The unprofessional act may be apart from professional training and activities. For example, a dentist with an excellent reputation in dentistry was convicted for abetting abortions. This was grounds for suspending his license to practice dentistry. Criminal tax evasion is another example.[6]

DEFINITION OF THE PROFESSIONAL NURSE

In addition to setting up licensure requirements, state bodies have undertaken to define the legal boundaries of the nursing functions. According to nursing practice acts, the function of the *professional registered nurse (RN)* is the performance for pay of services to a patient that require the application of nursing principles depending on the biological, physical, and social sciences. There is a hierarchy of responsibility extending from the professional nurse to the practical nurse and finally to auxiliary personnel. We shall discuss each of these in turn.

Dependent Function

The professional nurse works both dependently and independently. Her *dependent function* consists of giving treatment and medication to the patient in compliance with the physician's orders. This is the traditional definition of nursing, and many court decisions have so limited it. However, with the growth of professionalism, nursing has come to include many areas not delegated directly by the physician but rather characterized as independent nursing functions.

Independent Functions

1. Supervision of the patient. The nurse is responsible for the patient's safety and well-being. This includes (1) maintaining the security of the patient's physical environment, such as positioning him properly on an operating table, (2) determining the patient's physical and mental ability to care for himself, and (3) evaluating the relationship between patients. The last is important in deciding, for example, whether a patient should be restrained or whether full- or part-time attendance is necessary.

2. Observation and interpretation of symptoms and reactions. The nurse is required to know the typical symptoms and to be alert for their variations in her patient. She must also observe closely her patient's reaction to medication and treatment administered, record the information, and interpret his reactions accordingly. On the basis of her interpretation, she may recommend to the physician that he modify his orders.

3. Supervision of the nursing team. Closely allied to supervision of the patient is supervision of practical nurses and auxiliary person-

nel. This aspect of nursing is becoming more and more important today, with the increasing use of nursing teams. The professional registered nurse must appropriately divide and delegate portions of the total nursing service among practical nurses, nursing students, nurse's aides, and other personnel. She does this from her knowledge of the personal skill and experience of each, as well as the functional and ability level of the group within the nursing team they represent. She must also remember limitations imposed by law, prudence, and institutional policy.

By understanding the differing areas of function for the professional registered nurse and the licensed practical nurse as described in statute or case law, supervisory personnel can better describe the function of unlicensed personnel who are part of the nursing team and the degree of supervision required for each. In determining the responsibilities of nursing subordinates, the nursing leader must display the good judgment and reasonable prudence expected of someone who is given such a responsibility. Therefore, she is expected to act with caution when assigning relatively untrained or inexperienced help; i.e., they must be under the direction and personal supervision of one who is known to be competent and reliable. It further means that they can be assigned unsupervised duties only when they have had time to develop expertness in that particular duty, when no danger to patients is foreseeable, and when particular procedures are so simple and ordinary that no special instruction is required. These duties might include making a bed and taking temperatures.[7]

In the ANA's Code for Professional Nurses, statement 15 points out that the nurse has an obligation to protect the public by not delegating to a person less qualified any service which requires the professional competence of a nurse. The law therefore expects the professional nurse to select the specific patients who do not need her special scientific acumen. She can delegate responsibility for them to a practical nurse, carefully determining the latter's scope of action. Further, the law requires her to supervise, by observation, the practical nurse's execution of nursing tasks assigned. The professional nurse is also expected to be available to answer questions and settle doubts. All of this is to be, of course, on an individual basis. So, an experienced practical nurse who has proved to be more reliable may be assigned to more complex cases than one who is less qualified or less highly regarded.

When the care of a patient requires constant observation and recording of blood pressure, temperature, pulse, and respiration, the professional nurse is responsible for performing these duties. The licensed practical nurse may assist her by satisfying other needs of the patient.

STATUTORY LIMITS ON PROFESSIONAL NURSING

The nursing practice acts are negatively constructed, in that limitations predominate. Besides prohibiting nurses from practicing medicine or dentistry, they clearly indicate that the nurse who independently undertakes treatment, as distinct from care, of a patient's pain, injury, or physical condition is exceeding her authority, except where it is rendered on an emergency basis. The professional nurse may undertake any act of nursing. By advising and training, she may also assist in programs which are educational and preventive, but she is still limited in certain respects. She may not undertake diagnostic, surgical, and prescriptive procedures independently, nor may she usually accept such responsibilities from one who is authorized by state law to perform these acts. Wherever she undertakes activities which require substantial training and/or specialized skill, even though these rightfully belong within nursing, she must be prepared in conscience and in fact to carry them out.

Whatever the negative construction of the nursing practice acts, the professional nurse's field of action is continuing to expand. This is discussed more fully in Chapter 4. This is also true of her subordinate, the practical nurse, whose actions are still more sharply circumscribed. In considering the practical nurse, we must establish the essential difference between the two: the professional nurse, by education and training, must evaluate and interpret facts to decide what must be done. The practical nurse must not.

While there are an estimated 600,000 professional registered nurses currently practicing their profession in the United States, there are easily 300,000 more who are not nursing now for one reason or another. The AMA Committee on Nursing [8] stated that there are 285,000 inactive registered nurses as potential relief for the shortage. In view of the great shortage of nurses, methods are being considered to encourage the return of inactive nurses to their profession. However, it is recognized that encouragement is not enough; reeducation and retraining programs are also needed.

Regardless of why a nurse leaves her profession, so long as she has a valid license in the state, she has a legal privilege to resume her nursing duties and administer drugs. She must remember, however, that she is still subject to practice with such reasonable care, knowledge, and skill that are commonly possessed by nurses of the same privilege in the locality.

DEFINITION OF THE PRACTICAL NURSE

Licensed practical nurses (LPN's) have defined their role as "persons trained to care for the subacute, convalescent and chronic patient requiring nursing service at home or in institutions, who work under the direction of a licensed physician or registered professional nurse. . . ." [9] While discussing practical nurses, one authoritative source [10] points out that a base figure of approximately 360,000 practical nurse licenses were in force in the fifty United States and the District of Columbia, and that since well over 1,000 licensed practical nurse programs are presently in effect, the licensed practical nurse represents a substantial resource "in planning to meet the present and future needs of patient care. . . ."

In general terms, the practical nurse, operating under the supervision or direction of a professional nurse, physician, or dentist, may undertake care of the ill, injured, or infirm insofar as such acts may be properly entrusted to, or delegated to, her with due regard for the extent of her knowledge and training. (These descriptions, however, may be subject to change when legislators and board officials are in a better position to interpret the general rise in the LPN's skill, education, training, and stature.)

In some areas, the term *practical nurse* is replaced by other official terminology. In certain states she is known and licensed as a *vocational nurse*. In the Saskatchewan Registered Nurses' Association Act *nursing assistants* are described as "persons trained to care for convalescent subacutely ill and chronically ill patients and to assist registered nurses in the care of acutely ill patients." If employed to perform their duties in a private home, they must be under the direction of a registered nurse or a physician, unless they are doing only simple household chores. Improper use of this title is a punishable offense.[11] This statute does not prevent the nursing of the sick for hire or otherwise by any person who does not claim to be a registered nursing assistant.

The National Federation of Licensed Practical Nurses indicates its view of the utilization of the LPN in an approved statement published by *The Bedside Nurse* in 1968:

> The licensed practical nurse is prepared to nurse under the supervision of the registered nurse, physician or dentist in all nursing situations. The licensed practical nurse is a member of the nursing team and participates in meeting the objectives of the patient care plan. Administrative and supervisory personnel who have an understanding of current practice make it possible for the L.P.N. to develop her maximum potential for service.

STATUTORY LIMITS ON PRACTICAL NURSING

The practical nurse's functions, in accordance with the nursing practice acts, obviously involve fewer prerogatives than those established for professional nurses. The acts point out that the function of the LPN is limited to performance for pay of those duties required in the physical care of a patient and in carrying out those medical orders prescribed by a licensed doctor that require an understanding of nursing but not professional service. This would seem to indicate that where any of the specific portions of the professional nurse's function are involved, the practical nurse may be exceeding her authority and by implication her training and understanding. According to statutory guidelines, practical nurses are prepared primarily to give nursing care under reasonably direct supervision to patients in circumstances relatively uncomplicated by subtle or serious physiological or psychological potentialities.

In the states where the practical nurse may administer medication, she should not dispense it; nor should she undertake responsibility for independent recording and observation unless particular circumstances justify it under appropriate professional supervision. If she gives any injections, they should be administered under direct order and supervision of the authorized practitioner. She should generally not give intravenous injections, anesthetics, or drugs that are potent or dangerous to administer.

There are, of course, conflicts between statutory definitions and realities of practice. Therefore, interpretations of the nursing practice acts, since they are, as previously described, negatively constructed, will tend to be subjective. A damaged plaintiff and his counsel will no doubt see much less latitude for a practical nurse's actions than her hospital employers or the physician who has confidence in her as an individual from his own experience and observation. If this interpretation becomes a courtroom issue, the gray area of practice, which may, in the opinion of a plaintiff exceed and therefore violate regulatory restrictions or ordinary prudence, is evaluated in terms of the surrounding facts. These would include the levels of professional and nonprofessional education, skill, and experience of the defendant.

Cases have illustrated that juries, with the aid of expert nursing evidence, may better define nursing functions than a nurse's professional supervisors. In a classic case, a doctor, who had relied heavily on his practical nurse of long standing to determine how promptly he should attend a patient, found himself and his nurse sued for substantial damages following the death of an infant in his office.[12]

A registered nurse testified for the deceased child's parents that the history and symptoms available should have indicated a need for immediate medical attention. Further, she felt that competent and prompt nursing attention for the child, who strangled in his own vomitus, could have prevented the death. The independent nursing acts called for here were not those that a nursing act comtemplates for LPN's. The court ruled that the nurse's negligence, also imputable to her employer, could have contributed to the death of the infant.

UPGRADING THE STATUS OF THE PRACTICAL NURSE

The "Statement of Functions of the Licensed Practical Nurse" issued by the American Nurses' Association, urges that LPN's have "representation and participation on committees and in conferences relevant to personnel and nursing care," so that they can develop a total staff approach and mutual understanding of their responsible role in nursing service.

There is general agreement about the quantitative need for licensed practical nurses, or vocational nurses, as permanent members of the nursing team. There is also a substantial feeling that it may be unwise to approve, in a blanket manner, that more responsibility in nursing care may be assumed personally or authorized legislatively for practical nurses. These judgments must be made in individual circumstances or for particular licensed practical nurses or particular groups of practical nurses who have graduated from a relevant course of instruction. This means that in determining the limits of utility for the LPN, the functional, ethical, and legal basis for such delegation should be derived from the superior's knowledge of the nurse's basic preparation in practical nurse educational and training programs, as well as further education through in-service programs.

Various surveys have been made by interested associations and qualified educational and practitioner observers. They show that formalized programs of instruction for practical nurses, both pre- and post-licensure, are now incorporating into their curriculum, though in lesser detail and scope, areas previously reserved for the registered nurse. These include pharmacological principles and the administration of medicine, bacteriological concepts that aid comprehension of diseased states, and prophylaxis and patient hygiene needs. They are also being taught specialized areas of nursing care, such as geriatric nursing and rehabilitative nursing.

A survey conducted by the National Federation of Licensed Practical Nurses for one state chosen as typical (Ohio) showed that, in general, its hospitals were increasingly using LPN's for ordinary hospital services and activities. However, less than 2 percent of the hospitals had actually expanded LPN use into the higher-level tasks of the registered professional nurse or other licentiates. The areas of almost total exclusion were service in the recovery or emergency room, in private-duty nursing in the nursery, in oxygen therapy, in physiotherapy, in charting duties, and in sterile techniques, to name a few. On the other hand, there was a greater use of the LPN or licensed vocational nurse in giving bedside care in medical, surgical, and obstetric departments; in giving medications; in team positions in intensive care units; and in assuming responsibility as charge nurse.

NURSING CODES OF ETHICS

The Code of Ethics adopted by the National Federation of Licensed Practical Nurses in 1968 serves as an excellent guide to ethical, moral, and legal conduct for all members of the nursing team as well as for service aides and technicians. It is reprinted in the Appendix for that reason. However, the nurse should bear in mind that most codes are not intended to describe legal latitudes or limitations for those who adopt them.

The ANA Code for Professional Nurses, likewise revised in 1968 and reprinted in the Appendix,[13] considers, in addition to the ethical and moral responsibilities of the nurse, conduct and procedural guidelines that relate very closely to the principles of legal compliance discussed at length in this text. It should be borne in mind that the ANA Code is intended to apply to all registered nurses, regardless of education, who are in practice.

AUXILIARY PERSONNEL

Auxiliary nursing personnel are defined by the American Nurses' Association as *unlicensed staff employed and trained to perform tasks which involve specialized services for patients under the direction of professional and licensed practical nurses.* The Association's statement of April, 1962, "Auxiliary Personnel in Nursing Service," [14] deserves comment inasmuch as we shall cover the legal import of these relationships in detail throughout the following chapters. This statement separates auxiliary personnel from other supportive personnel whose employment, training, and supervision "should not be the responsibility of the nursing service." The statement refers, therefore, to nurses' aides, whose titles may be within the circumstances of their function "designated as nursing assistants, ward attendants, orderlies, nursing aides, etc."

As the national professional organization for registered nurses, the American Nurses' Association has on many occasions studied, both singly and jointly with other interested parties, the role of their auxiliaries and the propriety of interrelationships to be sought with auxiliaries. Its 1962 statement says: "The assocation believes therefore that the quantity and quality of nursing care rendered by the nurse can be increased by delegation to auxiliary workers tasks related to nursing in the care of the patient." One should note that there are public, as well as individual patient, benefits resulting from utilization of auxiliary personnel. More important than the monetary economy is the economy of skilled persons.

It seems further as a well-accepted principle of practice that ongoing evaluation as well as education can help professional nurses assign patient-care duties that may be safely and effectively performed by auxiliary nursing personnel. These may be best described as duties necessary to support either the professional or the licensed practical nurse's services. Since the auxiliaries' functions are so determined, they should always be directed and supervised by professional nurses.

The ANA statement contains a list of suggested duties for these workers that is not all-inclusive, and it offers guidance as to in-service education. It points out that misuse of auxiliary workers may jeopardize a nursing service, and, if it develops into the practice of nursing by unlicensed persons, "is illegal and violators are subject to prosecution. The auxiliary worker should be taught to understand the nature of his personal responsibility and the danger to himself and patients should he attempt to practice nursing." Elsewhere the statement stresses that "tasks performed by an auxiliary worker should include only those that do not require the preparation and judgment of a registered nurse or a licensed practical nurse."

NURSING ASSOCIATIONS

Growth of Professionalism

Perhaps the strongest forces to establish a progressively improving public image of the nurse as a trained and responsible member of the health team have been the national and local *nursing associations*. These associations are a logical outgrowth of the development of professional nursing in the twentieth-century United States. The great improvements in hospitals and medical practice at the turn of the century created a demand for the professional nurse. Hospital nursing developed. So did private-duty nursing, which led to the establishment of nursing registries. Finally, public health nursing developed. As medicine became more specialized and the number of students and schools increased, nursing education also began to specialize.

States used the police power clause to begin registering nurses (starting with North Carolina in 1902), passing nursing practice acts and establishing state boards of examiners. As the number of nurses, both professional and practical, increased, nursing associations were formed; they founded and disseminated nursing publications. The first of these was the *American Journal of Nursing,* founded by the American Nurses' Association in 1900. Other titles are *Nursing Outlook,* the official organ of the National League for Nursing, and *Nursing Research,* a specialized journal sponsored by the latter organization, to name but two.

Nursing associations proliferated between World Wars I and II. To provide liaison, interorganizational or "joint" committees and services were formed. As the structure became more unwieldy, six of the major nursing associations in the early 1940s began to study ways of restructuring the groups. Raymond Rich Associates, a research organization, was commissioned to make the study. Their findings, compiled in the Rich Report, were published in 1946. The report called for (1) a reorganized American Nurses' Association and (2) a new National League for Nursing. This plan was accepted by all nursing associations at their 1950 Biennial meeting and implemented in 1952.

Objectives

Among the objectives of nursing associations are the following:

1. To promote high standards of nursing education and practice in order to provide improved service to the public and thereby uphold the dignity of the profession of nursing
2. To interpret nursing to the public
3. To promote the social and economic welfare of the members of the association
4. To stimulate the members of the association to participate in local, provincial, national, and international nursing activities

In Canada, the roles of nursing associations are variously defined, but there is a rather succinct description in the bylaws of the Registered Nurses' Association of Ontario: [15]

A professional association is made up of individuals who have banded together to perform functions which they could not do alone. Its activities are designed to allow for:

The professional growth and development of individual practitioners.

The maintenance of the honour and status of the profession.

The profession's contribution to society.

The Association's bylaws provide a structure through which members of the nursing profession may promote these activities.

In some areas, associations serve a semiofficial function in that they carry out the specific definitive legislation that aids in administering the profession. So in terms of the bylaws of the Registered Nurses' Association of Ontario, a nurse is "a person who is or has been registered or is eligible to be registered under Section 4 of the Nurses Act 1961–1962 and whose registration with the College of Nurses of Ontario has not been suspended or cancelled."

The American Nurses' Association is the national professional association for registered nurses in the United States. It is aimed at improving professional practice, the welfare of nurses, and local and national health needs.

The National League for Nursing is the national association for the community interests of nursing. Through it, all persons engaged in the health sciences, agencies providing nursing education and services, and members of the community can work together to promote excellence in nursing service and education. It also serves as the national accrediting agency for all basic nursing education programs whose purpose is to qualify students as registered professional nurses or licensed practical nurses.

The National Federation of Licensed Practical Nurses is a national association for licensed practical nurses.

All of these groups are made up of constituent associations. The working relationships that exist between them and the national organization is reflected in understanding, cooperation, support, and development of educational programs on the constituent levels.

Guidelines for the Operation of Nursing Associations

From the practical legal approach, nursing associations have to be wary of several undesirable consequences that may result from their various activities. For one thing, they must not establish a qualification for membership that is unfair or exclusionary as measured by constitutional rights and commonsense business morality. This is of special importance when membership becomes either prerequisite or corequisite to licensure, employment, job status, or promotion.

An individual does not have an ironclad right to membership in a voluntary association of professionals or technicians, such as a nursing association. Where membership in such an association is an economic necessity, however, an applicant may not be rejected arbitrarily or capriciously. So, when a voluntary association has in effect a monopoly on a particular status or designated title, it must admit an applicant who is qualified. If the association rejects him, it must be on a reasonable basis.[16]

While associations have often dedicated themselves to upgrading standards and qualifications and to redefining functions, they should be aware that these very activities must keep pace with current medical practices, public attitudes, and medical legislation. They cannot be so out of step with reality that they jeopardize the nurse's "ordinary care and skill" pattern essential to defense in litigation. On the other hand, if their delineation of these factors reflects a credible consensus to the court, the court will probably use it as a measure of the range of duty, qualification for assignment, and quality of performance.

It seems, therefore, appropriate for nursing groups to continue to upgrade understanding of the major factors of qualification—selection, education and training, and experience. However, when they are knowingly avant-garde in this or in setting standards or guideposts for the nursing function, they must frankly state that their positions are not yet generally accepted or ordinary. A nursing association publication may describe a particular nursing assignment in terms of an individual nurse. For example, Nurse Y is in charge of the cardiopulmonary unit at X Hospital. She has certain experiential and educational qualifications and thinks all nurses who staff such units should have them. The publication must take care, in such a case, not to generalize from a single experience. It may also be important to disclaim any inference that this publication best portrays nursing practice. A court might well consider that commonly known and publicized "best nursing practice" ought to be "ordinary and usual nursing practice." While this is probably the point of view of the association as well, it may place a nurse defendant in an unwarranted and uncomfortable position.

CASE CITATIONS

1. *Whittington v. Levy,* 184 So. 2d 577; 226 A. 2d 87, 860 (1966).
2. *United States v. Murphy,* 61 F. Supp. 415 (1948).
3. *Board of Medical Examiners of Oregon v. Mintz,* 378 P. 2d 945 (1963).

4. *Arkansas State Board of Pharmacy v. S. W. Patrick,* Supreme Court of Arkansas, No. 4350 (1968).
5. *Sherman v. United States,* 356 U.S. 369 (1958).
6. *Wasem v. Missouri Dental Board,* 405 S.W. 2d 492 (1966).
7. *Lewenstein v. Curry,* 42 S.E. 2d 158 (1947).
8. Report of the A.M.A. Committee on Nursing, *Journal of the American Medical Association,* May 29 (1967).
9. National Association of Practical Nurses.
10. Etta B. Schmidt, *Modern Hospital,* **108**(1):82 (1967).
11. The Registered Nurses Act, 6 Elizabeth 11, ch. 82, 17A (1957).
12. *Crowe v. Provost,* 374 S.W. 2d 645 (1963).
13. A.N.A. Code for Nurses (1956).
14. A.N.A. Statement, "Auxiliary Personnel in Nursing Service" (1962).
15. Bylaws, revised (1966).
16. *Mable v. A.P.T.A., Inc.,* 35 L.W. 2350 (1966).

CHAPTER 3

THE NURSE AS AN AGENT, AN INDEPENDENT CONTRACTOR, AND AN EMPLOYEE

As we have noted, the legal and ethical responsibilities and privileges of every member of the health care team have been determined by tradition as well as by governmental recognition and definition. In many instances, these guidelines have been set through consensus by the practitioners for themselves, and then they have been formally adopted or informally adhered to. This, of course, holds true for the nurse. However, as in the case of every other individual, the application of these guidelines depends on her apparent or recognized status and on the individual circumstances that occur in the particular nursing situation.

Thus, there is an almost infinite area of possibility for diverse legal relationships with patients, supervisors and those supervised, fellow employees of every description, and professionals with whom the nurse comes into contact when carrying out her duties and assignments. While it is impossible to predetermine her legal position in every instance, it is necessary to examine the major bases that relate to her likely assumption of duties either as an independent contractor, an agent for a principal, or an employee for an employer. Within these general categories of action we can give some definition of her legal status so that she can better understand her rights and responsibilities in case of accident or behavior that involve her in the legal process.

The basic rule to remember, however, is that when a nurse errs in any aspect of patient care, such negligence may be imputable to a physician or nursing supervisor, *but every nurse,* like every member of the health care team, *is liable for her own failures.*[1]

AGENT

An *agent* acts on behalf of another party, called a *principal,* and by agreement between them is subject to the latter's control.

In a principal-agent relationship, control is a necessary element. Ordinarily the physician employs, engages, or prescribes so that the nurse may perform her function in assisting him. This is a usual principal-agent relationship, and it includes the element of controls. However, when control is lacking, the relationship may not be claimed. For example, a nurse who was visiting friends met a doctor at the house who asked her to drop off a tissue specimen for him at the hospital. She was not carrying out an order or a duty; she was doing him a favor voluntarily. Hence, when her vehicle struck another as she was leaving the friends' house and the case went into litigation, the court severed the physician from the suit, where he had been named a codefendant as principal. The court held that there was no control of the nurse by the doctor and no legal relationship which could make the doctor vicariously liable for the nurse's negligence.[2]

INDEPENDENT CONTRACTOR

Any person who undertakes to perform a service or a job as his own boss is an *independent contractor.* He can do a good job or not, depending only on his personal contractual liability to carry out the agreement, whether on a short- or long-term basis.

In theory, an employer is not liable for the negligence of an independent contractor. This contemplates an agreement with someone who possesses some special capacity for the assignment. The work must be neither unlawful nor dangerous to others; it must be done according to the contractor's own methods and pace and not be subject to the employer's control or orders except as to results to be obtained. In such circumstances the employer will not be liable for the wrongful or negligent acts of the independent contractor or his servants. The public, of course, has a right to look to an independent contractor for recovery if he is the cause of their harm. In practice, an employer may be held liable for harm caused by an independent contractor if he was careless or unreasonable in selection or assignment. Most doctors, dentists, osteopaths, podiatrists, lawyers, and the like function as independent contractors. Most nurses do not. However, any professional or practical nurse who undertakes an assignment voluntarily in which only she determines the quality and quantity of her nursing job can be considered an independent contractor. As such, she alone warrants satisfactory performance of the nursing contract she has entered into, and she alone will be liable for any breach of the agreement. A nurse, therefore, can be an independent contractor provided she is not subject to the control or the direction of another and is paid for the total job in some agreed fashion.

The concept of the physician as an independent contractor has undergone some modification where the physician is an outright employee of the hospital. Perhaps because of the greater role the federal and state governments have taken in reorganizing the compensatory system among hospitals, physicians, and many classes of patients, this concept will undergo even greater change. At present, however, this is not the rule. In a case in California,[3] the court evaded the resolution of this issue when it found the surgeon and anesthesiologist free of negligence—the court refused to consider the hospital a principal.

EMPLOYEE

An *employee* is a person who is hired to perform duties or services for another, the employer. The employee is paid for his performance and, to maintain his position, his performance must be substantially responsive to the control and direction of the employer. Unlike an agent, his authority to act in the place of his employer has not been spelled out, but his duty to perform for his employer is implicit in his employment contract. Contracts of both agency and employment last as long as the parties live up to their agreement in a manner acceptable to both.

For practical and most legal purposes, every employee is an agent and every employer is a principal. However, since relationships other than employment may create agency, not every agent is an employee. For example, the sole owner of a nursing home may employ a nursing supervisor, who is both agent and employee. The owner's wife or child, however, may make purchases or interview prospective patients as his agent, even though they are not employees. Also, if ownership is in the form of a partnership, each partner is legally an agent for the other. Another example: A nursing registry is asked to supply a nurse for special duty; the registry is an agent acting on behalf of a patient, but it is not an employee of the patient. Also, volunteer organizations that provide unpaid assistants in hospital operations are principals, but the volunteers who report for duty are not employees in any sense.

Two questions apply to all these examples. First, what type of relationship do the parties intend to establish? Second, how does this relationship appear to those who come into contact with it? The answers to these questions will determine, in a court of law, the relationship of the parties.

EMPLOYER'S DUTIES TO EMPLOYEES

An employer must carry out his contract of employment, whether it is oral or written and whether it is expressed in the terms of the agreement or implied from usual arrangements in such activities. He must provide the pay he promised for the work described. He is expected to provide proper surroundings and equipment that will make doing the job as safe for the employee as is reasonable. Employees' rights are limited by obvious assumption of risk and known occupational hazards. Although assumption of risk cannot be rigidly defined, it is generally considered to be a willingness to expose onself to some degree of danger while possessing sufficient information to realize the seriousness of such a choice. Not only will clear assumption of risk tend to negate a suit where a nurse is injured, but an employee's own negligence or poor judgment will be interpreted as contributory negligence and bar recourse against the employer.[4]

CIVIL RIGHTS OF EMPLOYEES

There is much interest in the long-range effects of the Civil Rights Act of 1964 on employer-employee relations in the hospital and health professions. Under Title III, the federal government is given authority to sue state and municipal officials on behalf of complainants. Title IV applies where schools of nursing and technology are based in governmental institutions or are supported mainly by federal funds. On petition from one who feels excluded for reasons of race, religion, or ethnic background, the Attorney General may bring an action in his behalf.

Under Title VI, federal funds may be withheld from a discriminating hospital, if not a discriminating physician. Physicians have been assured that they will retain their traditional right to select their patients. This has been so under the Hill-Burton, Kerr-Mills, and Medicare laws. However, court decisions have indicated that even a private hospital's acceptance and use of these federal funds render it an instrument of government and thus prohibit it under the Fifth and

Fourteenth Amendments from discriminating against patients, employees, and professional staff on the basis of race.

A recent case before a federal circuit court of appeals upheld a complaint against alleged discriminatory practices by a private hospital. Although partially financed by federal funds, the hospital had excluded Negro professionals from its staff and assigned hospital rooms on a racial basis. The court saw as prima facie evidence of discrimination the complete absence of Negro physicians on the staff, even though numerous licensed and board-certified Negro physicians practiced in the locality. The court also decided that a hospital that required a newcomer to gain approval of three-fourths of the staff in a secret vote was "loaded" to produce racial discrimination. In granting an injunction against the hospital, the court further pointed out that it was common knowledge that a hospital can be certified by the U.S. Department of Health, Education, and Welfare as meeting statutory desegregative criteria and yet not be in true compliance.[5]

In a landmark decision,[6] it was judicially emphasized that hospitals receiving federal assistance are subject to the constitutional prohibitions against racial discrimination (Fifth and Fourteenth Amendments). This holding was reiterated in *Smith v. Hampton Training School for Nurses*.[7] Nurses who had been discharged for desegregative acts in the hospital were reimbursed in accordance with contract law. They received reinstatement and all the back pay they had lost minus actual earnings they had gained while discharged.

However, the burden of proof to establish a charge of racial, religious, or ethnic discrimination is upon the one who asserts it. Where government agencies are not legally constituted to assist assertion of such claim in a particular locality, the expense of bringing such an action will probably have to be borne by the applicant.[8]

Title VII of the Civil Rights Act deals with equal employment opportunity provisions, much like New York State's Fair Employment Practice Laws. Certain practices of hiring, firing, promoting, or compensating employees because of their race, religion, national origin, or sex are forbidden. But sex or religion may be a legitimate job qualification and therefore permissible under proper and understandable circumstances.

Every professional has the right to refuse to perform a service for one who seeks his professional aid. However, this right has been qualified in certain states. In New York, Article XXI of the Education Law, which deals with unprofessional conduct in the practice of the professions, under Rules of the Board of Regents, states in paragraph 268:

The refusal of any practitioner holding a license or certificate issued by the Department, pursuant to the provisions of the Education Law, to provide treatment or other professional service to any person on account of race, religion, creed, color, or national origin, shall be deemed unprofessional conduct in the practice of his profession.

PERSONAL AND STATUTORY RIGHTS OF EMPLOYEES

In discussing the obligations of the principal or employer, we touched upon many of the rights that an employee enjoys as a result of her employment. Some of these rights are inherent and some are spelled out in statutes for her benefit.

As an example of the former, subject to certain limitations, no one has the right to obstruct her in her efforts to practice her skills and earn her livelihood. She shares the protection offered all individuals from those who may slander her character or impugn the quality of her work. On this basis she can take action against former employers, patients, and co-workers who make untruthful statements or give malicious or prejudiced accounts of her activities which lead to loss of employment, promotion, and reputation. As to statutory privileges, in addition to those afforded her by her legal status or licensure, she may be qualified to receive particular protection under workmen's compensation laws and similar employee benefits.

ASSUMPTION OF RISK BY EMPLOYEES

The employer must realize that nursing personnel, technicians, or others cannot voluntarily assume risk unless they are fully aware of the potential hazard involved. Where a nurse is injured by the patient's action and the nurse's superiors had actual knowledge of the patient's dangerous potential prior to the attack, the nurse could hold these superiors liable.[9] Courts have held that a nurse, either as an employee or as an independent contractor (private-duty nurse), assumes limited risk unless there is an express assumption of nonlimitation to the contrary.[10] In accordance with the master-servant concept and except as enlarged or modified by statutory provision, the employer is bound, within reason, to foresee and protect the employee from physical harm. If he fails to do this, he can be held liable for his negligence. Those placed in supervisory positions by the employer as his agents share this obligation in law and in practice.

It is the duty of one who employs a youthful or inexperienced employee for a service involving dangers known to the employer, but unknown to the employee, to explain to the employee the perils and to instruct him on how to avoid them. A nurse supervisor or a hospital that assigns an inexperienced nurse to attend a patient who suffers from a contagious disease is bound to inform her of the dangerous character of the service.

Since the Federal Tort Claims Act excludes actions brought by civilian employees of the government for on-the-job injuries or by military personnel for injuries incidental to their military duties, it would seem that federal nursing, medical, and technical employees are working under the assumption-of-risk doctrine. However, this is not quite the case since, although they cannot look to the superior for their damages, they can take action against particular tort-feasors whom they deem responsible under the Federal Employees' Compensation Act. A noteworthy exception permits retired military personnel, dependents of military personnel, and even active military personnel being treated for injuries of a nonmilitary nature to bring suit under the Federal Tort Claims Act.[11]

Nursing staff may expect the hospital to provide them with a safe place to work. The hospital must adhere to reasonable standards of cleanliness and safety. Employees should be warned of any unsafe conditions known to exist. Employees can assume only those risks that they expressly or implicitly acknowledge. There is not assumption of risk for every possible harm that may befall a hospital employee.[12] In such cases, the courts will examine the diligence with which cautions were given and warnings posted. Therefore, supervisory personnel must be certain that, whether hospital personnel, patients, or others are involved, linguistic and sensory handicaps are taken into account. In a recent case, two Spanish-speaking laborers failed to comprehend the meaning and significance of a skull and crossbones and a warning not to touch a certain strong pesticide without gloves. They handled the dangerous chemicals and died within days. The court held the employer and the manufacturer liable and said they should have made sure by action and language that the language barrier to the workmen's safety had been overcome.

With foreign exchange programs and domestic programs which seek to enlist newly emigrated Latin Americans in hospital and nursing service, the language problem has become of great importance. To this purpose many hospitals in the larger urban areas of the United States and Canada carry on programs, sometimes aided by the cities, designed to assist those who do not speak Spanish or French to communicate with those who do speak and understand these languages primarily. To further aid communication, similar programs of study to develop speech and understanding in English for the foreign born to whom it is strange have been established. In cases concerning employee safety, courts have taken the position that the employer has an obligation to prepare for foreseeable dangerous circumstances and to forestall them by whatever physical requirements are essential. The principal and his agent, therefore, would have a stronger defense in court if they could show that they provided such necessities. In performing this task, the employer must be aware if an employee is so hard of hearing, or so nearly sightless, or so dim-witted, or so noncomprehending of the language as to be unreasonably and foreseeably handicapped in his ability to preserve life and limb. This is equally true in hospital and nonhospital nursing situations.

A principal is obliged to defend his agent against any loss or liability incurred in the latter's carrying out of his assignment. Where statutes exist to benefit the employee, the principal is responsible for compliance with those of a mandatory nature, such as Social Security and workmen's compensation. In recent years, the employer has also been further required to abide by certain civil rights regulations.

RESPONSIBILITIES TO VISITORS, PATIENTS, AND EMPLOYEES

The principal is responsible for maintenance of a building. He must be certain that the proper signs are posted, the lights are bright enough, the ceilings are safe, the exits are clearly marked, the stairways are uncluttered, the floors are safe for walking, etc. To this extent, he is responsible to the visitors, patients, and employees in a hospital. Although for all practical purposes he may have delegated these responsibilities to an appropriate agent or employee, a court of law will hold him responsible under the doctrines of respondeat superior and master of the ship (see Glossary).

Visitors

Briefly put, a person comes onto the premises or into the house or office of another person in one of three classes of legal status: a trespasser, an uninvited licensee, or an invitee.

A *trespasser* does not warrant any care or precautions from the principal and his agents and employees. The law merely requires that the latter refrain from taking positive steps to harm a trespasser. This does not mean that one cannot put barbed wire around a fence or spiked points on surrounding gates, since these are visible means of protection. One cannot, however, set traps or spring guns or the like to catch a trespasser unaware and harm him.

A second class of visitor is a *licensee*, who, though uninvited, is tolerated. A licensee is neither a patient, a client, an employee, nor a trespasser. He is on the premises in his own interest. He has a right to expect that the premises will be in safe condition and that he will be warned where dangers exist. Many who enter the premises by a right to inspect them for building defects or fire hazards enter as licensees. The law frequently considers social guests in this category if their presence is of no benefit to the interest of the owner of the premises.

The third class is the legal status that makes the greatest demands upon the owner to maintain the safety of his premises. Persons in this group are classed as *invitees,* and the owner's duty is to keep the premises in a safe condition for them by the exercise of reasonable care and ordinary prudence. An invitee is owed the right of entering premises that are in reasonably safe condition and a warning of any danger. An invitee is actually one who is essential to the operation of those premises or for whom those premises have a purpose. Thus, a private-duty nurse attending a patient in a hospital has been held to be an invitee.[13]

Patients

A hospital patient is an invitee on the premises of that hospital, with the exclusion of those areas where she has been warned not to enter, or which obviously have not been set aside for her use. In short, her room or ward is an area of invitation in which she enjoys invitee status. But if she decides on her own to pay an unauthorized and unexpected visit to the boiler room of the hospital, she may well be considered a trespasser.

The same is true for employees and subordinate help and for those who come to visit patients or service the hospital. In general, they are entitled to have positive measures taken for their safety only when they are in those areas allocated to their use or employment and are doing what they are permitted and expected to do. According to the theory of many decisions,[14] a visiting nurse may bring an action against a landlord, a homeowner, and possibly a tenant, if she is unreasonably exposed to danger and harmed upon entering the area of invitation for her services. In this same action the nurse's husband could recover damages for loss of his wife's services

Employees

Some responsibilities of an employee to her employer may be derived from the above cases. In many actual situations, members of the nursing team are the contacts between the principal and those who come to his premises. They also serve to select, instruct, and supervise his lesser employees. Often it is the nurses who advise and remind those who are of superior professional status but less familiar with the necessary information for maintaining the safety and efficiency of the premises, its personnel, and the equipment.

Nurses, technicians, and hospital personnel in general have overriding responsibilities to the public as a whole. As agents, however, they owe particular obligations to their employers. The law expects an agent to be faithful and loyal and to follow instructions carefully to prevent damage or loss. Also, in accordance with agency requirements expressed in past common-law decisions by the Latin phrase *uberrima fides* ("utmost faith"), the nurse undertakes to care for equipment and money entrusted to her control as a fiduciary. She is expected to exercise that reasonable degree of care, skill, and diligence in performing her duties to which she has pledged herself and that is ordinarily exercised by others who are similarly engaged.

Nursing personnel must be careful not to expose themselves, their subordinates, and their patients to dangers that exist on the premises from radiation or contagion, for example. They should be alert to their legal and moral responsibility to warn visitors, city inspectors, unknowing hospital personnel, and others of such hazards. They must also store dangerous objects in safe quarters, away from areas where they may tempt adults or children. It is important that glassware, used syringes, drugs, and tubing be disposed of in a manner prescribed either by ordinance, by policy, or by common sense.

There are some instances when hospital nurses, office nurses, or other personnel must enlist the aid of the parents of a patient, those who accompany him, or even persons who happen to be nearby. Even though these are extraordinary circumstances, prudence is required in keeping with the probabilities of danger. On her own behalf and out of a duty of proper and faithful conduct to her employer, the nurse must not expose these temporary nonemployee assistants to any foreseeable danger. She must not have them assist in tasks which call for the special skills and the awareness of danger possessed by other members of the nursing team.

An agent has a duty to inform his principal of any matters which either come to his attention or are brought to his attention if such matters may affect the interests of the principal. Should the agent fail to do this and the principal suffer a loss, the agent may be liable to the extent of all or some of that loss. As an example, a nurse in charge of a nursing home or sanatorium may be advised by professional or governmental officials that the place will not be allowed to continue functioning unless certain requirements are met. She has a duty to let the owner know so that he can remedy the situation.

If she fails to do this, and, as a result, the owner's premises are forced to be vacated with loss of money and reputation, he can take steps against her for her failure.[15]

The nurse or other employee has a duty to care for equipment entrusted to her and to report to the employer when it is damaged or otherwise defective. We shall note related underlying principles when we discuss negligence in Chapter 5, but where a hospital uses defective equipment, it cannot easily defend its action by saying that the nurses failed to let their superiors know of the defect. On the other hand, if the hospital knowingly allows imperfect equipment to be used, even with the knowledge of the user nurse, they may both be liable for a consequent injury to an innocent third party under the doctrine of foreseeability. So, central-supply or surgical nurses who realize they have inadvertently bought an inferior supply of suture material and advise the surgical staff of this but ask them to use it until a replacement is made are creating joint responsibility.

Depending on their functional status, which is derived from their hiring, employees may have in terms of agency and respondeat superior a further responsibility to both the public and their principals or employers. They must act in the place of their employer in a manner calculated to discharge his duties properly. Under the law this means that the employee, as well as the employer, undertakes to assure the proper selection and supervision of subordinates so that the patient gets proper care, and that safe, careful conduct is practiced by all concerned. Thus, where someone with lesser skill or professional stature is utilized by a nurse, unwise direction, unreasonable selection, or supervisory neglect could make the nurse liable for the errors of that individual. We shall examine this duty in terms of delegation in Chapter 4.

Although we have been discussing the employee's responsibilities in terms of institutional employment, these same conditions also apply to smaller units of practice. Therefore the nursing employee has a duty to her superior as well as to the physicians, dentists, or other practitioners she assists. Many times these responsibilities arise from her role of communicator between the patient and the doctor either in the hospital or in the office. It is one thing for her to shield the physician from nuisance calls or messages but another to insulate him from those calls which may jeopardize the patient-physician relationship. A nurse who fails to report to the doctor serious warning signs that may cause a patient to be permanently disabled will be held jointly liable with the physician and will be subject to demand for indemnification.

A doctor's schedule is necessarily tight, and frequently his nurse is responsible for maintaining it. She must also react with common sense to circumstances that call for changes in schedule. For example, in a recent federal court decision, a physician was held liable for amputation of a patient's leg when an infection followed the reduction of a compound comminuted fracture. When the patient had called for an earlier appointment because the cast was moist around the fracture site, the odor was foul, and he was febrile, he was told to await his scheduled appointment.[16]

WORKMEN'S COMPENSATION LAWS

In most North American communities as well as in Europe and Australia, nurses are covered by the general type of workmen's compensation laws we know in the United States.

Purpose of the Laws

The purpose of workmen's compensation laws is to obviate the need for proving fault in order to obtain liability. It is a kind of statutory liability that ignores fault, so long as the injury arose out of employment and was incurred within the scope of employment. There are certain very definite exceptions to workmen's compensation coverage. While negligence of either nurse or employer is not at issue in workmen's compensation, injuries brought about by willful and intentional wrongdoing or self-harm may be barred. As a general rule, a hospital employee injured within the scope of his employment may recover compensation for such injury regardless of the kind of injury sustained.[17] For a nurse to collect workmen's compensation, her employment must be covered by the state act and her employer must have made the necessary contributions.

Status of the Independent Contractor

A nurse working as an independent contractor cannot collect workmen's compensation. Therefore, the status of nurses in independent assignments, such as special-duty nursing, often makes for legal controversy in terms of workmen's compensation. Today, if the circumstances can be construed as favorable to the nurse, the workmen's compensation board or the courts will strain to grant her an award.

Frequently, however, a private-duty nurse's claim for workmen's compensation benefits will be denied. In a recent case,[18] a practical nurse was engaged through a nursing registry to provide daily care for a patient in a nursing home. As a matter of convenience, she was paid by the nursing home from funds supplied by the patient.

In holding that she was not entitled to workmen's compensation, the court pointed out that an employer-employee relationship exists within the meaning of the law when there is a right to control and supervise the nurse in her performance and manner of working, to hire and fire her, and to subtract from her pay all standard deductions such as withholding tax and insurance. If a nurse works in an office for several doctors, they are jointly liable for compensation benefits.

Compensation for Occupational Disease

In Pennsylvania, a nurse contracting tuberculosis "in the occupation of nursing in hospitals or sanitaria involving exposure to such disease" is fully covered under the Pennsylvania Occupational Disease Act.[19] This model act specifically provides: "If it be shown that the employee, at or immediately before the date of disability, was employed in any occupation or industry in which the occupational disease is a hazard—it shall be presumed that the employee's occupational disease arose out of and in the course of his employment, but the assumption shall not be conclusive."

From time to time stiffer views of what a court regards as an occupational disease have been voiced. For example, in one case the appellate court of New York said that an occupational disease is an ailment which arises out of a distinctive feature of the kind of work performed by the claimant and others similarly employed. The court held that it is not an ailment caused by a peculiar place in which the particular claimant works or by ordinary contact with a fellow employee.[20] In another New York case, a nurse sought compensation for tuberculosis contracted from a tubercular patient under her care. Her own particular health circumstance thwarted monetary recovery. The appellate court, in denying her claim, held that no compensation could accrue where expert testimony held the condition to be endogenous and due to reactivation of previous infection.[21]

Third-Party Liability

Where an employee has been injured in compensable activity due to the fault of a person other than his employer, he has the option of claiming compensation or proceeding to sue the other party. If the employer pays the compensation, he (his insurer) is subrogated to the employee's rights against the third-party wrongdoer. Therefore, the employer should take action against the third-party liable. The act generally provides that the employee demand that his employer bring his suit against the third party within a specified period of time, such as thirty days. If the employer fails to comply with this demand, the employee can sue on his own.

A release that the employee has signed as a condition precedent to receiving the compensation settlement releases only the parties named in the agreement. Since the third party who actually caused the harm is not named, his future is determined by the party injured or those who can sue on their rights through him.[22] Hence, although her employer has covered her under the state workmen's compensation act, a nurse may recover both compensation and damage, although not from her employer. Recovery under workmen's compensation acts does not bar an action to recover damages from another person whose negligence brought about the nurse's injury, as, for example, a manufacturer of defective equipment.[23]

Limits of Compensable Activity

Most often it is held that a nurse need not be involved in a particular nursing or patient-care function on the occasion that gives rise to the claim. So long as her activity is incidental to her employment and is reasonably expected within its context she may be in a position to assert a claim. The narrower view is that she must be participating in compensable activity within the scope and course of her employment. Most frequently the employee's injury occurs on the employer's premises, but this is not essential for compensation. So long as the injury "arises out of" and "in the course of" the employment, it is compensable. This has been taken to include reasonable periods of time before and after working hours, so long as the activity is still connected with the employment. This covers the nurse who injures herself in the shower or in the locker room of the hospital as she cleans up and the nurse's aide who slips and falls on the brick sidewalk of the hospital while walking to or from her car in the hospital parking lot.

An injury inflicted upon a hospital employee engaged in her hospital duties, whether it results from an assault, prank, mutual fight, or willfully negligent act of a co-employee, is regarded as compensable under some state workmen's compensation acts.[24] But damages from "fight" injuries in many jurisdictions may not be recovered. However, if the "fight" and ultimate damage caused by it are really work-related, then workmen's compensation will be available. For example, Nurse A orders an aide to do a certain task. While closely supervising the aide's work, Nurse A becomes critical, whereupon they argue. They grapple and are finally separated after some pulling and scratching. As a result, Nurse A's back becomes sore and painful and she cannot work. Needless to say, an action in assault and battery might also result.

Applicability of the Laws

In determining the applicability of the workmen's compensation acts, the circumstances of the injury are viewed with various degrees of elasticity. Questions to be raised are the following:

1. Did the act occur out of or incidental to the employment, or did the conditions of the employment create the causal relation?
2. Were the time and place of the act during the period of employment and within its normal geographical area?
3. Was the accident a sudden and unforeseen occurrence?

Therefore, while the objective of the statutes is to provide a system of recompense for accidental injury in the scope of employment, courts usually will not use them to preclude suits in tort where the employer or a third party flagrantly abuse or harm the employee. In an unusual Midwestern case,[25] an employer paid his employee's nurse the cost of an influenza shot, since the administration was gratuitous and encouraged by the employer. The court held that the allergic reaction prompted by the injection was limited to recovery under the workmen's compensation act, because it was an unforeseen occurrence or accident within the scope of the employment and the meaning of the act. The employee had desired to sue the nurse and the employer (respondeat superior) for negligence. On the other hand, an employee may disclaim the benefits of the workmen's compensation law where injury was caused by willful or intentional wrongdoing on the part of her employer, and she may bring her suit in a court of law.

Instituting a Compensation Claim

The statute provides for the filing of a workmen's compensation claim against the employer without reference to his liability or non-liability. Acceptance of compensation benefits releases the employer from further suit on the account. However, it does not release third persons whom the employee seeks to hold accountable for causing his harm, nor to subsequent wrongdoers, as previously noted.

In brief, by filing for and being awarded compensation, the employee has elected to have the rights provided by the statute for all compensable consequences of the injury. If he has asserted his rights against the wrongdoer in a court of law and is victorious, or if the insurance carrier asserts his claim in his behalf, he is entitled to damages awarded beyond the insurance settlement.[26] Whenever malpractice occurs, the employee has the compensation payments and the additional statutory right to pursue the third parties if the insurer does not do so. The defendant physician or nurse can interpose the traditional malpractice defense, via expert medical witnesses, that the physician has exercised the degree of skill and followed the procedures ordinarily employed by physicians in the community.

The presentation and type of evidence admitted in workmen's compensation hearings are very different from those in civil or criminal trials. Most state courts interpret the law and the admission of pertinent evidence very liberally in favor of the employee where circumstances warrant.

The workmen's compensation board may rule on the basis of "substantial" evidence, which can include secondhand, or hearsay, comments. They may select from among conflicting medical opinions. Where the board refuses workmen's compensation on the ground that the disability is not causally connected to the work, the claimant may seek to prove his point in a regular civil lawsuit. However, he must understand that because of tighter rules of evidence it may be harder to develop the case with respect to a causal relation between the injury or disease and the nature or hazards of the occupation.

Among the various issues that arise in workmen's compensation cases are the time of readiness for return to work and professional advice about how to rehabilitate the injured party. Here, physician and nursing reports may be critical. They must be complete, factual, and unbiased.

If, for example, a disabled claimant can become partially or completely enabled to return to work through special treatment or surgery, the nature of the recommended treatment, the probability of success, the danger, the pain, and the inconvenience involved will continue to determine whether the claimant may refuse the treatment and still receive disability benefits.[27]

DOCTRINES GOVERNING NURSING PRACTICE

Doctrine of Respondeat Superior

Because the public identifies the employee or agent and his actions with the principal or employer, it looks to the latter for damages. The doctrine of *respondeat superior*, literally translated as "let the master answer," finds the principal or employer responsible when his agent or employee causes harm to the person or property of another party. It does not generally matter whether the harm was intended, whether it occurred by the agent's action or by his failure to act, or whether the "master" himself was present or out of sight, hearing, and control of the situation.

Responsibility of the Agent

It is important, however, whether the wrongdoing occurred outside the scope of the agent's or employee's duties or beyond the normal time and place of his duties. Also important is whether the employer can show that the harm resulted from the agent's or employee's willful disregard of his instructions. As we will note in our later discussion of contracts, it matters if the act complained of was illegal on its face, because no employment or agency agreement can countenance the doing of an illegal act. Therefore, while a nurse is authorized by the law of agency and the contract of employment to perform all the normal or delegated acts essential to fulfill her category of nursing service in the place and during the time of employment, she has no right to do anything prohibited by law or by the employer's instructions at the time she takes the position or thereafter. We should mention here that the principal may expect his instructions to be carried out by the nurse, but the public equally expects that he will fulfill his responsibility by properly selecting and instructing his agents and employees.

As far as the patient is concerned, anyone who provides him with nursing care can be held to have the proficiency of a nurse in executing that function. This is true whether she is a student, a trainee, or any other member of the nursing team.

Where a nurse, a student, any other hospital employee, or an institutional trainee exceeds the delegated functions, and where the employer through his supervisor knows this, or ought to know this, or appears to be aware of this, then the public has the right to feel that the employee has apparent authority to perform these functions.

Responsibility of the Subagent

Within the cloak of agency is the circumstance of subagency. The *subagent* is the agent of the agent, and he can bind the principal just as the agent can, where the subagency is apparent and necessary or has the authority and sanction of the principal. For example, the nursing director, acting on the general instruction to keep the corridors clean, may hire someone to come in evenings and scrub them. If the employee leaves the hall floors slippery and wet, he is a subagent creating a dangerous situation that may result in lawsuits. Another example is the hospital administrator who is an agent of the board of trustees of a nonproprietary hospital. On the authority of his position, he decides, or accepts the decision of one of his subordinates, to have all the hospital's laundering done by an outside service. That launderer becomes a subagent of the hospital.

On the other hand, a doctor's orders to a nurse he knows to be in charge of a particular patient may be delegated in some details to nursing students, orderlies, technicians, and even volunteers. This may be done with or without his knowledge of the acts or of the people involved. Thus, a nursing home or any other employer of nurses may be rendered liable under terms that the nurse never considered contractual and regardless of the fact that there was neither written nor oral authorization for subselection, subassignment, or subdelegation.

Litigation Involving Respondeat Superior

An interesting case that illustrates the court's view of the agent-principal relationship and the doctor's responsibility in delegation involved a patient who claimed that he received severe burns and electric-shock damage while undergoing x-ray treatment. The treatment was given by an experienced x-ray technologist who was an assistant to the roentgenologist in charge. The latter was not present when the incident causing the alleged harm took place. The patient and the x-ray tube came into contact, and the patient claimed to have suffered shock and burns.

In denying the roentgenologist's request that the case against him be dismissed since he was not responsible for the technician's action, the court pointed out that it was the roentgenologist's name and professional standing, not the x-ray technician's, that had brought the patient to that particular hospital for treatment.[28]

In a recent California case, the appellate court upheld a lower court's decision to revoke a pharmacist's license and his wife's pharmacy permit. The revocation of the wife's pharmacy permit was based purely on the doctrine of respondeat superior. As owner of the permit to operate that pharmacy, she had failed, in the opinion of the court, to exercise the degree of prudent supervision that would have stopped her employees from filling prescriptions illegally. The pharmacist's license to practice was revoked on evidence showing that he had accepted oral authorization to fill prescriptions from the nurse of an absent doctor. To complete his record, he had then written out the prescription and signed the doctor's name to it.[29]

Where members of the nursing team are employed and paid by the hospital, the hospital obviously assumes liability under the doctrine of respondeat superior. This is true when the employer is a doctor, a dentist, or any other professional person practicing either as an individual or in partnership.

In legal situations that are not quite as simple, however, other theories are advanced. For instance, we previously noted the circumstances of subagency, where the principal is often liable for an act performed by someone whom he has had no opportunity to select, hire, or instruct. In such cases, so long as he actually or by implication delegated to an employee the right to select, hire, and instruct this person, he will be held responsible.

Where an employee has exceeded authority or acted contrary to instructions, the chain of respondeat superior liability would stop at that employee. For example, P, the employer, is informed by his nursing supervisor that she wants to hire two more male attendants. She tells him that Mr. John and Mr. Abner are available, and he approves her hiring Mr. John but tells her he knows that Mr. Abner is a habitual drunkard and he does not want to hire the latter. The nursing supervisor, in desperation, hires Mr. Abner too, without telling P. Mr. Abner lives up to P's expectations, and, after drinking heavily, strikes a patient. As we shall discuss later in terms of tort responsibility, Mr. Abner will be liable for his own assault, the nursing supervisor will be liable under the doctrine of respondeat superior, but P may not be held liable when he establishes the facts we have described.

In a Delaware case based on respondeat superior,[30] a patient sued for damages because he claimed to have sustained a permanent drop of the left foot and atrophy of the musculature of the left calf. The proximate cause he alleged to be two injections given by a nurse which he claimed had been given beyond the upper outer quadrant of his left buttock, where such injections were to be given. He had had immediate pain and doctors asserted that the plaintiff's sciatic nerve had been damaged by the injections into it.

The patient named the nurse and the hospital as defendants. The court held for the plaintiff on two counts: the nurse should have been skilled enough to give the injections in the proper place and manner, and the hospital should have employed a competent nurse to perform the service which would be expected to be necessary. While in some jurisdictions it is held that the physician is generally not responsible for the actions of hospital nurses in performing ordinary nursing duties after the patient leaves the operating room, such holdings are far from universal.

More Than One Master

Another group of complex legal circumstances arises out of the realities of modern hospital procedures. For example, the nurse, who is an employee of the hospital, is involved in an allegedly tortious happening as a consequence of assisting or carrying out the orders of a visiting or attending physician. The visiting physician is an independent contractor, and the hospital would not normally be responsible for his actions or those of his agents or employees.

Insofar as federal employees are concerned, their liability for a tortious act committed by one of their subordinates is strictly construed to include only situations where they directly ordered it, participated in it, or, in a present supervisory capacity, could have stopped it. Such cases are resolved more on the evidence and the particular surrounding circumstances than on any doctrine or theory of law. We shall, therefore, note some of the latter and then cite a number of illustrations from actual cases in which application was either accepted or refused.

Borrowed Servant Theory

An attending physician is sometimes said to have "borrowed" a nursing employee from the hospital for his purposes, since she is assigned to the care of his patient and expected to follow his direction and instruction. While engaged in such activity, she is sometimes held to be his temporary agent and employee.

In one case, the court went so far as to advise the physician that where he alleged that his written orders for the patient were carried out negligently by an intern and two nurses, his only recourse was to sue the latter for a joint contribution to the plaintiff's award against him.[31]

In another case, the court reviewed application of the *borrowed-servant* theory and summarized its view by stating that the hospital employer is liable under the doctrine of respondeat superior for the negligence of an employee in the performance of his ordinary duties. Assisting physicians in treating patients is, for example, an ordinary duty of an intern.

A hospital employee may at times be temporarily under the exclusive control of the treating physician, and, when this is demonstrable, the hospital may not be liable for the employee's negligence at such time. Whether this situation exists is often an issue of fact for the jury to consider in the light of the circumstances and evidence received.[32]

Federal Employees

Federal professional and paramedical staff are often assigned to assist local and state programs of disease prevention, study, research, teaching, and the like. This is done on the premise that it serves the general welfare regardless of intranational geographical boundaries. However, under ordinary circumstances, courts will regard these personnel as borrowed servants, and the local unit will be liable for their negligence or other tortious behavior. This is true even if federal monies are carrying out the plan to implement some overall federal policy or program. In unusual circumstances where these persons are actually under federal control and supervision when doing the act that is the subject of the complaint, a contrary ruling is possible.

Master of the Ship

The *captain* or *master-of-the-ship theory* is generally applied to surgical situations; it holds that the surgeon is in charge of the operation much as the captain is in charge of the ship. Therefore, in theory, he has control and supervision of all who assist him. As they cumulatively aid his success, he must be liable for their failure.

LIMITATIONS ON RESPONSIBILITY

In the jurisdiction where this theory has been applied, the courts have whittled away at its blanket responsibility. For instance, they found a separation of authority when a board-certified cospecialist, such as an anesthesiologist, was concerned. An anesthesiologist interprets the surgeon's anesthesia requirements and adapts them to the patient's physiological condition and needs. Especially in performing this latter duty, the anesthesiologist has been found by the courts to have acted independently.

In some cases, the nurse may not be held to be the servant of the operating surgeon. Situations occur in which his selection, direction, and supervision are so limited that she is in no sense his employee. This has been held true for a scrub nurse, who prepares the operating room before the operation, unless she is proved to be the surgeon's employee.[33] The surgeon has been found not liable for negligent harm done to another part of the patient's body by someone else while he is concentrating on the task at home. He has also been found not liable for treatment administered by floor nurses and interns in the regular course of postoperative services which are ordinarily furnished by the hospital.[34]

The ultimate test seems to be whether the physician has supervisory control and the right to give orders to the employee in question that apply to the very act the employee performed negligently.

A physician understands that he is liable for a charge of negligence if he does not properly instruct the nurse or others who are to care for the patient. The same would be true of any nursing superior on the health team. It is agreed that the duty of the attending physician or surgeon to use reasonable care for the safety and well-being of his patient also includes the duty to warn and instruct persons having the care of the patient, if they are ignorant or inexperienced, as to the performance of the duties which they are to perform.

ASSUMPTION OF NURSES' COMPETENCE

If the doctor is performing his duties in a modern hospital that has experienced nurses and attendants, many courts have held that he should be entitled to take for granted that his subordinates will attend to their customary duties without instructions. For example, if a doctor instructs the nurse to see that a patient is kept warm, he can expect the nurse not to burn the patient if there was nothing to show that the nurse was incompetent or that the surgeon knew of this.[35] However, even in such a situation it is clearly his duty to give instructions which are essential to the safety and well-being of the patient when there are unusual features in the case or its treatment.

When an emergency requires all the doctor's attention, it is clear that he must leave minor details to the nurse. Thus a physician endeavoring to save a patient from heart failure may not be held responsible for the negligence of a nursing assistant who burns the patient at that time.

Frequently a patient is still in jeopardy after his intensive treatment has ended and possibly after he has been discharged. If the patient himself must observe certain precautions to avoid aggravation of a present injury or a reinjury, the doctor will be liable unless he gives the patient the necessary warning and advice about the care required. If the doctor transmits this information to a nurse to give to the patient orally or in writing, the nurse can be held liable for failure to provide such information or for giving incorrect or incomplete information.

The extent and degree of instruction required for a superior to give a subordinate will vary for the same patient condition depending on the experience and qualifications of the subordinate. However, in hospitals, instructions for routine care may not need to be given since it is reasonable to assume in most instances that persons entrusted with the tasks are sufficiently trained and experienced. When there is reasonable basis for doubt or when special procedures are required, greater care in selecting and instructing the assistant is in order.

In a Pennsylvania case,[36] the court used the master-of-the-ship theory and the borrowed-servant rule to analyze a situation where a transfusion of the wrong blood type that was provided by the hospital's blood bank employee caused the patient's death. This case exposed a curious situation that can find the *real* master and the *temporary* master liable in the same instance. The hospital, as employer of the technician, settled with the plaintiff out of court for $60,000, and no suit was instituted. The plaintiff brought suit against the doctor and ultimately gained a judgment of $89,318.

JUDGMENTS AGAINST TORT–FEASORS

Our judiciary systems recognize that, when a plaintiff joins in his complaint a number of defendants who may be liable as individuals or collectively, the court may decide on pro rata shares for each of the wrongdoers, or *tort-feasors,* as they are called.

Pennsylvania provides for contribution among tort-feasors at the time the judgment is granted (so does New York and other states). In our present case, however, contribution was not available because the plaintiff did not name the hospital as a defendant, since they had settled out of court. The physician did not establish the hospital's joinder as a codefendant, which might have been possible under both state and federal rules of practice.

The court found the physician vicariously negligent for the technician's error under the master-of-the-ship theory, thus accepting the premise that one can at the same time serve two masters. Here the technician was a borrowed servant under the control of the physician, while at the same time an employee of the hospital. Since they were not joined in the trial, the issue was not raised, but, on the court's reasoning, a plaintiff could collect from each master for the same servant's negligence.

APPLICATION OF THE FOREGOING THEORIES

As an exercise in doctrine surrounding the relationship of physician and nurse, examine the following situation from a Connecticut case.[37] A doctor examines an elderly patient in his office and finds that she needs an adenoidectomy and tonsillectomy. Her family is anxious, and the physician assures them that he will have her admitted to a good hospital and will take care of everything necessary to ensure her safety. As part of her preoperative preparation and again postoperatively, the physician directs that she receive a total of three intramuscular injections into her buttock. A nurse who is a hospital employee gives these injections according to the physician's directions, but in his absence. The patient complains of paralysis in her left leg, and her medical expert advises that it was due to penetration of the hypodermic needle in or about the sciatic nerve. The physician is the named defendant because the hospital cannot be sued. It enjoys charitable immunity in its broadest form under Connecticut law, which we shall examine in detail in a later chapter.

1. Should the court find the physician liable on grounds of respondeat superior?

The court answered in the negative since it was shown that the hospital nurses were not in his employ, that he did not even know who carried out his orders at the time, and that he did not at any time exercise control and supervision over the negligent nurse.

2. Could he be held liable under the borrowed servant doctrine?

The court held again in the negative because the plaintiff could not show even transitory control over the nurse while she administered the injections.

3. What recourse did the harmed patient then have?

She could have sued the nurse. She could have sued the doctor for breach of his oral contract made in the course of reassuring the patient and her family.

She chose the last course since, as a practical matter, the nurse without insurance did not represent a good collection possibility. The plaintiff won on the breach of contract claim in the lower court, only to have it reversed on appeal on the grounds that the oral contract was strained in such an interpretation.

A similar case occurred in Pennsylvania, but in this case the hospital was found liable. A student nurse injected iron dextran using the Z-track technique in the presence of a nursing supervisor. The court held the nursing student and her employer, the hospital, liable since she was selected by the hospital and controlled by it for the action.[38] Perhaps some additional details of this action are helpful. This case was tried in the federal court, and was based on injury allegedly stemming from a physician's order for a series of injections to be given by nurses to an infant. The final injection of the series was administered by the student nurse under the supervision of a registered nurse. The injection apparently penetrated the sciatic nerve causing immediate intense pain and inflammation and subsequent paralysis of the little girl's leg.

There are several things of interest in this case. First, note that the federal court in a particular district applies the legal principles that are usual in that state. Therefore, since Pennsylvania recognizes the master-of-the-ship doctrine, it could be applied. As we have seen, this doctrine holds the surgeon liable for improper acts on the part of his own staff or hospital personnel working under him during surgery and even in preoperative and postoperative procedures. The court noted that this was not a surgical procedure, and the doctrine should not apply.

Second, the physician gave particular and illustrative instruction to the charge nurse about the injection, pointing out that it was to be done in the infant's buttock utilizing the Z-track technique. In that hospital all nurses were trained to give such injections as a standard and regular part of the hospital service. When this situation is established by the evidence, it accomplishes two things. First it removes the physician's responsibility since he would be justified in relying on the nurse's skill in carrying out the order. Second, it does away with any defense of claiming only average skill and average responsibility of the average nurse in that community. Here we see admittedly better than minimal standards in practice.

The case, however, was still ultimately decided on agency and respondeat superior principles.

CASE CITATIONS

1. *Wood v. Miller,* 158 Ore. 444 (1938).
2. *Mohr v. Schmitt,* 189 So. 2d 46 (1966).
3. *Dunlap v. Marine,* 51 Cal. Rptr. 158 (1967).
4. *Good v. W. Seattle Hospital,* 335 Pac. 2d 590 (1909).
5. *Cyprus Case,* 375 F. 2d 648 (1967).
6. *Simkins v. Moses H. Cone Memorial Hospital,* 323 F. 2d 959 (1963).
7. *Smith v. Hampton Training School for Nurses,* 360 F. 2d 577 (1966).
8. *Cypress v. Newport News General and Non-Sectarian Hospital Association,* 251 F. Supp. 667 (1966).
9. *Sealey v. Finkelstein,* 206 N.Y. 2d 512 (1960).
10. *Burrows v. Hawaiian Trust,* 417 P. 2d 816 (1966).
11. *Watt v. United States,* 264 F. Supp. 386 (1966).

12. *Thigpen v. Executive Committee of Baptist Convention,* 152 S.E. 2d 920 (1966).
13. *Kerwood v. Rolling Hill Corporation,* 225 A. 2d 918 (1967).
14. *Dini v. Naiditch,* 20 Ill. 2d 406; 86 A.L.R. 2d 1184 (1960).
15. *Darling v. Charleston Community Memorial Hospital,* 211 N.E. 2d 253 (1965).
16. Recent federal court decision, 420 F. 2d 661.
17. *Filotel v. Carney,* 98 N.Y. Supp. 174 (1961).
18. *State v. LaDuke,* 202 A. 2d 913 (1963).
19. *Neary v. Carbondale Hospital,* 181 Pa. Supp. 189 (1956).
20. *Paider v. Park East Movers,* 19 N.Y. 2d 373 (1967).
21. Case noted, 153 N.Y. Supp. 2d 50 (1956).
22. *Steeves v. Irwin,* 233 A. 2d 126 (1967).
23. *Orth v. Shiely Petter,* 91 N.W. 2d 463 (1958).
24. *Terry v. Mixon,* 361 Pac. 2d 180 (1961).
25. Lampkin case, 407 S.W. 2d 894 (1966).
26. *Turner v. Guiliano,* 216 N.E. 2d 562 (1966).
27. *Watts v. J. S. Young Company,* 225 A. 2d 865 (1967).
28. *Gray v. McLaughlin,* 179 S.W. 2d 686 (1944).
29. *Rundle v. California State Board of Pharmacy,* 240 Cal. App. 2d 254; 17 A.L.R. 3d 1408 (1966).
30. Nichols case, Supreme Court No. 96 (1964).
31. *Campbell v. Preston,* 379 S.W. 2d 557 (1964).
32. *Parmerter v. Osteopathic General Hospital,* 196 So. 2d 505 (1967).
33. *Clary v. Christiansen,* 83 N.E. 2d 644 (1948).
34. *Shull v. Schwartz,* 73 A. 2d 402 (1950).
35. *Morrison v. Heanke et al.,* 165 Wis. 166 (1917).
36. *Mayer v. P. Lipshutz,* 360 F. 2d 275 (1966).
37. *Bria v. St. Joseph's Hospital,* 220 A. 2d 29 (1966).
38. *Honeywell v. Rogers,* 251 F. Supp. 841 (1966).

CHAPTER 4

DELEGATION

In 1968 the author was called upon to mediate a dispute between nurses and physicians at a hospital center. The dispute was based upon delegation to nurses by physicians, in one division of the hospital, of functions the nurse believed to be exclusively within the practice of medicine. This situation was brought about by (1) the extreme shortage of physicians available to practice this particular specialty, (2) the large number of patients who would not be helped unless the nurses assumed some of the duties involved, and (3) the fact that a federal grant of funds for research in this particular area encouraged the institution to overcommit its facilities and personnel.

The nurses selected to staff this program had all had experience in a related area of practice and were to receive some in-service education. They were asked to see the patients and their parents or friends who might accompany them, to examine prior physician findings about these patients, to write out a formal diagnosis using certain standard physician terminology, and to initiate treatment on the basis of standing orders. In some instances the last duty required prescribing and dispensing drugs from stocks made available through the hospital pharmacy.

The nurses felt that they were being asked to assume too much responsibility for the patient, that they were vulnerable to prosecution for practicing medicine without a license, and that they were potentially liable for patient lawsuits as well. The physicians felt that the public needed this help, and that if it were provided by knowledgeable professional people, even without physicians' assistance, it was better than no help at all. They felt that if nurses, who were better qualified than any but physicians, refused to undertake it, then they would have to seek nonprofessional assistance to the detriment of all concerned.

Following the author's presentation of the issues involved, made during his mediation of the dispute between nurses and physicians at the hospital center, it was mutually agreed that nurses selected and assigned to this duty would be pretrained for it to supplement their background experience and their ongoing education. This pretraining would deal with the specific needs for observation, technical and medical language, method and purpose of reporting. Furthermore, the nurses would list their impressions and assessments on the chart rather than as a formal diagnosis. At frequent and stated intervals a team headed by a physician would go over these and formalize them into a diagnosis with the physician's signature if approved. Nurses would not prescribe medication. Finally, it was agreed that the entire matter would be formalized and communicated to the appropriate hospital authorities for their acknowledgement and approval.

Although the matter was settled to the mutual satisfaction of all, the author had to advise them to continue to add all possible safeguards and improvements to this structure because it is impossible to guarantee freedom from prosecution or litigation where duties defined in nursing practice acts are exceeded.

PROBLEMS INVOLVED IN DELEGATION

The foregoing situation illustrates two problems: (1) the doctor's increasing delegation to the nurse of medical functions, and (2) the resulting ambiguity about the duties of the nurse in this transitional period. The problem does not end with the professional nurse, though we shall deal primarily with her in this chapter. As one action produces an equal and opposite reaction, so the professional nurse, with her newly acquired responsibilities, is forced to delegate some of her traditional functions to practical nurses, nursing students, and auxiliary personnel. This has created another gray area where responsibilities are not traditionally or statutorily fixed entirely. The following discussion will give some idea of the dimensions of the problem.

As a historical antecedent to the matter of delegation, we must remember that many procedures presently part of medical and surgical practice were performed by lay persons of special training and experience, and were frequently predicated on lengthy apprenticeship. This was true in the areas of surgery, bleeding, treatment of skin conditions, and midwifery. However, we are considering delegation that has evolved from a shortage of physicians, interns, and residents in the United States and Canada and has increasingly called upon nurses to perform various medical procedures.

These questionable transfers of authority represent potential malpractice suits, often devoid of insurance protection since they arise from what may be illegal actions. They range from giving injections to ordering the refilling of prescriptions, and they include dispensing of drugs by nonpharmacists.[1] Thus, the increase in the delegation of duties has led to a series of considerations for all members of the health care team. These considerations affect contract law, tort law, and criminal law. For example, they may create liability in negligence (tort) because they show carelessness or ignorance of skills; they may involve statutory crime because they violate nursing practice acts or ignore criminal statutes; they may create liability by breaching implied or express contracts to the public, professionals, or employees.

Responsibility of the Physician

It should be borne in mind that the right to practice a profession such as medicine is a personal privilege. Where a physician delegates a part of this personal privilege, his justification to do so rests on the premise that this element is still under his personal supervision. If the task is a mechanical or a common technical act that will be promptly reviewed and interpreted by the doctors, delegation may be reasonable and permissible. But if medical judgment and discretion are involved, only the physician can undertake the task, unless he has a trained, experienced agent performing it under his direct supervision.

The physician must also determine foreseeable danger to a patient, and the number of times that a dangerous situation has arisen is not, of itself, a valid measure of foreseeability. For example, in prescribing drugs, the physician would be wise to forbid an agent to order a prescription orally that he would not allow her to place in writing. If he will not permit her to write a prescription and sign his name, why let her give the prescription orally?

Ambiguous Position of the Nurse Delagee

Professional nurses are being upgraded to perform some physician tasks that require a high order of skill. These include giving intravenous solutions and injections of various types, as well as using x-ray equipment and the new and sophisticated equipment of the operating room and the recovery room.[2]

Nursing associations have divided nursing functions into those which are dependent and independent, and the associations are justly concerned about those functions which are really medical acts, though they may fit into either category. This occurs when licensed physicians delegate duties to nurses with substantial disregard of the nurse's education, training, and limitations. It has been said: "The nurse to whom the application and execution of legal orders of a physician is entrusted should be able to comprehend the cause and effect of the order." Using this general rule as a yardstick, since there is no specific statutory mention of which medical acts are delegable, we can see that some of these assumptions far exceed prudence. Therefore, where the superior entrusts such duties to her, the nurse must advise the superior of her own uncertainty and, in many instances, suggest that the assignment is not safely delegable. If these preventive steps are not taken and the patient is harmed, both nurse and superior are culpable.

We are concerned here primarily with delegation on a more or less permanent basis. However, if the nurse has been delegated physician tasks in an emergency, her ethical and legal position is somewhat different. The nurse should realize that emergency delegation represents only the danger of acting negligently or unreasonably. It is within the more regular pattern of undertaking procedures beyond the scope of her licensure and training that the nurse's real danger ensues. So it is one thing for a nurse, unable to reach the attending physician or the resident in time, to deliver a woman of her child, and it is quite another for her to do this numerous times throughout the year.

Need to Redefine Nursing Practices

In reference to permanent delegation, the A.N.A.'s Committee on Nursing Practice has stated: "Where a doctor delegates a medical act to a nurse, she does not in fact have a legal right to initiate it— unless state law also gives her this right. The legal right to perform medical acts must be granted by statute." Even though these delegations seem valid responses to necessity, the legal implications of the assumption of new duties or the delegation of duties will call for new transmissions of responsibility and new transfers of training.

In a legal sense, there is a need for redefining nursing functions since court actions based on malpractice and negligence will, in all probability, take a much more conservative view of the rationale for these changes, and decisions will be based on patients' rights rather than on hospital or professional needs or on economics. It would therefore seem that nursing practice acts need to be rewritten and that those provinces or states not requiring licensure will need to introduce such a requirement to ensure that their nurses are qualified to assume expanding responsibilities in the public welfare. This will also be true of the downward flow of delegated responsibilities. State health authorities will have to undertake the burden of verifying individual fitness for technical work and patient care by setting up certification procedures based on eligibility through education and experience. New York State has recently done this in relation to responsibilities of x-ray technologists.

IMPORTANCE OF PROPER DELEGATION WITHIN THE NURSING TEAM

The responsibilities involved in delegating downward are repeated within the nursing team. One independent function of the professional nurse is assigning tasks to the practical nurses, nursing students, nurse's aides and attendants with whom she works. Where a nursing supervisor delegates nursing duties to anyone who has lesser functional status and fewer skills than a nurse, whether it be a nursing student, orderly, technician, or nursing assistant, the supervisor has the responsibility for making a good choice and providing competent supervision. In the case of a nursing student or trainee, this responsibility is shared with the nursing instructor.

Generally, lay people have no means of knowing the limitations of a nurse's education, experience, and licensure. They cannot differentiate among the proper functional distinctions of various members of the nursing team, nor even among those of various members of the entire health team. In a practitioner's office they address anyone uniformed in white as "nurse," even when she is actually his receptionist. Therefore, whether he is catheterized by a student nurse, has stitches emplaced or removed by a nurse, or has a nurse examine him and send him home, the lay person usually cannot judge whether that individual is exceeding her rights within the act of health care.

Although there are no written statutes covering the subject, court-room law recognizes that so long as the act would not raise a question of ordinary lay prudence, the lay person has the right to expect that whoever performs a service for him is in every sense qualified to render that service. Therefore, even the supervisor's assignment of a licensed trained nurse to a specific job only at first glance satisfies the proper standards for delegation of duties. The nurse must be assigned because, by the exercise of good judgment and ordinary prudence, her superior feels she is qualified.

Selecting Qualified Personnel

Where a special qualification of training is essential, law and common sense both dictate that especially capable nurses may be required. This is true for nurses who serve in intensive-care units, coronary care units, isolation and rehabilitation wards, operating rooms, and recovery rooms.

In especially vulnerable places such as recovery rooms, the supervisor should make a competent professional nurse primarily responsible, and the employment of any less skilled persons should be under the close supervision, care, and training of the supervisor and the professional nurse to whom she has delegated responsibilty. After all, in the recovery room the nurse must be alert to note changes in muscle flexion (foot drop in a patient treated for hemorrhage), patency of airways, signs of cerebral hypoxia, management of drainage tubes, and pupillary signs (bloody).

Hospital and office assignments require differing backgrounds of instruction and experience, as well as differing temperament and personality patterns. Compare, for example, the positions of the operating room (OR) nurse and the pediatric ward nurse.

The patient's age, sex, and physical condition may largely determine the consideration that will have a bearing on the choice of nursing personnel. Therefore, when delegating jobs among all members of the nursing team, the supervisor must consider the propriety of selection from a mental and physical point of view and according to the extent of training that the duty requires.

A rather infamous example of inadequate training is seen in an Illinois case where a patient died following an operation.[3] A student nurse and operating room supervisor were implicated in this case. Testimony developed the fact that death was allegedly caused by leaving a laparotomy sponge in the patient's abdomen after a cesarean section had been performed. A student nurse with four days' experience in the operating room had been delegated the responsibility of the sponge count, although she maintained no one had even told her that a final count was necessary, much less checked with her to see if it had been done. The operating room supervisor was found liable for the judgment of damages.

Oral medication may be administered by a nurse's aide if it is so uncomplicated that a hardy patient might self-administer it. A simple and conservative test is to ask if this is the kind of dosage, medication, and administration that a prudent physician would direct the patient or a member of his family to administer. If so, the task may not require a registered nurse. But the time that it is administered and the patient's reactions might be recorded by a professional nurse.

FORMALIZING DELEGATION

As nursing education develops, tasks more recently being assigned to nurses are evaluated for addition to the curriculum. While this does not make such tasks certain of being accepted as ordinary nursing practice in a court of law, it does lend some color of community standard. Perhaps most importantly, the evaluations may lead to extended nursing training to include the particular functions. But the physician shortage is becoming more critical, and the nursing associations must be alert to the dangers of delegation dictated solely by economic necessity. Therefore, they should, and do, confer with physicians and hospital authorities in reviewing mutually acceptable avenues of nursing extension.[4]

Canadian Practice

As an example, in Canada a listing of "Approved Medical-Nurse Procedures" was published after consultation between the Executive Committee of the Registered Nurses' Association and the Provincial Liaison Committee on Nursing, composed of representatives from the Medical Society of Nova Scotia, the Nova Scotia Hospital Association, and the Registered Nurses' Association of Nova Scotia.

They agreed that the nurse "could" or "might" do the following:

1. Insert a Levin tube, if so instructed
2. Remove sutures and drains postoperatively
3. Syringe the aural canal
4. Remove packing, particularly vaginal packing
5. Vaccinate and inject gamma globulin, subject to the usual requirements of a doctor's orders

They also noted that nurses should be able to apply and remove certain types of traction after the doctor applies the initial traction.

Female nurses should be capable of catheterizing male patients when a male nurse or orderly is not available. This would seem to indicate that the Canadian groups believe that an orderly can catheterize patients. Some physicians and patients might not agree.

As to intravenous therapy, the Canadian associations agreed that "selected registered nurses" could do this provided their practice meets with the approval of the chiefs of medicine and the nursing and medical administration; also, each hospital must be amply protected with requisite liability insurance. It is assumed that "selected" means registered nurses qualified by special training and experience—but no mention is made of direct physician supervision.

Certain procedures, they advise, are never to be undertaken by a nurse because they are clearly outside her training and function. These are as follows:

1.   Injection of anesthetic solution into the epidural tube
2.   Removal of casts
3.   Injection of I.V.P. dye
4.   Pronouncing a patient dead in the absence of a physician

The "Joint Recommendations on Medical-Nursing Procedures," set forth in 1965 by the British Columbia Hospital's Association and the Registered Nurses' Association of British Columbia after consultation and agreement with the province's College of Physicians and Surgeons, is more detailed and therefore generally more restrictive. Portions of the statement are reproduced in the Appendix. Certain packings and drains are to be inserted solely by the *physician;* these include packings in plastic surgery, those generally inserted to prevent or control hemorrhage, and those in scrotal or rectal areas. Any removal or shortening of drains is not a nursing function, and a physician should instill and irrigate T-tubes and other tubes that go into such organs as the kidney or gall bladder. Nurses are precluded from performing all suturing in emergency departments as well as removing sutures from highly vascularized areas such as the inside of the mouth or the area near the eyes. They are not to remove sutures following plastic surgery, stay sutures, or sutures from a tracheotomy incision while the tracheotomy tube is still in position.

On the doctor's orders, graduate nurses may remove ordinary skin sutures and colostomy rods, and they may change uncomplicated dressings and cleanse (not debride) decubitus ulcers. They may not change burn dressings, nor may they cleanse or debride burn areas or areas in which plastic surgery was done. Only a physician should undertake debridement of any wound. Nurses are not to undertake IV therapy or blood transfusions unless specially trained and qualified in hospitals which approve such procedures.

The nurse may not do a cutdown; she may add drugs only as approved and directed into the bottle. Only a doctor may inject a drug directly into the vein or tubing or administer an ergot-type of drug IV.

Certain obstetric limitations are notable, such as a nurse's preclusion from performing a vaginal examination or initiating a Pitocin infusion.

The nurse may not apply a cast or traction for a fracture or splint a limb (other than for first aid).

She may not perform tasks usually assigned to an anesthetist, such as administering anesthetics or changing tracheotomy tubes.

She may not insert a Levin tube in patients who are unconscious, those who have had gastric surgery, immature newborns, or pediatric patients. She may not break up barium impactions with vulsellum forceps and proctoscope.

Responsibility for informed consents, postmortems, and abortions is placed solely upon physicians.

United States Practice

In the United States, two sets of guidelines have been established for the nurse in the gray area of delegation: joint statements and statutes.

JOINT STATEMENTS AND DEPENDENT NURSING FUNCTIONS

Included in the Appendix is a joint statement on non-nursing activities carried out by nursing personnel in some hospitals and issued by the British Columbia Hospitals' Association and the Registered Nurses' Association of British Columbia (1966). The study included observations about utilization of the nurse in performing functions of other departmental staff members; it proved that nurses are involved with actual work or supervision of dietary, housekeeping, pharmacy, laboratory, x-ray, and social service departments. It is human nature for nurses to resist dietary or housekeeping functions with more vigor than other functions, since the latter require a specialized type of skill that, if developed, increases the nurse's stature and importance to the hospital employer.

Purposes of Statements

Joint statements have numerous purposes. The most obvious is to set limits to guide nurses in problems of practice within the dependent functions of nursing. The American Nurses' Association defines the dependent function of nursing to be "the administration of medications and treatments prescribed by a licensed physician or dentist." Within this area of function there are many responsibilities and activities that doctors have sought to pass on to the nurse —with varying purposes and varying degrees of success.

Another purpose of the joint statements is to lessen the possibility of violation of medical practice acts and prosecution thereunder. At the same time, when the statements have been issued in a particular state or province, they alert nurses to avoid undertaking functions not covered by them and therefore having no authority whatsoever. A nurse who is asked to perform a function not mentioned in the joint statement has sufficient basis to refuse, and the state nursing association will probably support her.

It is important that nurses be acquainted with the scope and substance of joint statements of their state or province of practice. Copies of these are generally available from the state or provincial nursing association.

How Statements Are Formulated

The procedures by which joint statements come into being are generally fairly similar from state to state. For example, the California Nurses' Association invites professional, administrative, and legal representatives of appropriate California associations with vital related interests (e.g., California Medical Association and California Hospital Association) to attend joint meetings. These groups, through liaison committee action or discussion among the representatives, prepare the joint statement, which is submitted to the boards of each interacting organization for approval. After complete agreement is obtained, the joint statement is published and distributed.

Examples of Practices Covered by the Statements

Sometimes joint statements disapprove of a suggested nursing practice. For example, a joint statement issued a few years ago by the California Nursing Association opposed the use of hypnosis by a nurse.

Often the joint statement allows and disallows according to the ground rules and circumstances envisioned by the groups. For example, a few years ago the New York State Nursing Association, the Medical Society, and the Hospital Association of New York State jointly stated that the administration of anesthesia during labor is a medical procedure to be delegated by the attending physician only to a qualified physician or nurse-anesthetist. Therefore, a registered professional nurse who is not qualified should not undertake, or be permitted to undertake, such a function unless all concerned are willing to assume the risk.

Colorado's 1966 joint statement regarding defibrillation discusses the practical and institutional considerations as to whether such a function should be allowed. It then outlines certain prescribed conditions under which the procedure can take place.

The following extract from the Colorado joint statement can also be applied to similar tasks that were never previously regarded as nursing acts.

> 3. Registered professional nurses assigned to the care of such patients being monitored are specially selected and have had specific instructions. Specific instructions include theory and demonstration in the use of the monitoring system, interpretation of this system and subsequent necessary defibrillation and practice in the use of these techniques under direct medical supervision.
>
> 4. Registered professional nurses perform this treatment only on the order of a licensed physician for a specific patient.
>
> 5. Each registered professional nurse must exercise professional judgment in determining her qualifications and competency to perform this treatment.

Effectiveness of Statements

As stated previously, lawyers tend to feel that joint statements do not positively protect the professional groups against litigation or prosecution; such statements are, however, influential. In 1967 the California Nursing Association pointed out that "when under the Joint Statement, the medical, nursing, and administrative staff of an organization have established the required written criteria, and the nurse has followed the criteria, there has never been an indictment brought against her by the Board of Medical Examiners."

No matter how many associations concur in a joint statement, however, the nurse is still responsible for her own acts. For example, the California joint statements repeatedly emphasize that the procedures and activities of some functions require elaborate training and experience and are subject to the exercise of prudence and judgment. Such functions would include glaucoma screening tests;

closed chest cardiac resuscitation; and intravenous administration of fluids, including the addition of drugs.

United States Practice

JOINT STATEMENTS AND INDEPENDENT NURSING FUNCTIONS

Among the commonly recognized independent nursing functions (discussed in "Independent Functions," Chapter 2) are the following:

1. Evaluation of the patient's condition with respect to his ability to care for himself as well as the personal, adequate nursing attendance required
2. Interpretation of the environmental and psychological needs of the patient
3. Observation of symptoms and reactions
4. Recording and reporting of facts and evaluations upon which medical care and treatment may depend
5. Supervision of nonphysicians engaged in patient care
6. Application and execution of nursing procedures and techniques

These are readily differentiated from those functions performed under the legal orders, direction, or supervision of licensed physicians, dentists, and, in some instances, nurses of higher professional or employment status. The fact that a dependent or independent nursing function has preceded the act complained of by a plaintiff does not in itself decide whether malpractice or negligence is involved.

Purpose of Statements

Nursing associations are also interested in making available standards of care relating to independent nursing functions. Statements have been issued jointly by state nursing, medical, and hospital associations to place guideposts within the gray areas between traditional nursing functions and those covered by medical and dental practice acts. Nurses have also effected joint position statements with pharmacy groups and others for the same purpose. These statements have come about through professional education as well as private litigation. The latter focused attention on the fact that the nurse's employer often examined only the short-range implication of a particular duty the nurse was asked to assume within the area of dependent nursing function; that is, he failed to consider that special professional competence might be required to safeguard what might seem simple, or at most technical, procedures.

Examples of Practices Covered by the Statements

HANDLING OF DRUGS

The nursing and pharmacy associations of several states including Pennsylvania, Arizona, and Michigan have recognized the complexity and poetency of drugs in present use and have asked nurses and pharmacists to observe statutory and ethical safeguards.

> Therefore, professional nurses are educated and subsequently duly licensed only to administer medications: administration is the giving of a unit dose of medication to a patient as a result of a physician's order. Administration affects only one patient. . . . The pharmacist is educated and duly licensed to dispense medications. Dispensing is defined as the issuing of one or more doses in a suitable container such container being properly labeled by the dispenser as to contents, and directions for use. . . . Pharmacists are licensed to dispense . . . not to administer. Therefore, nurses, as well as all other persons not properly qualified, should not be required to, nor be permitted, to dispense drugs or perform other pharmaceutical functions.

> Both associations believe that implementation of the recommendations can reduce medication errors and provide safe care for patients.

In its discussion of the nurse handling drugs, the statement makes a number of important cautionary points. For example, the nurse's qualification and concern about drugs involves the act of administration, which is defined as giving a single dose to a patient pursuant to the order of a doctor or dentist. For this purpose, removal of this single dose from the pharmacy to the nursing station is included in administration.

Registered professional nurses may now administer intravenous medications in a number of states, New York included. However, intravenous procedures other than those permitted are illegal and in criminal and civil violation of the medical practice acts if carried out by any person other than a physician. The attorney general of New York stated: "Intravenous procedures limited solely to those involving venepuncture by needle which do not involve incision into or incision to reach a vein, reasonably can be considered to be encompassed within the language of the statute giving a registered professional nurse authority to carry out treatments and medications prescribed by a licensed physician." The nurse must, however, be qualified by training and experience sufficient to justify undertaking such a procedure.

Selection, purchasing, dispensing, and preparation of all drugs, along with dilution of IV solutions and narcotics control, are pharmacists' functions which should normally be taken over only by a physician. However, in many modern areas of nursing practice, the nurse finds that her handling of drugs has expanded from their administration to buying, storing, repackaging, and dispensing them. This is especially true in smaller institutions, clinics, industrial installations, and even physicians' offices. To accommodate the performance of these non-nursing functions, the role of the nurse as an agent of the physician must be expanded. The entire concept of the nurse as the physician's agent is being examined closely in state law and current decisions. Several states, such as Wisconsin and Washington, have taken hard positions to limit "emergency" circumstances where a nurse may extend her handling of drugs.

The law does not ordinarily contemplate that a pharmacist may administer drugs or that a nurse may dispense them. If they do these things in other than genuine emergency situations or without the direct supervision of a physician, they are in the area of illegal actions. The nurse is expected in law to administer drugs according to her legal status, training, and experience, and under direct orders from a licensed practitioner.

Any person engaged in handling drugs to be used as medicine is bound to exercise a high degree of care. Drug laws in the United States and Canada are generally formulated as criminal statutes. Since only a physician or a pharmacist may legally dispense drugs in an independent fashion, the nurse is on safest ground if she only administers medication—that is, she gives one dose of a drug to a designated patient.

In the province of Quebec, in accordance with the Pharmacy Act, registered pharmacists are the only legal distributors of drugs to the public. Where patients would suffer hardship because a pharmacist is not available, dispensing physicians may discharge that function. This is the accepted rule in many other localities.

When a medication error resulted from a misunderstanding between the prescribing physician and the administering nurse, a Louisiana court stated: "We believe it the duty of a nurse when in doubt about an order for medication to make absolutely certain what the doctor intended both as to dosage and route." Also, it is noteworthy that a contributory cause of the infant patient's death in this case was assumption of the dispensing function by a nurse with insufficient knowledge to realize that she had selected an erroneous and more potent form of the prescribed drug.[5]

A nurse today must resist, to a reasonable extent, such non-nursing tasks and forms of "medical assistanceship" as the above which are not realistically incidental to her legal and moral responsibility for providing nursing care for her patient. Such tasks should not be confused with the so-called "independent nursing functions," since the latter are included in the framework of the language of the nursing practice acts for both professional and practical nurses.

Today there is almost no prescribed drug that can be refilled by the pharmacist without written instruction to that effect on the original prescription. It may also be refilled if the physician telephones the pharmacist and authorizes the renewal and, depending upon the nature of the drug and the state's legal requirements, follows this up in a stated period of time with written confirmation of the renewal order or with a new prescription.

Can the physician's agent telephone a prescription to a pharmacist or authorize a renewal? The answer depends on the agent's qualifications. If the agent is also a physician, there is no problem. If the agent is a registered nurse with sufficient training to enable the physician to delegate this task to her under his direction and if the physician signs the prescription or the written confirmation of renewal, the transaction should be safe. Where, however, an oral prescription that need not be signed or confirmed is involved, the pharmacist is within his rights and on safer ground to ask that the physician personally telephone him. He may also request that the agent's recital of the actual prescription be preceded by the doctor's verbal assurance that she is conveying the information on his authority.

All narcotic drugs should be directly prescribed by the physician, whether he writes it on his prescription blank or the patient's chart or order sheet as hospital requirements may demand. Prescribing narcotic drugs should never be delegated even where they can be prescribed orally. If such a task is improperly delegated, it is questionable whether the pharmacist will receive and fill such an order.

Today's pharmacist realizes that the federal food and drug acts, narcotics laws, and laws affecting dispensation of barbiturates, tranquilizers, and similar drugs capable of abuse are all criminal laws. He is careful, therefore, to protect himself from the enforcement of these regulations, and a physician must measure very closely and realistically the amount of power he ought to delegate to an unlicensed practitioner or lay person.

EXTERNAL CARDIAC MASSAGE

Opinions may differ somewhat about the legal implications of external cardiac massage, an emergency method of cardiac resuscitation,[8] and other emergency procedures that are primarily within the physician's realm. The A.N.A. Committee on Nursing Practice has recommended that a nurse be prepared to assist rather than initiate the procedure, since it requires a medical diagnosis of the type that is excluded from the practice of nursing.

TESTS

Questions are frequently raised about the delegability of various tests that are interpreted by physicians, but not necessarily performed by them. The Attorney General of Oregon in 1966 offered an opinion in connection with some proposed licensing statutes that sought to distinguish diagnosis, which is unquestionably an act of medical practice, from technical performance of laboratory tests.

Diagnosis is defined by statute as the examination of a person for the purpose of determining the source or nature of a disease or other abnormal physical or mental condition. For example, the examination of body fluids to determine the presence or absence of an infectious agent is considered a diagnostic function. *Technical performance* of laboratory tests is limited by statute to the examination of human or animal body fluids, secretions, or excretions.

Under federal law, diagnostic agents and chemicals are drugs, even though their use may never require contact with a human or animal. Copper sulfate that is intended to be used to test urine for sugar and antibiotic sensitivity discs would both be considered drugs. However, it is only when drugs are introduced into the animal or human body that they must be labeled for use by or under a physician's supervision.

LABORATORY TESTS

Error

Dr. D. J. Sencer, director of the National Communicable Disease Center, stated while testifying before a U.S. Senate subcommittee in 1967: "Erroneous results are obtained in more than 25% of all tests analyzed. . . ." This statement was based on figures supplied from studies at the Center and elsewhere. It included bacteriological testing by tube dilution, discs, and plates; blood grouping, typing and hemoglobin measurement, c.b.c.'s, and differentials; and basic clinical chemistry analyses and measurement of serum electrolytes. While this high figure has been challenged and may not be truly indicative of the overall percentage of error in the United States and Canada, admittedly test results are not nearly 100 percent accurate.

Neither country has uniform regulations to determine personnel qualifications or to assure testing quality in terms of material and performance. Some states, including New York, do have licensure requirements, and many universities are now training medical technologists to supply quality manpower for this critical area of patient care.

Responsibilities of the Physician, Nurse, and Technician

The responsibility of a physician who accepts and acts upon erroneous test results is not clear-cut unless he knows or should reasonably conclude that he has placed the testing responsibility on a person of questionable training, experience, and competence. The attending physician cannot be held liable for acts over which he had and could have had no control.[7]

The physician is responsible for informing the nurse of factors that may interfere with the reliability of these determinations. He should tell her the procedure for obtaining and handling the particular specimen. And, if she delegates this duty to another, she should forward the instructions accurately. Very often the timing of the collection of blood or other body fluids is crucial. The nurse should record such data as therapeutic and diagnostic clues to which she can refer the physician. For example, the physician will expect specimens to be collected for glucose or lipid determinations before a meal, lest they be misleading. If taken after a meal, the nurse should bring this to the doctor's attention. Similarly, if the nurse observes that the patient has had a row with a visitor, another patient, or a member of the staff, hormonal measurement and glucose and cholesterol readings can well be misleading. Glucose, lactic acid, and serum protein readings may be unreliable if they are based on specimens collected when the patient has just returned from the hydrotherapy or physiotherapy department.

Once they are collected by the technologist or nurse, the specimens cannot be neglected without fear of prejudicing the analysis. Even temporary delays may require refrigeration or freezing in special instances, such as where serum or plasma for acid and alkaline phosphatase tests are concerned. In other tests, such as the test for serum glutamic oxaloacetic transaminase, cells must be initially separated by centrifuge to avoid hemolysis. Insofar as laboratory procedures are concerned, only registered laboratory technologists should perform routine tests and take specimens of blood or gastric contents. Unfortunately, this is not a uniform or general practice throughout the United States and Canada.

Since the nurse records the time, quantity, and names of drugs administered to the patient, she serves as a reminder to the physician that many common tests are affected by specific drugs. Natural and synthetic opiates influence serum amylase measurements, and dextran chemically interferes with bilirubin determinations. Of course, drugs used as contrast media in gall bladder studies and intravenous pyelography will invalidate tests of thyroid function.

ELECTROCARDIOGRAPHY

Most often physicians delegate to their assistants the patient's preparation for electrocardiography. The instrument is a quartz string galvanometer that photographs the passage of minute electric currents produced by the human heart in the course of its activity. However, for an accurate reading, the skin current, which is of higher amplitude than the heart current, must be overcome. Since skin current varies both among individuals and within the same individual, this preparatory adjustment must be made at the time the machine is used. The nurse or technician may or may not have had instruction in this, and, thus, she may not understand its significance. If she does not, it is the physician's duty to instruct her. If she performs poorly, or merely uses a standard voltage she believes to be equal in amount but opposite in polarity, the findings may be distorted.

Practitioners will usually agree with lawyers and jurists who have said that the ultimate objective in defining the scope of professional practice should be protection of the public. A rule-of-thumb evolving from this objective is that any activity which can be performed by nonphysician personnel without increasing the risk of harm to a patient, even though such functions were traditionally carried out by physicians, should be acceptable when it does not endanger the public's safety. Necessity has carried this principle to extremes to meet wartime or military needs, national disasters, and the like. It is now being extended in civilian and ordinary circumstances as well.

There are two approaches to the problem of increasing delegation. One is essentially an ethical and professional approach. Here, to satisfy public need, physicians delegate certain of their erstwhile functions to nonphysicians. Such delegation has certain basic requirements:

1. The delagees must have been trained and educated to undertake the functions assigned.

2. They must be supervised and directed, and their work must be reviewed.

3. No functions are to be delegated that a nonphysician could not and should not undertake even under such conditions.

4. Delegating a task should never endanger the patient's welfare.

5. The physician should feel reasonably certain that it is not feasible to perform the task in another way, that other physicians are not available, and that the plan would not outrage his professional judgments or the public's sense of fairness.

NURSING PRACTICE ACTS

Second is the legal approach, which is essentially more rigid. The joint statements on dependent and independent functions constitute the nursing profession's protection and self-regulation; nursing practice acts are their statutory counterpart. The acts state that a nurse who undertakes a physician's duties or prerogatives is practicing medicine without a license. A physician who has her do this is guilty of an unprofessional act: abetting nonphysicians in practicing medicine without a license. An institution that sanctions such an act will be held liable for any harm that is allegedly proximately caused by it.

Medical Practice Defined

Let us examine the medical practice act as it applies to nurses. Following is an excerpt from Handbook 13 of the New York State Education Department. (The italics, for emphasis, are the author's.)

ARTICLE 131

Medicine; Osteopathy; Physiotherapy

§ 6501. **Definitions.** As used in this article:

1. "Board" means the board of medical examiners of the state of New York.

2. "Medical examiner" means a member of the board of medical examiners of the state of New York.

3. 'Medical school" means any medical school, college or department of a university, registered by the regents as maintaining a proper medical standard and as legally incorporated.

4. *The practice of medicine is defined as* follows: A person practices medicine within the meaning of this article, except as hereinafter stated, who holds himself out as being able to *diagnose, treat, operate* or *prescribe* for any human disease, pain, injury, deformity or physical condition, and who shall *either offer or undertake,* by any means or method, *to diagnose, treat, operate* or *prescribe for any human disease,* pain, injury, deformity or physical condition.

5. "Physician" means a practitioner of medicine.

6. Physiotherapy and/or physical therapy is defined as the use of actinotherapy, hydrotherapy, which shall include under hydrotherapy, electric baths of all types, medicated baths of all types and the giving of colonic irrigations; mechanotherapy, which shall include all types of therapeutic exercise, thermotherapy, and electrotherapy, exclusive of the x-ray.

7. "Physiotherapist", "mechanotherapist" and "physical therapist" have the same meaning and effect. (*Amended L. 1964, ch. 548*)

§ 6502. **Qualifications for practice.** *No person shall practice medicine, unless registered and legally authorized prior to September first, eighteen hundred ninety-one, or unless licensed by the regents and registered under article eight of chapter six hundred sixty-one of the laws of eighteen hundred ninety-three* and acts amendatory thereto, *or unless licensed by the department and registered as required by this article. . . .*

Following is a punishment clause. It must be remembered, however, that these unlawful acts may be considered felonies rather than misdemeanors in some jurisdictions.

§ 6513. **Penalties.** 1. *Any person shall be guilty of a misdemeanor* who shall:

a. Sell or fraudulently obtain or furnish any medical, osteopathic or physiotherapeutic diploma, license, record, or registration, or aid or abet in the same; or

b. Practice medicine, osteopathy or physiotherapy under cover of any diploma, license, record or registration illegally or fraudulently obtained or signed or issued unlawfully or under fraudulent representation or mistake of fact in a material regard; or

c. Advertise to practice medicine, osteopathy or physiotherapy under a name other than his own or under a false or assumed name.

2. Any person shall be guilty of a misdemeanor who not being then lawfully licensed or authorized to practice medicine, osteopathy or physiotherapy within this state shall

a. *Practice* or advertise to practice *medicine,* osteopathy or physiotherapy; or

c. In the prosecution of any criminal action for violation of this article by the attorney-general or his deputy, said attorney-general or his deputy shall exercise all the powers and perform all the duties with respect to such actions or proceedings which the district attorney would otherwise be authorized or required to exercise or perform, and in such actions or proceedings the district attorney shall only exercise such powers and perform such duties as are required of him by the attorney-general or the deputy attorney-general so attending.

6.   The display by any person of a sign or an advertisement bearing a name as a practitioner of medicine, osteopathy or physiotherapy in any manner or by implication or containing any other matter forbidden by law shall be presumptive evidence in any prosecution or hearing of a holding out and of the practice of medicine, osteopathy or physiotherapy by such person for each separate day such sign or advertisement is anywhere displayed by anyone; but such presumptions shall be rebuttable by the defense. It shall be necessary to prove in any prosecution or hearing under this article only by a single act prohibited by law or a single holding out or an attempt without proving a general course of conduct, in order to constitute a violation.

7.   In any action for damages for personal injuries or death against a person not licensed hereunder for any act or acts constituting the practice of medicine, osteopathy or physiotherapy, when such act or acts were a competent producing proximate or contributing cause of such injuries or death, the fact that such person practiced medicine, osteopathy or physiotherapy without being duly licensed shall be deemed prima facie evidence of negligence.

8.   All violations of this article, when reported to the department and duly substantiated by affidavits or other satisfactory evidence, shall be investigated and if the report is found to be true and the complaint substantiated, the department *shall report* such violation to the attorney-general and request prompt prosecution of such violation.

From the punishment clause we can see the following:

1.   Diagnosing and prescribing are acts of medical practice in state law to be undertaken by physician

2.   When assisting physicians, nurses are carrying out the *dependent nursing function*

3.   A nurse who works without medical supervision must be acting in the realm of recognized independent function.

Nursing Practice Defined

Now we shall compare these observations with the Nursing Practice Act in the same state.

ARTICLE 139

Nursing

[As amended to the close of legislation, 1962]

§ 6901. **Definitions.** 1. "Board", as used in this article, means the board of examiners of nurses of the state of New York.

2. The practice of nursing is defined as follows:

a. A person practices nursing as a registered professional nurse within the meaning of this article who for compensation or personal profit performs any professional service requiring the application of principles of nursing based on biological, physical and social sciences, such as responsible supervision of a patient requiring skill in observation of symptoms and reactions and the accurate recording of the facts, and carrying out of treatments and medications as prescribed by a licensed physician or by a licensed dentist and the application of such nursing procedures as involves understanding of cause and effect in order to safeguard life and health of a patient and others

b. *A person practices nursing as a licensed practical nurse within the meaning of this article who for compensation or personal profit performs such duties as are required in the physical care of a patient and in carrying out of medical orders as prescribed by a licensed physician or by a licensed dentist requiring an understanding of nursing but not requiring the professional service as outlined in paragraph a.*

§ 6902. **Qualification for practice.** In order to safeguard life and health, any person practicing or offering to practice nursing in this state for compensation or personal profit shall be required to submit evidence that he or she is qualified so to practice, and shall be licensed as hereinafter provided. It shall be unlawful for any person to practice or to offer to practice nursing in this state or to use any title, sign, card or device to indicate that such a person is practicing nursing unless such person has been duly licensed and registered under the provisions of this article.

The nurse, therefore, in accordance with the Nursing Act and the nurse's function, undertakes the observation of symptoms and reactions, the accurate recording of facts, and the administration of treatments and medications prescribed by the doctor.

§ 6909. **Construction of article.** *1. This article shall not* [negative limitation] *be construed as conferring any authority to practice medicine or to undertake the treatment or cure of disease, pain, injury, deformity or physical condition in violation of article one hundred thirty-one of this* *chapter, nor shall it be construed as conferring any authority to practice dentistry or to undertake to diagnose, treat, operate or prescribe for any disease, pain, injury, deficiency, deformity or physical condition of the human teeth, alveolar process, gums or jaws in violation of article one hundred thirty-three of this chapter,* nor shall it be construed as prohibiting the care of the sick by domestic servants, housekeepers, nursemaids, companions or household aides of any type, whether employed regularly or because of an emergency of illness, provided such person is employed primarily in a domestic capacity and does not hold himself or herself out, or accept employment as a person licensed to practice nursing for hire under the provisions of this article, or preventing any person from the domestic administration of family remedies or the furnishing of nursing assistance in case of an emergency; nor shall it be construed as including service given by attendants in institutions under the jurisdiction of or subject to the visitation of the state department of mental hygiene if adequate medical and nursing supervision is provided; nor shall it be construed as prohibiting such performance of nursing service by students enrolled in registered schools as may be incidental to their course of study; nor shall it be construed as prohibiting or preventing the practice of nursing in this state by any legally qualified nurse of another state, province, or country whose engagement requires him or her to accompany and care for a patient temporarily residing in this state during the period of such engagement provided such person does not represent or hold himself or herself out as a nurse licensed to practice in this state.

Nursing Diagnosis

Nursing diagnosis is an independent function. A nurse's diagnosis would include performing the following activities:

1.   A general assessment of the nursing care that the patient will need. This would require examining the doctor's admission note, questioning the patient and his family, and considering any objective and subjective factors involved. Note that a medical diagnosis by a physician precedes these nursing activities.

2.   A plan of care to be carried out by the nurse or her assistants, e.g., cold compress, foot soak, alcohol sponge.

3.   A projection of the normal expectancy with items 1 and 2 in mind. In a sense, this is a nursing prognosis.

Some hospitals, such as rehabilitation hospitals, have the nurse make a preliminary diagnosis and recommend measures that would make the patient comfortable. However, no action is taken on either activity until the patient is seen by a physician and the nurse's findings and suggestions are corroborated.

Standing Orders

Within the hospital, standing orders enable a nurse to follow the doctor's directions for a specific patient, or in some instances for a class of patients, without having to await his presence or personal order. The standing orders depend on the nurse's acuity and ability to observe and assess. She is required to make a judgment that certain signs are in evidence that suggest the need to initiate the therapy indicated by the standing order. Her judgment may be subject to a fixed time schedule or to the physician's actual review. Within the hospital, where responsible members of the medical and nursing staff see the need for standing orders and devise, supervise, and review them, the nurse who puts the orders into effect is generally on safe ground; the patient is, too. Both are on safer ground, however, if standing orders are current and if their usefulness is shown when the physician is actually present and available.

Many times in professional work in the field, public health nurses and mental health nurses, for example, make diagnoses to institute standing orders. The nurse who observes, for example, that a child has a cold, the chickenpox, or a reaction to immunization will follow a standardized regimen. Here, for obvious reasons, she is not on such safe ground as is the hospital nurse.

The best way to ensure the safety of the nurse is to train her specifically for the judgments she will have to make. This training should be followed by education that will reinforce the nurse's abilities and allow her to review personally her performance and decisions. The latter should also be reviewed by her superiors on a regular and timely basis. Here, as in any other service where she undertakes tasks that may be considered extensions of nursing duties and prerogatives, she must be taught and encouraged to ask for physician assistance or to refer the patient to a physician if she has the slightest doubt about her own sufficiency in any given circumstance.

Emergency Medical Diagnosis: Limits of the Nurse's Function

To observe a patient's symptoms and perhaps to correlate these to case history information and other objective data available for the purpose of making a diagnosis presupposes a need for more than mental acuity. These activities require professional training and education, often specifically addressed to foreseeable needs and circumstances.

There is no doubt that in some circumstances that preclude a careful review by her superior, a nurse must make such diagnoses.

But except for such emergency measures, the determination of therapy is usually held to be exclusively in the province of the physician and outside the limits of nursing practice.

As Dr. B. Dixon Holland of the A.M.A. has put it:

> In other than emergency cases where a physician is not present, diagnosis is not a function of professional nursing and treatment by nurses is restricted to the execution of orders given by and under the direction and supervision of a physician.
>
> Furthermore, the nurse should only execute legally valid medical orders which she is qualified by training and experience to perform. . . . It is axiomatic that the practice of medicine may not be delegated to nonphysicians.

On the other hand, the physician is considered an expert in the scope and quality of nursing practice. Therefore, what comprises nursing is in a sense determined by what physicians think should be included in the practice. By custom and practice, nursing is dependent for definition and direction on medical practice and physicians. Therefore, where a sizable minority or any sizable class of reputable physicians creates a new standard or new extension for nursing practice that is not imprudent or indifferent to the public's needs and welfare, it will have a strong chance of acceptance.

Under such circumstances, nursing practice might be construed to include not only emergency diagnoses and treatment but other medical acts, techniques, or procedures which are commonly performed by qualified nurses under physicians' orders. These might in time be legislatively added to the language of the nursing practice act and the nurse's functions. Therefore, as a practical necessity and under the direction or supervision of physicians, nurses today are performing numerous procedures which were formerly performed exclusively by physicians. These have been limited by the nature of the relationship between the medical and nursing professions in the community, the scope of the nurse's educational training, and the nurse's individual experience and proficiency.

SUCCESSFUL DELEGATION OF MEDICAL FUNCTIONS

There are many examples of successful delegation of medical practices to nonphysicians. Midwifery was the subject of a recent study made at Johns Hopkins University and reported at the Spring, 1968, meeting of the College of Nurse-Midwifery by Dr. Lillian Runnerstrom, the director. The study indicated that a patient would have had difficulty choosing between nurse-midwives and obstetric residents on the basis of service and results. In fact, a larger percentage of cases handled by the nurses terminated pregnancy in normal spontaneous delivery rather than operative delivery.

In New York, nurse-midwives are specially licensed and, although there are only 50 of them, they deliver well over 2,000 babies a year. In at least one major hospital center, Harlem Hospital in New York City, nurse-midwives supervise student nurses undergoing this training, and they undertake a good deal of patient counseling. They serve in prenatal and postpartum care clinics and in clinics for supportive effort in the case of high-risk patients. This is indeed a special area of nursing.

In a similar vein, a pediatric nurse-practitioner program prepares RN's having a B.S. or M.S. degree to undertake some of the functions and activities of the pediatrician. Such nurses work in the offices of private pediatricians and in areas with inadequate health services. They provide comprehensive care to children who are well, and they identify, appraise, and temporarily manage certain acute and chronic conditions of sick children. This program has resulted in a realignment of functions performed by physicians and nurses so that each can assume responsibility for those aspects of the patient's needs that he can *perform most effectively.*

This program which gained statutory recognition in 1969, was developed jointly by the Department of Pediatrics of the Medical School and the Nursing School of the University of Colorado. It contemplates a one-to-one relationship: one pediatric practitioner to one pediatrician. It requires nurses to interview patients and parents in order to develop techniques they will use later for assessment. It teaches nurses to perform a complete physical examination, including inspection, palpation, percussion, and auscultation. They learn to use the stethoscope and the otoscope, and they are coached by a child psychiatrist in psychosocial and cultural forces affecting health and personality development. They develop proficiency in counseling parents in child-rearing practice (a 4-month course). They are reportedly able to give total care to more than 75 percent of all children who come to field stations where they may or may not have physicians with whom to consult.

The success of these transitional developments has been dependent upon the good will, good intentions, and good efforts of all concerned. This includes the relationship between the medical and nursing professions in each institution, geographic area, and community. It requires as a basic tenet the improvement of the quality and scope of the nurse's education, experience, and proficiency.

Although these extensions may be agreed upon by physicians,

nurses, and hospital administrators, they may still be rendered vulnerable from a legal and public viewpoint by not creating or maintaining appropriate standards. With all the foregoing considered, with perhaps additional background of a joint statement, with the knowledge and consent of the institution or agency when such is involved, with all such color of substance and authority, the extension must not be an affront to good judgment, professional or lay. It may not jeopardize the patient or diminish the physician's responsibility in terms of the physician-patient relationship. It must be cloaked with adequate supervision for the delagee and adequate safeguards for the patient.

LITIGATION

It is interesting to note that both diagnosis specifically and medical acts in general, when carried out by a physician, are usually immune to a plaintiff's allegations of malpractice and negligence, whether the complaints are directed against the physician, the hospital, or both.

When tasks are delegated, the defense of the physician's judgment is lost, and the court may consider the act administrative rather than medical. When this happens, any vestige of the immunity enjoyed by nonproprietary hospitals for negligent acts of their physicians is lost, and the doctrine of respondeat superior is invoked.[8]

How a Nurse May Protect Herself

A patient who sues a hospital for negligent treatment by its agent or employee finds the hospital liable if the agent's acts were performed within the scope of her employment. However, if a nurse, for example, performs a function outside of nursing, she might herself be liable or be liable to the hospital on a cross-claim for performing an act she was not hired to perform. Therefore, she should be certain that her hospital superiors are aware of the circumstances and will support her should the need arise.

There are ways to substantiate delegated duties that are seemingly in the gray area between practice restrictions and demands made by medical persons on their subordinates. There are also ways to indicate valid objections to overdelegation. For example, the joint statements we have discussed provide certain guidelines as to which activities are technically overdelegated, but are nonetheless considered practical and permissible in the judgment of qualified physicians and nurses.

If the task delegated is not covered by the joint statement in a particular state, a nurse may rightfully advise her superior to that effect. She may refuse to undertake the task on that basis or she may insist on some form of assurance that will satisfy a reasonable and prudent person that neither patient nor public welfare will be endangered, and that she will not be in danger of civil litigation or criminal prosecution.

In the preceding pages we have pointed out the legal liabilities involved for the members of the nursing team, those who give direction, and employers. We have also discussed the various ways to give certain delegated tasks some degree of authority, such as attorney-general opinions in some states, resolutions following studies by professional associations and societies, and even particular description within the hospital's by laws and other self-regulatory documents.

Nurses must remember that where the procedures are in fact the practice of medicine, the laws regarding such practice by one who is not licensed to practice medicine may be strictly construed. These laws can be applied not only as punitive measures for those who practice unlawfully, but also in negligence and malpractice suits that may be brought when a patient is harmed.

Acknowledged shortages of physicians and tacit or written interprofessional agreements such as that between the College of Physicians and Surgeons of Ontario, the Ontario Hospital Association, and the Registered Nurses' Association of Ontario would seem to protect nurses who carry out these procedures against charges by medical groups or persons. Hospitals may feel that they are not in danger since they are legal entities with power to enact bylaws governing the application of the extension of such prerogatives to registered nurses within the hospital.

Areas of Possible Litigation

A patient who feels that harm has befallen him because a medical procedure was performed by a nurse can question the circumstances and seek damages on several propositions.

First, if the procedures in question are generally acknowledged to be medical procedures, persons and groups with special economic interests cannot contract away the patient's right to expect that medical treatment will be given him by a physician. If such a situation exists, the patient deserves the right to be put on notice initially and given a choice, just as informed consent is required for any procedure not universally recognized as normal and prudent.

Second, it goes without saying that the issue of overdelegation usually arises only when injury has occurred. Therefore, those who direct and employ a registered nurse to perform a procedure or make a decision generally reserved to a physician must be sure that she has adequate training, experience, direction, and supervision to perform it with safety and efficiency.

Third, the nurse owes it to both her employers and the patient to be capable of doing the particular task at the particular time. She must not mislead her employers or the patient in this respect.

Fourth, the employers must be able to show their bona fide attempt to minimize risk by proper selection of qualified personnel and by a description of any educational and training programs for such employees. This description should include a log of the time actually spent on the program and the name and qualifications of the instructor(s).

It is important to remember that while these internal or interprofessional understandings allay fears of prosecution for violation of the medical practice act, they may nonetheless conflict with accepted tort principles and the modern requirements of informed consent on the part of the patient.

Litigation Resulting from Improper Delegation

In *Zophy v. New York*,[9] the court noted that a hospital "can be found liable for failure to provide experienced personnel." While this liability is in tort, it might be construed as a contractual issue. An individual who is hospitalized has a reasonable expectation, implicit in his agreement to become a patient, that he will be treated carefully by reasonably trained and experienced personnel.

In every jurisdiction, the plaintiff's attorney may draw upon precedent to demonstrate that delegating medical or surgical functions to assistants unauthorized by law to carry them out is unjustified. If a doctor, to the patient's damage, delegates to a subordinate tasks that require a physician's qualifications, his wrongful delegation will be relatively simple to prove. After describing the harm allegedly caused by the nonphysician, the plaintiff's attorney will show (1) that this act is one usually carried out by doctors in the community, so the defendant physician has departed from ordinary standards, and (2) that the state medical practice act and any licensure act affecting the delagee are violated.

In a recent California case,[10] the Board of Medical Examiners suspended for 90 days a physician's license to practice and placed him on probation for 5 years. The matter of delegation under direct supervision was involved. The charge against the physician was that he aided, abetted, and employed unlicensed persons in the practice of medicine. Those involved were a male nurse and Japanese and Mexican resident physicians whom the defendant brought in pursuant to the exchange-visitor program established under the United States Information and Educational Exchange Act. There were no claims of harm to patients.

The court held that, in the absence of prior approval by the Board of Medical Examiners to permit their practice in California, the foreign physicians' status was that of unlicensed practitioners giving medical treatment. Further, the court stated that supervision of the foreign residents by the defendant, a licensed practitioner, did not alter the situation.

In this case, testimony by a patient pointed out that a male nurse had been the only person to treat her during her entire hospital stay. In this situation, the courts will generally find the principal liable for cloaking his agent, the nurse, with apparent authority to perform a procedure where her responsibility exceeds the contemplation of the nursing act and where, through lack of judgment or employer pressure, she exceeds her authority and her purpose in accordance with the standards of her skill and prudence. In the case cited, the male nurse had no problems with the patient, so he was not involved. The board chose to prosecute only his employer.

The nurse may impress upon her employers the danger in delegating supranursing tasks to her by inquiring about her right to be protected in case of a lawsuit. If the employer includes her in his own insurance policy, rather than provide a separate one, the nurse must be certain that her own name appears or that a distinct class of persons of which she is clearly a member is stated. Violation of statutes and criminal acts generally invalidates insurance for both the hospital and its employees. However, this is interpreted variously depending on the circumstances and the insurance carrier.

IMMUNITIES

Many times, liberties are taken with laws affected by improper delegation. These liberties result from a feeling of immunity which may or may not be justified. We should therefore examine and explain the whys and hows of these immunities as well as their meanings, privileges, and limitations in law.

Government Immunity

It is an old and cardinal rule of law that the sovereign is above suit. The concept originated from the fact that, since the sovereign was divinely chosen and the "giver" of law, no court could entertain or deliver a judgment against him. Although the development of republican forms of government rendered this theory inapplicable, it was nonetheless desirable to retain it. Modifications that developed were permissive; the government would allow itself to be sued in special instances. In the United States this has been formalized to include certain types of suits.

FEDERAL TORT CLAIMS ACT

The willingness of the federal government to accept responsibility for the misdeeds of its employees is a relatively recent circumstance. The Federal Tort Claims Act became law in 1946, and with it the United States Government undertook liability, as a private person, for tortious behavior on the part of its employees while they acted within the scope of their office or employment. In short, the Government thus elected to be bound, in cases of torts, by the doctrine of respondeat superior.

Since actions under this statute must be brought in the federal courts (the district courts initially), the tort law used is that of the particular state involved. This is a generally accepted principle of common law, and it applies to the limits of the plaintiff's claim, as well as to the Government's defense.

The test of whether the wrongdoer is a Government employee is generally whether he is subject to the control and supervision of other Government personnel. The test for scope of employment is generally just as simple: Was the act complained of part of the routine or special assignments associated with the job?

Therefore, a resident physician based in a Government hospital is acting on his own authority while replacing a private practitioner during his time off. And a nurse who finishes her assignment and accepts a special-duty nursing position is likewise operating without protection.

Torts Not Covered by Federal Tort Claims Act

Not all torts are covered by the Federal Tort Claims Act. Those sometimes described as intentional torts (assault, battery, false imprisonment, and misrepresentation either fraudulent or negligent) are excluded.[11]

The act also does not apply to a claim based on the exercise or performance of a discretionary function or duty of a Government employee. This includes such administrative or discretionary acts as whether an ambulance is required or whether a patient should be admitted. However, once the patient is accepted for examination, a decision to treat him as an outpatient or to hospitalize him may be subject to another interpretation and go beyond the exclusion for discretionary acts. The Government employees would probably fare similarly to a proprietary hospital, where a patient is discharged before the appropriate time.[12]

The Eleventh Amendment to the U.S. Constitution rules out third-party malpractice suits against state institutions. The Amendment provides that no action may be brought in a federal court against a state by its citizens or the citizens of a foreign state.

The doctrine of government immunity, old as it is, has never been considered to be at variance with constitutional guarantees of a remedy for personal injury by due process of law. It is common law that an agency of the state is immune, as is its sovereign, from liability—and only a strictly construed statute imposing such liability can revoke that principle.[13]

Where such immunities have been set aside by the judiciary (and these cases are few), it was because the hospital had acquired or was able to acquire liability insurance. This seemed to eliminate the reason for immunity: conservation of public funds. Courts in some jurisdictions have interpreted statutes expressly waiving the immunity to mean that the Government unit could be held liable only for the amount of coverage on the policy issued.[14]

Delegation of Immunity to Municipalities

Since the state can maintain its right to immunity from suit, various courts have described the delegation of this privileged position to lesser governmental units and the hospitals they operate. Municipalities are frequently authorized by statute to establish and regulate hospitals. The administrative and nursing staffs may be chosen on the basis of civil service examinations, appointments, or regular hiring procedures. Generally, one or more persons specially qualified undertake the chief administrative duties, while a group of persons or board of trustees are responsible for the hospital's overall management and control. Since the legislature has delegated a portion of its inherent police power to permit the municipal unit to handle local matters, such a transfer of authority is proper. The city or town then delegates its authority to the board of trustees to do everything necessary for the hospital's proper management and control. This gives the trustees great power over the conduct of hospital business and the policy of hospital practices, except that they generally delegate to the medical staff the regulation of physician privileges. Even here, however, though it might prove embarrassing, they are within their rights to suspend or remove any professional from the staff, as they would an employee. They are responsible for the reputation, as well as the successful function, of the hospital.[15]

Unlike charitable immunity, if the doctrine of government immunity is abrogated in particular states, the courts usually are loath to change it by decision. Courts in some states, besides using the argument of insurance, have abolished the doctrine by reasoning that legislatures are generally apathetic about modernizing tort law. They have leaned on this conclusion, to which may be added their general distaste for unfair enrichment, to abrogate the doctrine of charitable immunity by judicial decree.

Nevertheless, courts in some states uphold government immunity. In Texas, for example, a nurse who fell while on duty in a county hospital could not collect for her injuries.[16] In denying her cause of action, the court stated that a city, in operating a hospital for the needy, is performing a government function. A government agency is immune from tort liability while engaged in a government function. So long as the hospital was properly established by the government district in accordance with the state constitution and the statutes, it was immune from tort liability. Because of the nature of the hospital and the fact that it cared only for needy and indigent residents of the district, this decision seemed to combine the doctrines of charitable immunity and governmental immunity.

In those jurisdictions which permit suit against the government unit, the right to sue is qualified. Thus a patient must give the city notice of a claim against it for injury caused by its employees' negligence within 30 days after the injury.[17] Those who are physically or mentally incapacitated by the injury have an additional 90 days in which to file notice. This is strictly construed by the courts.

Where actions must be taken against government institutions, as we have noted, various enabling acts must allow the suit in the face of the sovereign's immunity. Since the federal government has permitted itself to be sued in tort, negligence, and malpractice, some states have done likewise. Where a state consents to be sued, its consent is limited to suit in its own courts, not federal courts. However, where the cause of action arises out of a proprietary function of the state (as, for example, where it sells geyser or spring water), the doctrine of government immunity might be cast aside since a nongovernment function is involved.[18]

The states have the right to delegate such immunity in special circumstances where it is desirable. For example, in Massachusetts a school nurse or physician who, while participating in one of the prophylactic public health programs, injects vaccines or administers immunizing materials cannot be held liable in a civil suit for damages as a result of carrying out such duties.[19]

Charitable Immunity and Respondeat Superior

We have indicated that, as principals, hospitals may be liable for injuries resulting from the professional or administrative acts of their employees, whether they be doctors, nurses, orderlies, or technicians. This is a generalization, and employees must recognize certain exceptions. For instance, in a number of states, hospitals categorized as charitable are either totally or partially immune from suit. *This does not immunize their employees.* This charitable immunity is, however, being gradually discarded since insurance is available to all hospitals. In the most populous states, such as New York, California, Illinois, and Pennsylvania, it has disappeared completely. In March, 1965, the Pennsylvania Supreme Court repudiated the doctrine of charitable immunity. If, however, suits against an institution had been dismissed previously by court order based on the doctrine, and no appeal from that order was taken and pending, then the case would be closed. The doctrine of res judicata would apply since the matter had been terminated in "action adjudicated." [20] In other states, such as Texas, application of the doctrine depends on whether or not the claimant was a charity or paying patient.[21]

An older rule on hospital liability that is applied to charitable, educational, religious, and government hospitals in many states depends on the function of the individual(s). The courts will hold the hospital liable for harm ensuing from administrative acts, but not from medical acts. In New York, where this concept has outlived its usefulness, it is called the Schloendorff Rule.[22] Application of this line of reasoning is rendered extremely difficult by the fact that laboratory technicians undertake duties that are difficult to define as either medical or administrative.

For example, a patient in a charitable hospital was seriously injured by receiving a blood transfusion of the wrong blood type.[23] The physician had ordered the blood transfusion. A qualified laboratory technician employed by the hospital performed a test to determine the patient's blood type. In so doing, he made an error which led to the harmful transfusion. The trial court found the hospital liable because the negligent act was administrative. The intermediate appellate court reversed the decision on the ground that performing a blood test is a medical act for which that charitable hospital could not be held liable.

The New York Court of Appeals, however, upheld the lower

court's decision, reasoning that since the act had not been performed by a physician or professional nurse "in their professional capacities," but rather by a nonprofessional employee, it could not be considered a medical act. To do otherwise, the court opined, would create an escape from liability in almost every case.

As this defense, which is used by a multitude of church-oriented and other hospital organizations, fades away, it is increasingly clear that the old basis for the doctrine of charitable immunity as a part of public policy is unreasonable. It is an implied waiver of rights by the beneficiary of the hospital's services. Also, it conserves a trust fund that would be dissipated in suits by some, rather than used to provide care for the many which has been supplanted by general acceptance of insurance coverage. Texas and several other states continue to maintain the theory of charitable immunity. Idaho maintained the same barrier until 1966; it then decided that this stand was illogical and joined the vast majority of jurisdictions in total denial of the doctrine.[24] While the theory as enforced unquestionably benefits the institution, it never gives the same degree of protection to hospital personnel. Selecting and training employees require supervision and care. If good judgment is not used, the employee is still vulnerable to suit, although the hospital retains its immunity. Also, as stated by the Texas Court of Civil Appeals, an exception to the immunity doctrine may exist "if the charitable institution was negligent in retaining in its employment an employee who knew, or in the exercise of ordinary care should have known, of a condition of danger on the hospital premises and failed to correct it."[25]

It has been held that in order for the property of a benevolent organization to enjoy the benefits of charitable immunity, including the right to be tax-exempt, it must be used exclusively, rather than simply primarily, for benevolent purposes. Where there are any elements of personal advantage and profit to the association's members which differ from those inuring to the public, it loses the exemption. Therefore, if it operates an insurance plan that earns a profit or if it rents space, it is vulnerable.[26]

For years, hospitals that are chartered as charitable institutions have been exempt from the requirements of labor laws designed to allow unionization and collective bargaining by employees.

The right to recover damages against another who negligently inflicts injury is a property-right complaint in the Bill of Rights.[27] Charitable immunity doctrines seem to contradict this principle of common law. There are no vested rights in common-law rules. However, when common-law rules that alter private and property rights are changed, the changes must be reasonable and must satisfy due process. For years, the charitable immunity doctrine was held to be a reasonable and necessary method to encourage charitable hospitals and relieve the public and the state of many burdens. This has, for the most part, been terminated today because there are better ways available to safeguard patients and hospital funds.

State courts have defended against renewal of prior suits terminated because of the doctrine on the premise that it was not unreasonable in its time, and removal by legislative act or court decision is not intended, nor need be, retroactive.[28]

CASE CITATIONS

1. *Reed v. Kuzirian,* 88 A.L.R. 2d 1284 (1961).
2. *Journal of the American Medical Association,* **196**(2), p. 269 (1967).
3. *Piper v. Epstein,* 326 Ill. App. 400 (1945).
4. *Ibid.,* p. 269.
5. *Norton v. Argonaut Insurance Company,* 144 So. 2d 249 (1962).
6. *Canadian Nurse,* **61**(6), p. 471 (1965).
7. *Salgo v. Stanford,* 317 P. 2d 170 (California).
8. *Schloendorff v. Society of New York Hospital,* 211 N.Y. 125 (1914).
9. *Zophy v. New York,* New York Appellate Division, Fourth Department, 1967.
10. *O'Reilly v. Board of Medical Examiners,* 55 Cal. Rptr. 152 (1966).
11. *United States v. McCann,* 386 F. 2d 626 (1967).
12. *Denny v. United States,* 171 F. 2d 365 (1949).
13. *McCoy v. Board of Regents,* 413 P. 2d 73 (1966).
14. *Myers v. Droda,* 141 N.W. 2d 852 (1966).
15. *Koelling v. Board of Trustees of Mary E. Skiff Memorial Hospital,* 146 N.W. 2d 284 (1966).
16. *Arseneau v. Tarrant County Hospital District,* 408 S.W. 2d 802 (1966).
17. *Hirth v. Village of Long Prairie,* 143 N.W. 2d 205 (1966).
18. *Farners Electric v. Austed,* 366 F. 2d 557 (1966).
19. Massachusetts Laws, ch. 583, p. 587 (1966).
20. *Love v. Temple University,* 220 A. 2d 838 (1966).
21. *Molitur v. Kaneland District,* 18 Ill. 2d 11 (1959).
22. *Schloendorff v. Society of New York Hospital,* 211 N.Y. 125 (1914).
23. *Berg v. New York Society for the Crippled,* 1 N.Y. 2d 499 (1956).
24. *Bell v. Presbytery of Boise,* 421 P. 2d 745 (1966).

25. Fifth Supreme Judicial District No. 16, 737 (1966).
26. *South Dakota State Medical Association v. Jones,* 146 N.W. 2d 725 (1966).
27. *Sanner v. Enoch Pratt Hospital,* 278 F. Supp. 138 (1968).
28. *Ibid.*

CHAPTER 5

TORT LAW: UNINTENTIONAL TORT

Just as the American Bill of Rights, or a similar set of safeguards written into the codes of other countries, is meant to ensure the right of each citizen to life, liberty, and the pursuit of happiness, so tort law establishes rules of conduct that are intended to maintain personal safety.

WHAT IS A TORT?

A *tort* is a civil wrong arising from a person's failure to use care in his contact with other persons, or his failure to refrain from injuring the person or property of another. The tort-feasor—the person who has committed the tort—has usurped the rights of another person. Tort is not dependent on a contractual agreement; it is a breach of a duty imposed by law rather than one undertaken through agreement by the parties. Whereas a contract generally is made as a result of agreement between persons who thereby necessarily are not strangers, a tort generally arises out of an action that has taken place between strangers. The same act can be both tortious and a breach of contract where personal services are involved, and the remedy in both instances is the same: the claim of the wronged party is satisfied by payment of an award of money.

TORT CONTRASTED WITH CRIME

Tort will be more readily understood if is contrasted with crime (Table 1). A *crime* is a wrong punishable by the

Table 1. · **Types of Torts**

Intentional:	Malicious prosecution
	False imprisonment
	Fraud and deceit
	Invasion of privacy
	Assault and battery
	Libel and slander
Unintentional:	Negligence
	Product liability
	Malpractice
	Special forms

state. A special group of actions exist that are statutorily defined as crimes. Any infraction of the Federal Food, Drug, and Cosmetic Act, for example, may give rise to criminal prosecution; the element of criminal intent need not be established. The Drug Directorate of Canada has similar powers. In most other instances, an actual criminal intent—*mens rea*—must be present. By contrast, in a tort action a wrong may be perpetrated and injuries caused, yet the element of intent may not be present. A tort is committed against an individual, a crime is committed against the state. In a tort the complainant is an individual citizen, in a crime the complainant is the state.

The same action can be both tortious and criminal. This situation may occur, as in gross or criminal negligence, when a tort has been committed in circumstances that show the wrongdoer to have demonstrated such willful disregard for human life that he is considered a menace to society. In such a case, the wronged person can seek financial recompense for the damages he has sustained, while criminal prosecution proceeds that may result in the wrongdoer's being fined or imprisoned, or both.

RESPONSIBILITY FOR TORT

In common law, actions in tort did not survive the death of either the tort-feasor or the injured party, whereas actions arising out of contracts survived the death of either. In several states, e.g., Illinois and New York, this common-law rule has been amended by so-called "survival statutes." [1]

Individual responsibility for acts of negligence in medical treatment or care of patients extends to federal employees, although they do enjoy broader immunity than private practitioners. This principle of individual responsibility is followed in American, English, and Canadian law.

Respondeat Superior

The nurse charged with negligence must face the charge both as an individual and as a codefendant where the principle of respondeat superior applies.

Article 1053 of the Civil Code of the Province of Quebec sets forth this principle, and a corresponding principle exists in the United States.[2] "Every person capable of distinguishing right from wrong is responsible for the damage caused by his fault to another, whether by positive act, imprudence, neglect or want of skill." Further, a person "is responsible not only for the damage caused by his own fault, but also for that caused by the fault of persons under his control and by things he has under his care."

In judging the applicability and extent of the nurse's responsibility, the Quebec courts employ the established criterion of *"bon père de famille"*—the rational, intelligent, thoughtful, reasonably careful citizen.[3]

In both the United States and Canada, the test is whether or not the employee is subordinate to the managerial powers of the employer's organization. The employer's liability stems from his having chosen the staff and having available the power to dismiss any employee.[4]

MALPRACTICE AND NEGLIGENCE

Malpractice

The terms *malpractice* and *negligence* are sometimes used interchangeably, but there is a distinction between them. Malpractice is the form of negligence that occurs when a professional, in treating or caring for a patient, does not conduct himself with the prudence and skill which the public has a reasonable right to expect.

Members of the health team are expected to exhibit the same prudence as others of their class in the same locality, and to give those entrusted to their care the same degree of skill and knowledge that others of their class would. The nurse, like the physician, the pharmacist, the dentist, and the veterinarian, is expected to possess the degree of skill and competence usually possessed by others of similar licensure, status, and training who are working in the same location. Further, the nurse is expected to use her skill and training just as would any other skilled nurse in similar circumstances. Nonetheless, if, for example, the nurse promises to obtain particular results for the patient, or claims special expertness or ability in treating the patient, then the patient has a legal right to hold the nurse to the promise.

A professional person who has achieved a higher degree of skill in a particular area of medicine is expected to perform at the appropriate level: Just as the roentgenologist is expected to bring greater skill to a radiologic procedure than would the general practitioner, so is the intensive care nurse expected to perform at a level above that of the ward nurse.

Distinction between Malpractice and Negligence

Malpractice is negligent in character within the area of professional actions for which professional persons may be held liable; but since only professionals hold licenses, only they will be charged with malpractice, and nonlicentiates will be charged with negligence.

Another distinction between malpractice and negligence as viewed by many authors is that the licentiate may be held liable for malpractice only if the task that formed the basis of the complaint was of a professional character. There is no consensus on this point, however. In a few states a complaint may be made against a nurse for negligence only,[5] and the complaint of malpractice is reserved to physicians and others of comparable skill and training.

Nonetheless, the distinction between malpractice and negligence can be critical. In one instance [6] the Supreme Court of West Virginia ordered a new trial on the ground that the lower court should have considered the case to be one of negligence rather than malpractice, and the plaintiff's suit was disallowed.

Negligent examination and treatment, supported by sufficient facts, is cause for a claim of malpractice.

Negligence

The yardstick of reasonableness—what the reasonable, prudent man would have done in similar circumstances—is applied also to negligence.

Negligence may be regarded in several ways, according to the given circumstances. *Negligence* involves exposure of the person or property of another to an unreasonable risk of injury by a commissive action (doing something) or an omissive action (failing to do something). *Gross negligence* is characterized as a willful disregard for the person or property of another. The failure of a treatment or a regimen does not constitute negligence.

BASIC ELEMENTS OF A CAUSE OF ACTION IN NEGLIGENCE

Certain elements are essential to show negligence, and if any of these is lacking the case may be disallowed. These elements are sometimes described as the "four d's": duty, dereliction, direct causation, and damages. A duty must have been owed the plaintiff by the defendant; the defendant must have been derelict in his duty; this dereliction must have led directly to the damage suffered by the plaintiff; and the plaintiff must demonstrate the damage so that its validity and compensability may be correctly evaluated.

A claim of negligence (which applies also to malpractice) against a nurse must provide evidence of the following:

1.   That a circumstance or relationship existed in which the nurse owed a duty to the patient and failure in that duty would foreseeably cause harm to the patient or prevent the benefit that would otherwise derive from that relationship

2.   That the prevailing standard of care was breached

3.   That the lapse in duty, failure, or breach of care was the direct cause of the patient's injury or harm. The patient must prove a direct and clear chain of events leading from the nurse's wrongful act to the resultant harm; no intervening chance causes must be capable of having produced the harm or injury. If there were two or more possible causes of the injury, for only one of which the nurse could be held responsible, she will not be held liable unless the weight of evidence indicates that her wrongful act is the probable cause of the injury.

4.   That damages due the patient resulted from this breach of care

In some jurisdictions the plaintiff must prove the following:

1.   The degree of skill or knowledge possessed or the degree of care generally exercised by physicians or dentists practicing in comparable communities.

2.   That the defendant lacked this degree of skill and knowledge or failed to exercise this degree of care.

3.   That the patient suffered injuries that otherwise would not have occurred as a direct result of this lack of skill or knowledge or his failure to exercise this degree of care. In malpractice or negligence suits in all jurisdictions the burden of proof is initially on the patient.[7]

ORDINARY SKILL

A trial court usually will instruct the jury that a physician is not required to obtain perfect or nearly perfect results with his treatment, since medicine is not an exact science, and he is not liable for lack of success or an honest mistake in judgment, unless evidence is offered to the contrary. This guideline applies to nurses as well.[8] As one court has stated it: "When one possesses the requisite skill and ability and acts according to his best judgment, and in a careful and prudent manner, he is not chargeable with negligence." [9]

FORESEEABILITY

A person who recognizes a duty to another person can reasonably foresee why he should perform that duty, and, having ordinary foresight and judgment, he is able to foresee what might happen if he did not perform that duty. This is the concept of *foreseeability,* and it bears directly on proof of negligence.

Dangers that are considered foreseeable and preventable and yet occur in treatment may be enough to make out a prima facie case in negligence. For example, in a Michigan case where a former hospital patient claimed nerve damage during an operation, the attending resident physician and nurse testified that care must be exercised in strapping a patient to the operating table to prevent damage to the ulnar nerve. An appellate court ruled in the patient's favor.

There are limitations to foreseeability. Neither a nurse nor a physician can become a guarantor of a patient's safety. They are required to act reasonably and prudently to secure and maintain the patient's safety. When, for example, they know that the patient has suicidal tendencies, they are duty-bound to attempt to prevent a suicidal act.

But foreseeability would not apply, for example, in such an instance as the one that occurred when an employee left a cup of tea near the bedside of a sleeping patient. The patient burned herself with the tea, and the cup was found overturned on her bed. The court held that the hospital and the employers were not liable, inasmuch as the patient had not been restless or waving her arms.

Foreseeability would, however, apply in a case like this one: A convalescent patient at a city hospital died of burns received from a heat lamp that had been placed too close to his bedside, causing the mattress to catch fire. The court held that the fire was foreseeable, since in a previous treatment a brown spot had been burned into the bedclothes. This occurrence should have alerted prudent employees to the risk involved.

While the wrongdoer is liable for the foreseeable consequences of his tort, once foreseeability has been established the plaintiff may hold the wrongdoer responsible for all injuries resulting from the act, even though they may not have been foreseeable. In some cases, however, there are intervening acts of negligence or poor judgment that are so directly related to the patient's harm that they, rather than the original act, are regarded as the direct cause of the injury.

In most states, including New York, California, and Illinois, the original wrongdoer is held liable for all injuries that follow directly from his negligence. This liability includes damages resulting from misdiagnosis, and failure in care given by members of the health team. As a rule, the original wrongdoer who has caused the injury to another person is responsible also for aggravation of that injury through the negligence of physicians, nurses, and others who give treatment or care. The following example illustrates this situation:

A, a passenger in a car driven by B, is injured when B's car collides with one driven by C. M Hospital dispatches an ambulance. The ambulance attendants stanch A's bleeding, place him on an ambulance litter, and speed toward the hospital. On the way the ambulance collides with another car, driven by D, and A's bleeding recurs. The attendants do not stop, this time. A's bleeding continues, he loses much blood, and he arrives at the M Hospital in a state of shock. At this time A's claim is against B or C, whoever A believes was negligent in the first collision.

In M Hospital emergency room, the nurse does a venous cutdown and prepares an infusion of a pressor agent to raise A's blood pressure. Extravasation of the agent causes considerable slough, as a consequence of which a portion of the affected limb must be amputated. A's action against B or C still is valid; he can claim damages against either of them because of pain, suffering, and loss of limb. In addition, A can sue the hospital and the emergency room nurse who attended him. However, A can collect only that total amount that the jury believes is sufficient to compensate him for his injuries.[10]

If the injured person gives the original wrongdoer a general release, this does not automatically release other professionals who care for him subsequently.[11]

Where more than one tort-feasor is involved in causing injury or loss, the term *joint tort-feasors* is used. It is not necessary for the plaintiff to prove which of them was the sole or chief cause of his injury; he need only demonstrate that either or both of them were responsible. The joint tort-feasors can ask the court to determine each one's share of the damages on the basis of his share in causing them.

STANDARDS OF CARE

The plaintiff must present evidence indicating the standard of care that is required of a practitioner in the given circumstances, and then offer evidence that through ignorance, negligence, or lack of skill, the defendant failed to adhere to the standards cited.[12] The New York Court of Appeals has ruled that failure to exercise the standards of care required constitutes negligence, possibly even gross negligence. The negligent person is liable without regard to the employer-agent relationship for any injury resulting proximately from his negligence.[13]

NEGLIGENCE PER SE

SOURCES OF STANDARDS OF CARE   Existing standards of conduct provide a yardstick against which reasonable care may be measured. These standards are official when they are defined by legislative act or by regulation imposed through legislative authority. A violation of such a statute imputes a strong inference of negligence—*negligence per se*, that is, negligence in itself.

Another way in which standards of care may be violated occurs when such standards have been codified into local laws or ordinances. In general, such standards will be upheld under a challenge.[14] The New York City Hospital Code has prescribed specific standards for surgical and medical care. These standards were challenged as being oppressive and going beyond the statutory privileges of the city's Department of Hospitals, but the State Supreme Court upheld the standards.

Still another source for standards of care is private groups or associations or boards which exert influence in specific areas of practice through their accreditation function or similar authority. An action that contravenes the standards of care prescribed by such a group does not constitute statutory negligence, but would be given considerable weight as evidence.

Then again, there exist informal standards which have not been codified but which are followed generally by all the practitioners in a given locality. These practices, too, would be considered by the court.

PURPOSES OF STANDARDS OF CARE   Standards of care aid in defining duties and responsibilities. Their chief objective is to avert injury to the members of the public whom they seek to protect by limiting the possibility of harm to *unforeseeable* circumstances. In a court test, the plaintiff would be required to prove that the informal code had been violated, and, if the plaintiff is able so to prove, his case is greatly strengthened.

For example: The plaintiff may seek, through calling upon expert opinion, to establish the standard of care that is exercised in the preparation of cultures by physicians, nurses, or technicians. Such proof would be relevant where death or harm has resulted from localized or systemic infection, and would aid in determining the defendant's negligence.[15] On the other hand, inasmuch as medicine is not an exact science, the courts will not hold a doctor or dentist guilty of negligence for an incorrect diagnosis; but the courts do hold that "only if a patient is adequately examined is there no liability for an erroneous diagnosis." [16, 17]

Just as the physician is expected to exercise ordinary care and judgment in carrying out procedures and arriving at a diagnosis based on them, so are technicians or nurses employed and instructed by him expected to exercise such judgment. For example, the nurse must use special care where the patient is senile, has physical or mental impediments, suffers from hypotensive or hypertensive disease, or is sensorily handicapped.

The court will consider whether the professional defendant acted according to the standards set by his colleagues in the community. These standards, however, must be reasonable, progressive, and enlightening. Sometimes they are not, as in the case of a seventy-one-year-old woman who complained of stomach pains, general fatigue and syncope, and who was referred to the radiologist in the hospital for x-ray and fluoroscopy. Without taking any clinical history or making any inquiry of her, he instructed her to position herself on the x-ray table. While unattended, she fainted and fell to the floor.

Having suffered fractures, she also claimed aggravation of a preexisting vascular condition, and in the lower court, the standard of care by radiologists in the community eventually became the issue in the malpractice suit. Testimony pointed out that radiologists did not usually take clinical histories or try to discover their patients' preexisting or undetermined physical or mental limitations. The lower court held for the physician on the ground that laboratories fixed standards of practice in the community. In holding for the plaintiff, the appellate court found this an improper and unreasonable standard of care, therefore inadequate defense against the patient's claim.[18] It violated elementary principles of due care, ignored the premise of foreseeability, and abdicated the professional's responsibility to be sufficiently alert in preventing further injury to those who came to him for assistance.

In a similar case [19] the Circuit Court of Appeals for the District of Columbia was equally clear in holding for the plaintiff. Here, too, a patient complaining of dizziness and syncope was sent to the defendant radiologists in the local hospital for diagnostic roentgenography. She came to them with the usual radiology requisition slip, which contained neither reference to her condition nor precautions. Since she had come in for an intravenous pyelogram, the requisition form did note that she had diabetes with complications. Hypertension is a complication frequently associated with diabetes.

The patient's chart would have given adequate warning, had it been read by the radiologist. The requisition slip was the only thing the defendant radiologists and their x-ray technician saw that might, in the opinion of the court, be inadequate. A series of x-ray films was taken in the supine position; then vertical irradiation was begun. At this point the patient fell and fractured her left cheekbone.

The court instructed the jury that the hospital (by its requisition form used) and the radiologists and technician (by their technical acts) might establish with expert testimony that they had met locally acceptable standards of care. However, the jury was instructed to measure the actions that caused the injury by the criterion of what a reasonable person of ordinary prudence would have properly done, given the preliminary information, in the same circumstances.

While expert testimony is usually deemed essential to malpractice cases, courts in many jurisdictions find it unnecessary if the issue can be determined on the basis of lay knowledge and experience. Had a roentgenologist testified for the patient as to customs and standards of practice, that expert might well have recited the same standard which the jury's decision ultimately deemed inadequate. The case, however, was decided not on the basis of inexpert radiologic service or abrogation of standards, but on failure to use ordinary care.

In a recent landmark case,[20] a somewhat similar line of reasoning was adopted by the Illinois courts. They held that plaintiff could look to higher standards of care than those prevalent in hospitals in the community, such as national hospital accreditation standards, public regulations, and bylaws of hospital medical staff.

FAILURE TO GIVE DEGREE OF CARE REQUIRED   If knowledge of the patient's condition or prudent immediate observation establishes the need for attendance or instruction to the patient in rising from a bed or an x-ray table, a hospital may be held liable for a patient's fall when such care is not provided. In one case [21] a hospital failed to instruct the patient to call for assistance if she needed to leave her bed. Hospital personnel were also negligent in not putting up bed rails in accordance with general nursing practice to deter patients over sixty from leaving their beds. A jury found that these two circumstances, given the hospital's prior knowledge of the patient's disorder, constituted the proximate cause of the patient's fall.

FAILURE TO MEET SPECIAL STANDARDS OF PRACTICE   Special care is as necessary when the patient is in transit to and from a medical department as it is during the procedure. Straps, supportive material, and sufficient staff must be available.

Courts are customarily most sympathetic to handicapped patients, especially the old and the young. However, in the case of a nine-year-old patient who fainted and fell when she was left unattended after receiving an intramuscular penicillin injection for tonsillitis,[22] the court felt otherwise. The nurse gave the injection in the treatment room as ordered by the examining physician. She then instructed the child to sit in a chair, and left her. The patient fell from the chair and broke two teeth. In finding for the physician, the Washington court said that the local standard of practice—to leave a patient unattended after receiving an injection—had not been refuted by expert testimony.[23]

Special nurses, such as nurse anesthetists, are held to the standards of care of their specialty. In a recent case of paralysis following administration of a spinal anesthetic, an Oregon court noted the importance of a community standard of practice.[24] Expert testimony had stated that it was standard local practice to place a pillow under the patient's head when giving a spinal anesthetic, in order to prevent the possible rise of the anesthetic in the spinal canal. Here no pillow had been used. The court said the jury might infer that this omission was the proximate cause of the patient's paralysis.

A patient who feels an x-ray study should have been taken, or been taken sooner or of another area of the body, must always prove this by expert testimony. A 1967 New Jersey case [25] concerned a woman who had injured her back in a fall. X-ray films taken at the hospital by a physician and confirmed by the head of the radiology department showed no fracture. An anterior-posterior view was taken, but not a lateral view. After continued pain, the patient saw her personal physician, who referred her to another radiologist.

The latter examined a larger area roentgenographically and discovered a fracture.

The patient's physician testified that the time lost had contributed to her additional pain and suffering and probably extended the period of recovery. The crucial testimony, however, was that of the second radiologist the patient had consulted. He defined the standard of practice in this type of radiologic examination to include at least both an anterior-posterior and a lateral view in examination for sacral defect. Since the doctors at the hospital had failed to do this, the appellate court reversed the trial court's finding for the defendant physicians and hospital.

In *Schempp v. City of New York,*[26] where the city of New York was held liable for substantial damage, standards were examined for the transportation and treatment of cardiac patients. The patient had been required to dress and walk downstairs so that the ambulance could take him to the hospital. The court considered this a breach of standards.

This question of standards also involves the office nurse. She must often decide whether the patient who calls can come to see the physician, or the physician must make a house call. In one case, however, the hospital's emergency personnel had been called by the patient's private physician and told the nature of the emergency. Of twelve orders posted on the patient's order sheet by the ward physician on admittance, only four had been carried out. Oxygen was made available for administration ten hours after his admission (and five minutes before his death).

It was the estate's contention that he should have been stretcher-carried without delay to the ambulance, that electrocardiography and other diagnostic tests should have been carried out promptly despite the hour (2:30 A.M.), and that oxygen should have been administered early. The jury agreed.

In the case of a hospital nurse who gave intramuscular injections improperly (outside the upper outer quadrant of the buttock) the hospital was held accountable for damages and pain.[27] A medical witness' testimony was adequate to establish a deviation from standard. It should be noted that a medical witness is also competent to testify as to the proper procedure a technician should employ.

OPERATING EQUIPMENT   Negligence would be very likely if a certain therapy had been given to many patients over a long period, then unexpectedly and suddenly caused symptoms when applied to a particular patient. In an Oklahoma orthopedic clinic, a patient had received 50 treatments on her leg with a "Medcolator" after having undergone a laminectomy. .At the fifty-first treatment, she claimed a burn which developed subsequently into a chronic ulcer. She said the technician who administered the treatment had to readjust the machine and wet down the ground pad, and that it then stung and burned her ankle. The technician was supposed to turn off the machine and call her supervisor if she had any difficulty in operating it; this was standard procedure. The patient testified that the technician had had difficulty but called no one and instead made the adjustment herself. The patient's family physician testified that the injury was of a type that could be caused by a burn. His testimony, plus that of the patient, made out a prima facie case for negligence. Even though instructed to hold the defendants to only a measure of the care exercised by an ordinary prudent person, the jury found for the plaintiff and against both the orthopedist who ordered the treatment and the clinic that employed the technician.[28]

Standards of good hospital practice require not only the use of protective side rails for patients in various categories, but also their proper placement. In one case, where there was evidence that the side rails on the bed were up near the patient's head but slanted down toward the foot of the bed, the court felt an issue of fact was properly raised as to whether the patient might have left the bed in a dazed condition and fallen.[29] In another case, a substantial award was given by an Illinois jury to a plaintiff who, while under sedation following surgery, fell over side rails only partially raised.

Care in the use of operating equipment was defined by the *MacPherson v. Buick* case,[30] which has been upheld in many courts for more than half a century. From it, the following principle has been derived: One who allows imperfect equipment to be used, whether he is the manufacturer, leasor, or a member of the board of trustees at a hospital, becomes jointly liable with the person who actually uses the equipment for any injury to an innocent third party, such as a patient, a special duty nurse, or an attending physician.

It is the duty of the manufacturer of a potentially dangerous piece of equipment to use due care in its preparation. He is liable to persons other than the buyer and the immediate user. His duty is held to extend to *anyone* subsequently using it. It makes no difference if the part that caused the trouble was not of his own make originally, so long as he used it in assembling his equipment and sold it as part of his total product. In *MacPherson v. Buick*, the car in question had been bought second-hand. The wheel collapsed and caused the accident. It was made for Buick by a wheel manufacturer. The Buick Company was held responsible, even though it had never dealt with the owner.

The objective of such a holding and the resultant principle show how the court can establish a standard of care in the public interest. The court stated that a manufacturer must submit parts bought from other manufacturers to adequate tests, or else be directly responsible for the harm caused if adequate examination should have disclosed the defect. This principle holds true for all types of surgical and Roentgen equipment, syringes, and even drugs. Both the distributor and the manufacturer of component parts may be liable.

ATTRACTIVE NUISANCE   In Chapter 4 we discussed the duties of the owner or controller of a property such as a hospital, an office, or a home, to trespassers, licensees, and invitees. The doctrine of *attractive nuisance* creates an inference of negligence and responsibility upon persons who permit anything that might be the cause of injury or harm to be available in such a way that it might attract children onto or into it or might use it externally or internally. A discarded refrigerator from which the door has not been removed is an attractive nuisance; an unattended dumbwaiter or elevator is another; discarded medical equipment is still another.

PROXIMATE CAUSE (DIRECT CAUSAL EFFECT)   In a 1967 New Jersey case,[31] the trial court instructed the jury in defining *proximate cause* as one which in natural and continual sequence, unbroken by an efficient intervening cause, produces the result complained of and without which the result would not have occurred. *Intervening cause* is defined as factors which a defendant could neither control nor anticipate. The plaintiff must prove that the negligent act complained of was the proximate cause of the harm he suffered.[32]

We have said previously that the court must see the breach of duty as the real cause of harm. For example, a nurse and surgeon may lose track of a sponge and leave it in the patient's abdomen, thus breaching their duties of care. If, a few days later, the patient dies of lobar pneumonia, their breach of duty involving the sponge would not ordinarily implicate them in a charge of negligence for his death. In any complaint, the patient or his lawyer must prove causation and may do so by circumstantial evidence.

Where a nurse fails to strap a dizzy, hypotensive, and semisedated patient to an x-ray or examining table and the patient falls off and breaks a limb, that failure to secure him might be considered the proximate cause of the injury. On the other hand, in a recent case,[33] a summary judgment was granted against the claimant and upheld on appeal. The patient received a penicillin injection from a nurse and subsequently sued for damages, claiming she suffered a staphylococcal infection and osteomyelitis. Since the nurse showed that she had used a prepackaged sterile needle and syringe and never contaminated the needle, there was no proven connection between the injection and the later complaint.

NEED FOR EXPERT TESTIMONY   Since the practice of medicine and dentistry is not an exact science, a patient who alleges professional negligence must support it with expert testimony. This holds true for both routine and special procedures undertaken by a professional nurse. In a 1967 Pennsylvania case,[34] the court found that a dentist was not liable for the patient's loss of all her teeth following a painful root canal operation. It pointed out that without expert testimony to show that the act complained of was the proximate cause of the harm, the patient had failed to establish her case. The only exception to the need for expert testimony occurs where the subject matter is so simple and the lack of skill or care so obvious as to be common lay knowledge.

When a patient dies and it is alleged that a physician or nurse is guilty of tortious action, the one charged cannot raise conjectures as to what the patient's chances of survival would have been in the absence of negligence. The patient's survivors need not prove to a certainty that the patient would have lived if the defendants had promptly used proper medical or surgical techniques.[35]

ALTERNATE CAUSATION

In weighing the evidence to determine the proximate cause of injury, the jury may determine whether any possible cause other than the negligence charged was the more probable, less probable, or equally probable cause of the harm. If, however, one or more causes for the damage exist, the patient must generally show that the one he is complaining about contributed with the other act or acts to his injury.[36]

Where the evidence discloses two or more possible causes for the patient's injury, for only one of which the nurse would bear responsibility, she will not be held liable unless the preponderant evidence discloses that her action was the more probable cause. This is ordinarily a question to be decided by the jury, since it is a question of fact. Many higher courts have indicated that where more than one possible cause is offered, and as a matter of law none of these could be said to be non-negligent, it is the jury's duty rather than the judge's to determine which of the possible causes constituted negligence and which, if any, was the proximate cause of the injury.[37] It is important to note, however, that medical testimony for the plaintiff must be confined to reasonable medical *probabilities* to be accepted as evidence. The defendant can attack the claim of injury with medical proof based on *possibilities*.

A surgeon caring for a patient in emergency treatment necessitated by nose bleeding of three days' duration asserted he had ligated the patient's external carotid artery. The patient subsequently suffered partial paralysis. He based his claim for malpractice on testimony of two medical experts that it was the internal carotid artery that had been ligated. This error gave rise to paralysis and was tantamount to malpractice. The last statement was not denied by the defendant.

However, in support of the defendant's position, the patient's own medical expert testified that at least half a dozen other variables could have caused the paralysis. This made the plaintiff's allegation too indefinite for proximate cause of the injury, which admittedly could also have been caused by shock, muscle spasm, aneurysm, arteriosclerosis, or malformations of the peripherovascular system.[38] In this case there was such complete disagreement of medical testimony, all of which claimed expertness, that only a jury could resolve it.

In *Schulz v. Feigal*,[39] the doctor's nurse gave an elderly cardiac patient a vitamin injection, one of a series, to improve an eye condition. She immediately discovered she had used a syringe containing epinephrine instead, and informed the physician. The doctor thereupon laid the patient down and gave an injection of Sparine as an antidote to the epinephrine. The patient seemed to be recovering, so he returned to his schedule, admonishing her to remain on the cot where she had been placed.

While alone on the cot in the EKG room, the patient became nauseous. She tried to go to the bathroom to vomit, and fell. She sued, and the doctor defended on the premise, which was accepted by the trial court, that her injury had resulted from her own negligence in getting off the cot against his instructions. The Minnesota Supreme Court reversed the decision on the principle that "the succession of events, unbroken by any event for which the patient could be blamed, flowed from the original negligent act, injecting her with wrong substance." There was evidence from which the jury could find that her fall was the natural and proximate result of that act.

Even where it could be said that the nurse's or the physician's negligence was the proximate cause of a particular circumstance that the plaintiff is complaining about, it must be established that the harm thus caused will sustain a claim for legal damages.

There are some cases where a failure to successfully sterilize a patient after a physician has undertaken to do so results in childbirth. The birth of a healthy child, even if unwanted, by itself may be rejected as a basis for the recovery of damages. It may be sustained, however, if the patient suffered extraordinary pain and suffering with the childbirth or if her health was damaged.

For the past twenty years most courts have held that a child has a valid cause of action for injuries sustained prior to birth. Aside from the concept of viability—that a fetus is a living human being from the moment of conception—courts have acted on the belief that a child has a legal right to begin life with a sound mind and body. The existence of a cause of action depends on whether the child's congenital injury was caused by the wrongful act of another.

Courts have used this doctrine in making awards for malformation caused by teratogenic drugs. In a recent case, a physician was found to be negligent in failing to prescribe gamma globulin for a pregnant patient when informed she had been exposed to German measles.[40] If the physician had prescribed the product and it had been given— and because outdated or otherwise imperfect it failed in its purpose —a cause of action might lie in product liability. Pharmacists should be especially careful in dispensing drugs to patients (in the outpatient dispensary) during the first trimester of pregnancy, and nurses should check dating and dosage in administering them.

RES IPSA LOQUITUR

When negligence is "so apparent that a layman would have no difficulty in recognizing it" (as stated in Arizona law), the case is sufficient, other basic elements being shown, to send it to the jury.[41] This concept is obviously related to the theory of res ipsa loquitur in negligence and malpractice actions. Because the plaintiff sometimes faces great difficulty in establishing the direct cause of his injury, through either expert testimony or circumstantial evidence, he frequently has recourse to an old doctrine called res ipsa loquitur, sometimes termed the doctrine of implied negligence, literally, "the thing speaks for itself." This doctrine developed in English tort law.

WHEN APPLICABLE The doctrine maintains that a claimant who often cannot show the precise act or instrument that caused his injury may be entitled to infer that such an injury could not have taken place without negligence on someone's part. The defendant must undertake to explain to the court how the injury *could* have occurred without him or his agents or employees being negligent.

Where the instrument or process which allegedly caused harm is controlled by the defendant(s), and where an accident has occurred which as a matter of common knowledge does not ordinarily occur if proper care is exerted, the court expects the defendant(s) to explain satisfactorily their freedom from negligence. This presumption of negligence occurs where common knowledge, lay and/or medical, holds that the injury would not have occurred in the absence of negligence.

The doctrine of res ipsa loquitur applies in Canadian courts as well. As in the U.S. it applies most stringently to defendants who are shown to be in full control of the situation that caused the alleged harm and damages. Thus, in circumstances where the patient could not have interfered or even known what was occurring because of anesthesia or sedation or screening, this rule of evidence would be most apt to be recognized.

Most frequently, res ipsa loquitur is offered by a plaintiff when foreign bodies or material of hospital origin, such as surgical sponges or instruments, are left in the body or when there are new injuries to untreated areas of the body. For example, the plaintiff may show glove powder in his wound, or burns to his body after x-ray treatment or other applications of heat, rays, or electricity. Or, by showing that a piece of gauze had been left in his body, the patient may establish a prima facie case against the physician who operated on him, and the burden of disproving the plaintiff's contention is shifted to the defendant. If this piece of gauze lacked a precautionary radiopaque marking, it would constitute proof for the plaintiff against a hospital defendant.

A classic example is that of a female patient in surgery for a hysterectomy. In her room after the operation she discovers bad burns on her body. The surgeon and nurses had for use during the operation an electric cautery and inflammable sterilizing solutions. No one can tell her how she was burned. In her suit she names those present, and someone must explain away the inference of negligence and tell the court what occurred.

The patient who sustains infection through the use of an unsterile hypodermic needle usually pleads res ipsa loquitur. In short, common knowledge and experience teach that the result would not have occurred if the nurse had used due care, not only professionally but also as a normal prudent person.

The doctrine is also applicable to the use of equipment. In one case [42] a wheelchair leg rest supporting the plaintiff's previously fractured leg allegedly collapsed. The leg was badly fractured. The court held that since the patient had not touched the locking device, the leg rest would probably not have collapsed if the hospital had used proper care in its maintenance and inspection.

Res ipsa loquitur is useful not only to a plaintiff who has suffered harm by the defendant's act of commission during treatment or surgery. Consider the case of the aged paralytic with impaired vocal cords who hankered for the pipe he could neither fill nor light and which he could hold only with his teeth. He used to get attendants to fill it, light it and stick it in his mouth, and then remove it after a while.

One day, what started as an act of kindness ended with fire in his bed and bad burns on his body. The last person in his room was a hospital attendant. The court felt that circumstances were sufficient to make the doctrine of res ipsa loquitur applicable. The reasonable conjecture was that someone had left the patient smoking and unattended. Even though there was no conclusive proof that only hospital employees could have left the pipe in his mouth, the evidence did demonstrate that the hospital, through its employees, did have the opportunity to control the pipe and matches.[43]

The plaintiff can only attempt to assert this doctrine. It remains for the judge to determine whether it applies to the particular case on the basis of the facts presented to him. If he charges the jury to consider it and the defense feels his definition and instruction are unjust, it is a basis for appeal. If he rules it out, the plaintiff has the same option.

DEFENSE AGAINST RES IPSA LOQUITUR   While the plaintiff may achieve an inferential advantage from application of the doctrine, the defendant can respond by showing that the injury could have resulted from other probable causes. For example, a patient had a tourniquet applied to her arm and claimed that this was the obvious cause of resultant paralysis. Expert testimony introduced by the defendant demonstrated that this was not necessarily so. The defense pointed out that paralysis could occur without negligence in patients with latent circulatory and anatomic structural abnormalities, or in patients with individual susceptibility of an abnormal nature.[44] In any case, when expert testimony by the defense tries to nullify the plaintiff's charge, the burden of proof again shifts to the plaintiff. He must now prove, by a preponderance of the evidence, that the physician's action was negligent and the true cause of the harm.

Occasionally, liberal courts will associate the doctrine of res ipsa loquitur with the implication of breach of· standards of care and judgment, as in *Edelman v. Ziegler,*[45] where cardiac arrest resulted in severe brain damage. Res ipsa loquitur was held applicable against the anesthesiologist because arresting the action of the heart was fairly rare in abdominal operations and he was relatively untrained. Community standards of practice required special training to perform an endotracheal intubation. The surgeon was not implicated; the anesthesiologist, as an independent contractor, was completely liable. Had this been a nurse anesthetist, depending on the circumstances, either principal or both, that is, surgeon and/or hospital, would have been liable.

Sometimes courts will not allow the plaintiff to use res ipsa loquitur, since it is applicable in professional negligence if it can be said that it is common lay knowledge that harm ensues from the treatment or procedure only when negligence occurred. If the professional had undertaken a highly complex or scientific procedure, it is not likely to be common knowledge that injury has come from negligent performance.[46] The plaintiff, however, could present expert testimony that such injuries as those sustained could have occurred only with negligence. Thus, the plaintiff can then properly invoke the doctrine of res ipsa loquitur.[47] The doctrine may be invoked only against a defendant who was in control at the time. He would be liable for the negligence of his agents (e.g., nurses, interns).

The doctrine may not be applicable when the injury cannot clearly be shown to have resulted from an instrument or process controlled exclusively by the defendant. It may be turned aside by positive proof at best, and, at the least, by evidence which casts doubt on the origin of the inquiry. In one case,[48] a burn on the patient's back could have been caused by the friction of an improperly fitted back cast or by the application of heat with a lamp applied to the cast after the patient returned to her room. This becomes a question of fact for the jury to weigh.

CONTRIBUTORY NEGLIGENCE

HOW IT NEGATES A CLAIM   We have said that contributory negligence would destroy an assertion of advantage under res ipsa loquitur. What is contributory negligence?

Contributory negligence is conduct by the plaintiff which involved an unreasonable risk of harm to himself or his property that bears on his present suit against the defendant. Since contributory negligence offers a complete defense against the plaintiff, the latter must prove that he was *not* contributorily negligent. In several states, including New York, the plaintiff need not do this in a *wrongful death action* (death allegedly caused by defective mechanisms, accident, or institutional or individual negligence) since it would be unfair to those who fall heir to his rights, his testimony being unavailable. However, even in a wrongful death action, the defendant can take on this burden. If he proves the deceased was contributorily negligent, the case is concluded in his favor.

Respondeat superior also operates in contributory negligences. The contributory negligence of an agent or employee is imputed to the employer and nullifies the latter's cause of action.

Infants and children below six years of age generally cannot be held contributorily negligent. In some states, such as New York, the minimum age is four years, depending on intelligence.

HOW TO PREPARE IT FOR DEFENSE   Failure of a patient to comply with the professional's directions before, during, or after therapy is often held to constitute a basis for an allegation of contributory negligence. This is an important advantage to the defendant, since the plaintiff's negligence which proximately contributes to the harm that he complains of bars recovery in a suit based on negligence or malpractice.[49]

When a patient ignores or acts contrarily to the doctor's or nurse's instructions, it is important to record this since it may ultimately show the patient's contributory negligence to any harm he claims. In a Florida case a widow sued on the basis of improper diagnosis and treatment of her husband. When it was shown that he left the hospital against orders—and that the hospital did nevertheless call him at home to caution him to eat strained baby foods—the fact that his death was caused by fecal peritonitis proved he had acted against his own interests.[50]

This is true also in the many cases where patients leave the bed, take down side rails, go to the toilet—against express orders not to do so or with a warning to request an attendant. Disobedience of orders should be recorded in the nurse's chart and notes. The patient's cause of action would then have to overcome such a fact with good reason.[51] The patient might show that she could not wait the lengthy period for an attendant. In such a case she might show that guard rails were put up improperly and she was in a dazed and sedated condition of which the nurse was aware. In one case,[52] the court said the jury would weigh the facts and evidence and decide whether the nurse had rendered proper care.

Most U.S. and Canadian jurisdictions have ruled that the plaintiff must be free of contributory negligence to press his claim for the negligence of another, as stated previously, outside of the exception noted. In most states, including New York, as part of his presentation to the court he must declare and prove freedom from contributory negligence. Sometimes the plaintiff attempts to avoid the rule by claiming that the defendant ignored the doctrine of *last clear chance*. This doctrine creates an inference of negligence against the person who had the last opportunity to avert the harm.

COMPARATIVE NEGLIGENCE

About six states and some jurisdictions outside of the United States do recognize and practice the doctrine of *comparative negligence*, French in derivation, which permits a pro rata allocation of damages in accordance with the estimated percentage of the plaintiff's own negligence. Contributory negligence in these jurisdictions does not bar a suit, though good documentation and records can play a major part in reducing the award of damages. Comparative negligence operates on the theory that even if one has been careless in some slight manner, he should not be prevented from recovering some of the damages from the party mainly responsible for the harm.

For example, Nurse A is on night duty as a supervisor and checks wards on various floors. She takes the elevator up to the fourth floor, makes her check, and wants to go to the third floor. There are two stairways and an elevator. She walks to the end stairway, which will facilitate her check on the floor below. She opens the door to the stairway and finds that it is dark, apparently because of a defective light bulb. At this point, using due care and prudence, she should go back to the fourth-floor ward desk and advise the maintenance department to replace the bulb. She should then use the alternate stairway or the elevator to descend to the third floor. She does none of these things, but confident that she knows the flight of stairs, she uses it anyway. She stumbles into a large standing ashtray at the top of the landing and falls, causing herself various injuries.

A court might find that her contributory negligence had disqualified her from a successful suit against the hospital. In terms of comparative negligence, they might find both parties—the nurse and the hospital—at fault and pay the nurse, who suffered the actual harm, some fair amount of damages.

A recent malpractice suit against a dentist in New York sought to differentiate between negligence and dereliction from professional duty, attempting to get away from that state's strict observance of the contributory negligence rules against plaintiffs. As a result, they seemingly found a position where the comparative negligence doctrine could be applied. Finding for the plaintiff, the court held that while a patient's contributory negligence would bar recovery, in an action in negligence his failure to follow instructions may not defeat a suit for improper professional treatment. Given both contributory negligence and improper treatment, a jury might find that the improper professional treatment did in fact cause the injury, but would reduce the award of damage since the patient's failure increased the damage.[53] This was the decision reached by the lower court; a retrial, ordered because of a technical error, is pending at this writing. The court seemed to have believed the patient was treated so badly that the failure to follow directions had nothing to do with the injury.

DAMAGES

Damages has many meanings within the context of this discussion.

As an essential element of his case, the plaintiff must allege and prove that the tortious act complained of caused him harm on which he bases a specific demand for compensation. He could in theory make out a successful case, but unless his objective is merely satisfaction, and not recompense, without stipulating and proving damages it would be an empty victory. Symbolic awards such as one dollars, six cents, or one peppercorn are termed *nominal damages*.

Black's Law Dictionary defines *damages* as "a pecuniary compensation or indemnity which may be recovered in the courts by any person who has suffered loss, detriment or injury, whether to his person, property or rights, through the unlawful act or omission or negligence of another." When the court assesses damages for the plaintiff, it is considering actual and pecuniary damages. These damages are generally described as *compensatory*, since they are arrived at on the basis of what financial loss the plaintiff has had and will have from his injury to person or property. Awards frequently refer also to *special damages*. These are the actual or exacted consequences of the harm suffered but going beyond repayment for pain and suffering to some fair reimbursement for lost income.

Exemplary or *punitive damages* are separate from an award which would merely compensate the plaintiff for his loss or costs. They are intended to penalize the defendant for having acted in a malicious, fraudulent, or wanton manner. The intention is to discourage a repetition of such actions. At the same time, they compensate the plaintiff for the unusual trouble he has had. So, when an action involves gross negligence, the plaintiff's attorney will ask for punitive damages. If the judge has been shown evidence that ordinary negligence has been compounded by intent, recklessness, willfulness, or deceit, he will generally agree to submit such an issue to the jury.[54]

Appellate courts have sometimes questioned the wisdom of putting an issue of punitive damages to the jury, especially where there was no proof from which a jury might properly conclude that the defendants manifested deliberate disregard for human welfare. As a general rule, punitive damages are awarded as a result of a defendant's recklessness and/or callousness and like criminal complaints, this should be very clear from the evidence.

At the conclusion of the case the court awards the damages it deems just; this is the judgment for the plaintiff. Repayment must be made either by the professional who personally caused the damage or by a third party who has undertaken to pay for his derelictions, e.g., the insurer. We have previously noted that it may also be paid by one whom the law indicates or selects as responsible to the general public when the professional errs or omits, according to the law of agency and the doctrine of respondeat superior.

Damages and Mental Health

Traditionally, damages are based on personal physical injury or property damage. In tort cases, probable or possible adverse effects of an allegedly tortious injury are elements of damage. These add mental pain and suffering to the physical disability already incurred.[55] In *Ferrara v. Galluchio* (1958), the New York State Supreme Court reiterated the increasingly important policy of compensation for emotional distress and psychic trauma. However, most courts have recognized mental suffering only in conjunction with physical injury, even in cases where physical injury is relatively minor. Our discussion of proximate cause noted that in an earlier New York case,[56] it was held that "a wrongdoer is liable for the ultimate result, though the mistake or even negligence of the physician who treated the injury may have increased the damage which would otherwise have followed from the original wrong." In criminal law, the courts have followed such a policy for an even longer period of time. In *People v. Kane*[57] the decision stated: "It is only where the causal connection between the original injury and the ultimate damage may be said to be too tenuous, that the original wrongdoer will be freed from liability for the ultimate damage." The New York court used precedent from these two cases in finding for Mrs. Ferrara.

Where the action has been predicated on the wrongful death of a decedent, courts hold that his dependents and next of kin are generally entitled to recover pecuniary damages. This would be based on the amount of money the decedent would probably have given them, according to what he actually gave them in the past. His estate would also apply for damages for his pain and suffering. A husband has an additional action for loss of consortium and services. This last has resulted in large awards when the wife is a young mother and the husband will have to hire paid help to run the home and care for children.

Good Samaritan Laws

Many states now exempt from liability for damages doctors, and sometimes nurses, who in good faith render emergency care to an injured person at the scene of an accident or other casualty.

With the growing concern over negligence and malpractice suits and the impact of insurance rules and awards, many professional organizations have sought to limit their liability when their aid is proffered or solicited in emergency situations. This limited liability has taken the form of *Good Samaritan laws,* which exist in most states. These laws vary greatly in coverage of health professionals. Some cover only physicians; others include nurses. Still others include any persons who provide emergency assistance. Since the state of California enacted the first such law in 1959, many other legislative bodies have tried to provide some legal protection against suits resulting from emergency care.

RESPONSIBILITY OF THE GOOD SAMARITAN

Anyone may render first aid and emergency care, but under English and American law, no one is forced to do so. However, in the French Civil Code and other bodies of civil law it has influenced, one who fails to give such assistance, either personally or by summoning aid, can be criminally prosecuted. The only exception is risk or danger to the rescuer or other persons.

A nurse, like a physician, is not obliged to render assistance in an emergency. But once she does so, she must meet the standards of skill, competence, and prudence that society has a right to expect of her. Since she obviously knows more than a lay person, she is held more accountable than the former when she undertakes the role of the Good Samaritan. If she exercises normal competence even in a matter usually beyond her scope (justified by emergency need), she will be liable only for obvious imprudence, negligence, and carelessness. Some persons fear that the language of these statutes is open to broader interpretation than was intended.

Within the usual scope of her activities, every nurse in an emergency may be required (1) to determine the need for prompt medical attention, (2) to make a tentative diagnosis or assessment of the patient's condition, and (3) to employ necessary resuscitative and first aid measures. Nurses employed at industrial installations are expected to render first aid. However, they must be aware of the danger in failing to advise the patient of any need for further treatment. A jury could construe this failure as negligence and further deduce that the negligence caused the patient's damages.[58]

While common law did not make emergency assistance a duty, it did show great respect and consideration for the rescuer. If the latter is injured or suffers loss in giving aid, the law often recognizes an obligation to him, either by the person assisted or by a third party who created the disaster or predicament. In one New York case [59] a man who saved a small child from death from an oncoming train was himself killed. The court did not permit the defendant —the railroad—to challenge the claim for damages on the grounds of the decedent's willing exposure (assumption of risk) to the risk involved and possible contributory negligence.

In his *Lawmen, Medicine Men and Good Samaritans*, Professor Foster of New York University indicates a growing belief that the clamor for the protection of Good Samaritan laws is being utilized as an excuse not to get involved by helping those in distress. He further points out that professionals have a moral duty (symbolized by the oaths they take), if not a legal one, to be involved, and this serves as a proper example for others.[60]

LIMITS OF THE GOOD SAMARITAN LAWS

If a rescuer injures the person he is attempting to help, Good Samaritan laws will not give him blanket protection. These statutes cannot be distorted to deny a patient the right of redress for injury. If they are so distorted, they will not be allowed to stand.

Also, in spite of the doctrine of respondeat superior, common law still finds the doer liable for his own misdeeds. However, common law has also established that negligence might create liability when resulting not from carrying out a duty, but rather from a voluntary action. This held true regardless of whether the voluntary act was gratuitous or for compensation, past, present, or future. The purpose of this concept is the attempt to guarantee that where the health, safety, or property of an individual is in jeopardy, those who render voluntary assistance will proceed with as much care as they would where their aid was a matter of duty, contract, or responsibility. The law restrains the individual from doing harm, rather than requires him to do a good deed.

Records and Charts

Good records must be kept for the benefit of the physician, nurse, and hospital, and for the patient's safety and care. This applies whether he (she) is a surgical, medical, or gynecological patient. Records should show that complete and proper attention was given to the patient; that a full case history was taken; that a history of allergy was or was not present; that all necessary routine tests were taken in a timely manner; and that both ordinary and extraordinary findings were documented.

If tests and findings, no matter how ordinary, are omitted from records, an inference can be created that they were not done. When laboratory tests are inconsistent with clinical findings, the tests should be rerun or other tests made.

A mistake in diagnosis can be a basis for a charge of malpractice. However, the courts recognize that medicine and dentistry are not exact sciences and that sometimes diagnoses require a willingness to check and recheck as needed.[61] Tentative diagnoses are made to be confirmed or altered on the basis of various tests, and the history leading up to the final diagnosis should be carefully documented. Entries on the patient's chart should be qualified in an appropriate manner by the doctor in control. Failure to use such language will allow the chart to be subjected to another interpretation in court.[62] While there is no need for verbosity in record keeping, there is even more danger in brevity, in the "one-worders" or "one-liners" that betoken inadequacy. This is often a flaw in dental records (especially when they are not maintained concurrently with treatment).

Records should reflect advice given the patient, whether that advice was accepted and acted upon or rejected. They should also show that the patient was warned when failure to keep appointments created the possibility of jeopardy. Once records have been set down, alterations and additions should be dated and initialed so that they cannot be misinterpreted as admissions of second thought or fault.

The office nurse for a physician or dentist protects her employer. However, the occupational nurse, like a physician, can be found negligent in failing to advise the patient in time of his need for further treatment, where such negligence becomes the proximate cause of a worsening of the patient's condition or a new complication. She should keep a record to protect herself as well as her employer.

Many attorneys agree with educators in professional schools that the importance of keeping adequate records should be stressed. Record keeping tends to slacken as the professional grows busier. While this is especially true of dental and medical practitioners, it is also true of nurses. The busier and more active the practitioner, the less he can afford to prepare anything but an adequate record.

Unfortunately, for many busy private practitioners, the records are less records of care than accountancy and tax aids. Therefore, they often state the date of the visit and the fee collected. Obviously this is not a record that will help a defendant in a malpractice or negligence action. In fact, it might have the opposite effect.

Nurse's Assumption of Medical or Paramedical Duties

Can an industrial nurse at an industrial installation which operates without a physician order an x-ray study independently? Can she receive, either verbally or in writing, the interpretation of x-ray results for the patient? May the x-ray technologist give these directly to a nurse not acting as immediate agent for a physician? May a nurse give an intravenous injection of contrast medium for radiological procedures such as intravenous pyelograms and angiograms? These are some of the questions that are frequently raised by physicians, nurses, and x-ray technologists in practice. We need not look to the nursing practice act for an answer if we are concerned only with tort liability.

Let us take as an example a nurse who orders a chest x-ray examination of a patient at an industrial installation and examines it without a physician's intervening reading, advice, and direction. Perhaps she is attempting to discover whether the worker's complaints are due to silicosis or reactivation of a tubercular lesion. Ordering the examination for this purpose and reading it without having established a proper physician-nurse-patient relationship would in itself violate the state medical practice act and be punishable as a misdemeanor or a felony. A further complication in tort would exist if she lacks the requisite skill and experience. Whether or not she had read the chest plates properly, she might be held responsible for missing, or seeing and not reporting, other diagnostic signs on the plate. Widespread pulmonary alveolar disease usually is identifiable radiologically, as are numerous cardiac pathological changes.

Handling of Drugs

A nurse handling drugs must consider the liability of using prescription drugs without the authority of the physician-patient relationship. A doctor is expected to get an adequate case history and to record drugs that the patient is presently taking before prescribing others. A nurse who gives drugs to an employee would be expected to do the same as a matter of expected prudence. Therefore, if she gives cold tablets with antihistamine content to a worker who is already taking rauwolfia and phenobarbital for hypertension, an

injury inflicted upon himself by loss of alertness or a highway accident caused by falling asleep might be attributable to the nurse and
her employers.[63] In a Midwestern case,[64] a nurse at a utility company
dispensed a penicillin tablet to an employee. Antibiotics, penicillin
in particular, are known to cause many fatal and near-fatal reactions
of an anaphylactic nature. In this case, moments later, the patient
suffered cardiac arrest. There was no prior history of heart trouble,
and the court awarded the patient a 10 percent disability. In circumstances like these, the plaintiff's attorney investigates the manner in
which the proximate cause of the injury (in this case the penicillin
tablet) caused the damage to the complainant. As a result, the nurse
and all those responsible for her might be named codefendants,
and her authority to dispense or administer the medication would
have to be statutorily measured. Here, too, the nurse, like the manufacturer of the drug is vulnerable in circumstances where either his
product is claimed to be contaminated, ineffective, incompletely
described in his labeling as to directions, cautions, and contraindications, or in any other eventuality that could foreseeably create
danger with distribution of the product.

Relations with Other Professions

When two professionals are caring for the same patient, each will
be liable for his own acts, even though one is in a subordinate or
dependent position. For example, if a doctor writes a prescription
erroneously and the pharmacist fills it unquestioningly in the erroneous manner and the patient is harmed, the patient has recourse
against both parties: the doctor for his negligence in writing it in-
correctly, and the pharmacist for his failure to discover the error.
Every professional has a duty to prevent the negligent acts of another
professional which he has observed or ought to have discovered by
exercising ordinary professional prudence and skill.

Responsibility of the Nurse

A nurse is not liable for the malpractice of a physician, nor is she
liable if, in following the physician's orders, the patient is injured.
The physician alone is liable.[65] She would be liable if she deviated
from his directions without authorization; if she failed to carry out
the directions properly; or if she failed to question and seek the
physician's correction, advice, or explanation for any directions she,
as a nurse, knew to be dangerous to the patient. She may not abdi-
cate her own responsibility by ignoring her expert knowledge in
favor of the statement of her employer or nominal superior. Nor may

she delegate this duty to a subordinate in training or ability. In short, her joint or primary liability will stem from her own negligence in the practice of her profession, or from her own failure to exercise the standard of judgment and care the public has a right to expect.

Along with her legal responsibility, she must accept the moral responsibility that accompanies her professional status. Therefore, although her hospital, physician employer, or lay employer is responsible for her legal negligence, she too is responsible for the misperformance of her acts—although her financial resources being less than the employer's may act as protection. She is legally and morally bound to give her employer a quality of performance he has a right to expect.

However, the principal professional or independent contractor, employer, or superior must also undertake some responsibility for the negligent acts or omissions of his assistants or employees who act within the scope of their duties or employment. That does not relieve employees of their own responsibility. It merely assures the public that they may look to the employer for a remedy, even if the employer is ostensibly in no way responsible for the patient's injury.

Unless a physician actually employs the nurse or technician, he may not be liable for their torts. He will be, however, if they are functioning under his direct supervision and instruction. As an example of this principle,[66] a doctor performing an exchange transfusion on an infant in an incubator did not notice that the infant's foot was on a 150-watt light bulb. The covers were over the infant's foot and the doctor did not remove them or position her. Burns were so serious that amputation was required. The court of appeals held that he had not placed the infant on the bulb, and that it would exceed a duty of ordinary care to require him to inspect the positioning and preparation of the baby by the hospital's nursing employees prior to commencement of his work.

Persons on the medical health team are morally and legally bound not to abet the negligence, malpractice, torts, or crimes of other members of the team. Therefore, a nurse should discuss with her superior the facts, as she is aware of them, of any accident or mistake which adversely affects the patient. The deliberate concealment of this information may be considered evidence of admission of culpability; callous indifference is equally unethical. All too frequently, in an attempt to shield a particular person, she causes blame to be directed to another who is innocent, or to the hospital. Fraudulent concealment has other legal drawbacks, in addition to undesirable publicity. See the newspaper account of this Canadian incident.

GMC proceedings

DOCTOR WHO LEFT FORCEPS IN PATIENT TRIES 'CONCEALMENT'

A doctor who left a pair of forceps in a patient when he performed a gastrectomy was charged with infamous conduct in a professional respect before the Medical Disciplinary Committee recently. But Mr Paul Honingmann, for the GMC, stressed: "The charge is not one of carelessly leaving forceps in the patient's abdomen; the charge is essentially one of concealment."

It was said that William Albert Paine, registered as of Redwater Alberta, Canada, M.B., N.U. Irel 1943, an immigrant to Canada, on January 4, 1966, at the Sacred Heart Hospital, McLennan, Alberta, performed a gastrectomy on Mr Andre Erickson, at the conclusion of which a pair of Spencer-Wells forceps was left in the patient's abdomen. Dr Paine subsequently concealed the accident from the authorities of the hospital, and failed to record the fact on the patient's record.

Dr Paine, who was not present, said by letter he had nothing to add to what he had said at a disciplinary inquiry by Canadian doctors, except that he had been under the influence of a Dr Campbell Fowler.

Instruments

He had thought it was his duty not to communicate anything which happened in the practice outside—even to the chief of staff.

After the operation had been concluded, Mr Honingmann said, there was the usual routine check of instruments and swabs and it was discovered that a pair of Spencer-Wells forceps were missing from the operating theatre. One of the nurses must has suspected these were left in the abdomen.

An X-ray was immediately made and it was discovered that the instrument was inside the patient. The other superintendent telephoned Dr Campbell Fowler and Dr Paine. They immediately returned and decided to leave the forceps inside for eight to ten days.

There was evidence that Dr Fowler was interested that this incident should not come to the notice of other colleagues: there was rivalry between the doctors who practised in Falher and those who practised in the neighbouring small town of McLennan.

The patient seemed to make a normal recovery, and the doctors changed their minds and on the 14th day decided to discharge the patient without removing the forceps. Three months later he collapsed, and Dr Paine arranged for him to be brought back. When the patient was re-opened a large mass of gangrene was found around the forceps.

Four operations

After the second operation the patient had a stormy convalescence. A third operation was necessary when the anastomosis of the bowel broke down. It was not successful and a fourth was necessary.

Eventually, about three months after the original operation, it was decided to refer the matter to Dr Fish, the superintendent, who according to the by-laws of the hospital should have been informed at once. He arranged for the patient to be transferred immediately to the nearest large hospital, the Royal Alexandra, at Edmonton.

Explaining that the charge was of concealment which might have had much more serious consequences than was, in fact, the case, Mr Honingmann said the most serious aspect was the falsification of records. The fact that the forceps were left inside was not recorded on the chart.

False

Dr Paine's evidence was that he made two records, one false and a correct one which he kept at home. When the patient was re-admitted the records were again falsified concealing that the purpose of the operation was to remove the instrument and the gangrenous section.

The Legal Assessor, Mr Cyril Harvey, read to the Committee extracts from the transcripts of evidence from Canada, in which Dr Paine said that his reason for not informing the hospital authorities was loyalty to his chief.

Finding Dr Paine guilty, the committee directed that he should not be struck off in view of his earlier suspension in Canada.

SOURCE: *Pulse,* Woking, England, July 29, 1967.

CASE CITATIONS

1. *Butterman v. Chamales,* 220 N.E. 2d 81 (1966).
2. *Thomas v. Winchester,* 6 N.Y. 397 (1852).
3. E. Jacque Courtois, *The Canadian Nurse,* **60** (12), 1170 (1964).
4. *Cassidy v. Minister of Health,* in K. G. Gray, "Law and Nursing," *The Canadian Nurse,* **60**(6):545 (1969).
5. *Richardson v. Doe,* 199 N.E. 2d 878 (1964).
6. *Duling v. Bluefield Sanitation,* 142 S.E. 2d 754 (1966).
7. *Alaska Laws,* C. 49 (1967).
8. *Hopper v. McCord,* 153 S.E. 2d 646 (1967).
9. North Carolina Supreme Court, No. 624 (1966).
10. *Lurie v. Dr. Goldman and Mount Sinai Hospital,* 278 N.Y. 2d 549 (1965).
11. *Milks v. McIver,* Joint Tort-feasor Rule.
12. *George v. Travelers, Inc.,* 215 F Supp. 340 (1963).
13. *Thomas v. Winchester,* 6 N.Y. 397 (1852).
14. *Ferrante v. City of New York,* 271 N.Y. 2d 256 (1966)
15. *Artist v. Butterweck,* 426 P. 2d 559 (1967).
16. No. 18432, U.S. Court of Appeals, Fourth Circuit (1966).

17. *Frazor v. Osborne,* 414 S.W. 2d 118 (1966).
18. *Favalora v. Aetna Casualty & Surety Company,* 144 So. 2d 544 (1962).
19. *Washington Hospital v. Butler,* 384 F. 2d 331 (1967).
20. *Darling v. Charleston Hospital,* 211 N.E. 2d (1965).
21. *Mercy Hospital v. Larkins,* 174 So. 2d 408 (1965).
22. Washington Supreme Court No. 37, 630 (1966).
23. *Ibid.*
24. *Mayor v. Dowsett,* 400 P. 2d 234 (1965).
25. *Betenbaugh v. Princeton Hospital,* 235 A. 2d 889 (1967).
26. *Schempp v. City of New York,* 279 N.Y. 2d 183 (1967).
27. *Nichols v. Wilmington General Hospital,* Delaware Supreme Court 19 (1964).
28. *Orthopedic Clinic v. Hanson,* 415 P. 2d 991 (1966).
29. *Vick v. Methodist Evangelical Hospital, Inc.,* 408 S.W. 2d 428 (1966).
30. *MacPherson v. Buick,* 217 N.Y. 382; 111 N.E. 1050 (1916).
31. *Fernandez v. Baruch,* 232 A. 2d 661 (1967).
32. *Silvers v. Wesson,* 122 Ca. App. 2d 902 (1954).
33. *Cobran v. Harper,* 154 S.E. 2d 461 (1967).
34. *Lambert v. Soltis,* 221 A. 2d 173 (1967).
35. *Hicks v. United States,* 386 F. 2d 626 (1965).
36. *Gonzales v. Salveston,* 84 Tex. 3 (1892).
37. Case of Moore, 202 So. 2d 568 (1967).
38. *Horst v. Shearburn,* 233 A. 2d 236 (1967).
39. *Schulz v. Feigal,* 142 N.W. 2d 84 (1966).
40. *Sylvia v. Gobeille,* 220 A. 2d 222 (1966).
41. Arizona Supreme Court 79111 (1966).
42. *Martin v. Aetna Casualty Company,* 387 S.W. 334 (1965).
43. *Hospital Authority of the City of St. Mary's v. Eason,* 148 S.E. 2d 499 (1966).
44. *Beary v. Smart,* 51 Cal. Rptr. 306 (1966).
45. *Edelman v. Ziegler,* 44 Cal. Rptr. 114 (1965).
46. *Haase v. Delree,* 142 N.W. 2d 486 (1966).
47. *Shannon v. Jalles,* 217 N.E. 2d 234 (1966).
48. *Learch v. Ellensburgh Hospital Association,* 400 P. 2d 611 (1965).
49. *Shirey v. Schlemmer,* 223 N.E. 2d 759 (1967).
50. Florida Court of Appeals, Third District, No. 65-893, 894 (1966).
51. Wisconsin Supreme Court No. 108 (1966).
52. *Vicks v. Methodist Evangelical Hospital,* 417 S.W. 2d 137 (1966).
53. *Morse v. Rapkin,* 263 N.Y. 2d 428 (1965).
54. *Kelly v. Chillag,* 381 F. 2d 344 (1967).
55. *Mull v. Emory University,* 150 S.E. 2d 276 (1966).

56. *Milks v. McIver,* 264 N.Y. 267, 270 (1934).
57. *People v. Kane,* 213 N.Y. 260 (1914).
58. *Doan v. Griffith,* 402 S.W. 2d 855 (1966).
59. *Eckert v. Long Island Rail Road,* 43 N.Y. 502 (1871).
60. *Journal of the American Bar Association,* **50,** p. 223 (1966).
61. *Price v. Neyland,* 320 F. 2d 674 (1963).
62. *United States v. McCann,* 386 F. 2d 626 (1966).
63. *Kaiser v. Suburban Transport and Dr. Faghin,* 398 P. 2d 14 (1965).
64. *People v. Gilbert,* 145 F. 2d 925 (1944).
65. *Byrd v. Marion General Hospital,* 162 S.E. 738 (1932).
66. *Timmons v. Commonwealth of Virginia,* 129 S.E. 2d 701 (1963).

CHAPTER 6

TORT LAW:
INTENTIONAL TORTS

Intentional torts are those which occur "whenever a person [does] damage to another wilfully and intentionally, and without just cause or excuse."[1] We shall examine these in turn.

FRAUD AND DECEIT

Fraud has certain elements that the plaintiff must allege in his complaint and that must ultimately be found to have been present by the court. First, fraud is characterized as willful and intentional; the wrongdoer must be shown to have acted purposefully.

Second, the fraud must attach to *material* misrepresentations. That is, the deception deals with important elements of the understanding between the parties. For example, a salesman shows a log cabin at a lake resort to a prospective buyer, and the latter notes that the logs seem wet. He tells the salesman that the logs look to him like unseasoned and untreated timber. The salesman says, "Oh, no. The logs are seasoned and treated. It rained the night before." The fact that it did *not* rain the night before is irrelevant. What *is* germane is that the salesman said the wood was seasoned and treated when actually it was not.

Third, the misstatement or untruth must be known as such to the one perpetrating the fraud. This may include being purposefully unresponsive to an inquiry. For example, a nurse orders curtains for a sanitarium housing mental patients. She asks the seller whether they are fireproof, since she is required to provide them for the patients' rooms. The seller, who knows they are not fireproof, may

1. Say they are fireproof; that would be fraudulent.
2. Say he does not know; that would be fraudulent.
3. Say they are not fireproof; that would obviously be nonfraudulent.

The fourth and final element upon which a claim of fraud or deceit is based is that it did cause a loss or harm to the victim. Or, as we used the term in negligence, the fraud was the proximate cause of the damage.

There is an associated tort actionable in many states called *negligent misrepresentation,* which covers the same basic elements as fraud and deceit except that the wrongdoer does not definitely know that he is telling a falsehood. If the seller of the curtains did not know for certain that they were not fireproof and yet stated they were in order to make the sale, he would be committing negligent misrepresentation. The type of relief that a plaintiff gets in such a case is similar to that in a negligence action.

Also associated with fraud in medicolegal situations is the doctrine of *fraudulent concealment,* sometimes called the *discovery rule,*[2] which is not a cause of action in itself but is important in determining the statute of limitations. An allegation that the physician, hospital, or nurses had fraudulently concealed the cause of his injuries gives the plaintiff in many states the right to sue in the period starting from the time of his discovery. In some jurisdictions the statute has been considered to take effect from the time an ordinary prudent person should have discovered the concealment.

If a nurse misleads her employer as to her training, experience, and ability, and as a result causes harm to persons or equipment entrusted to her, mere discharge may not suffice. The employer may also establish fraud and seek to recover damages from her. Fraud or deceit not only allows recovery in damages but may also form the basis for annulling the terms of a contract from its time of inception. The nursing practice acts provide for prosecution and revocation of license where registration or licensure has been procured by fraudulent misrepresentation as to identity, education, age, or citizenship, for example.

ASSAULT AND BATTERY

Assault is the act of knowingly threatening another person with the likelihood of immediate harmful and offensive bodily contact.

If a man speaking to you holds his cane over your head and says: "Isn't that a beautiful cloud formation!" that is not assault. If the same man holds his cane over your head and says, "I am going to crack your skull," that is assault. While to a distant observer you may have appeared to be in jeopardy on both occasions, you can see that words often help determine what is or is not a hostile gesture. Sometimes assault is characterized as *justifiable* because it is in the interest of safeguarding oneself, one's property, or others. One is justified in raising a fist, an umbrella, or even a weapon to chase off a would-be intruder or thief.

Battery is the intentional harmful or offensive bodily contact with another person, either without consent or with consent exceeded or fraudulently obtained. Accidentally bumping someone is neither assault nor battery.

Assault and battery, which generally occur together, are a frequent and favorite avenue of suit against physicians. This is because it is so often difficult to get the expert testimony the plaintiff needs in a cause of action involving malpractice or negligence. While battery represents an unwelcome touching, specifically here by members of the health team, the intent and the capacity for intent will be measured carefully by the court. There are many occasions where members of the nursing team undertake medically justifiable procedures that may cause pain and apprehension to the patient, and yet not be characterized as assault and battery. Giving an injection, scaling teeth, and physical therapy are examples. However, other actions involving physical contact may well be considered assault and battery. For instance, in one case a mental patient with a diagnosis of dementia praecox was institutionalized in a state hospital. He had a compulsive desire to touch people with light taps on their shoulder. This was noted on his record. An attendant who was annoyed at being touched in this manner threatened to break the patient's jaw if he did this again. He subsequently carried out the threat. The court noted that this was neither battery in exchange for battery, nor justifiable assault, nor self-defense. The attendant knew that the patient was mentally ill and was no physical match for him. He had been told of the patient's quirk, or his supervisor had been remiss in not telling him. Further, the attendant and his employers had the primary duty to exercise reasonable care to protect the patient from hazards which his known condition had made reasonably foreseeable. Since the attendant's employer was a state hospital, the state was found liable for the patient's injuries.

Words alone, no matter how coarse or insulting, do not excuse assault or battery against a patient or fellow employee. The line between these torts and criminal acts is often very thin. This does not disqualify defending oneself against imminent danger that any prudent person would react to. In such cases, only the degree of force should be used that will defend against the other's assault and battery.

In restraining a child or an adult, therefore, the use of force requires a delicate balance of judgment. Needless force or harm to a patient is ethically and legally reprehensible. Assault and/or battery should be used to enforce discipline only in extraordinary circumstances. For this reason, courts have examined closely instances where a member of the health team may legally strike a patient in self-defense, and where it may be necessary to use physical force for the patient's benefit. These must not exceed reasonable bounds.

As an example, in *Croce v. Myers*,[3] a patient's relatives sued a hospital for injuries allegedly inflicted upon her while she was there. The patient had been hospitalized for a severe case of dysmenorrhea and suffering from nervous spells around her menstrual periods. During one of these spells, she had crawled under the bed in fear and refused to come out. In getting her out, those in attendance broke her arm. She was also black and blue, and parts of her body were swollen. Although the trial court had found for the defendant hospital, the appellate court reversed for the patient. The decision stated: "No reasonable person would contend that the breaking of the patient's arm was either necessary or desirable in treating her for her dysmenorrhea, nervousness, or insanity."

In another recent case, in Louisiana, a doctor was held liable for damages when he slapped a child to make her lie still while he removed sutures from her toe. However, when an infant clamped her teeth down on the finger of a physician examining her and would not let go, he was held not liable for exercising sufficient force to free his finger.

Consent

As previously stated, failure to obtain consent and exceeded, abused, or uninformed consent may result in battery. Further, the plaintiff may name as a codefendant every individual who participated in the unconsented touching. This may include the doctor, nurse, and x-ray technician, as well as the hospital or other overall superior. Anyone who assists in the examination of an adult, without his consent, or of a minor without the express or implied consent of his parent or legal guardian, is liable to a charge of assault and battery. This can come about by assisting in dressing, undressing, positioning, or whenever unauthorized touching takes place. In cases of medical or surgical procedure on a minor without the parents' knowledge and consent, courts have often changed the charge from assault and battery to professional negligence arising from a breach of duty to inform the parents.[4]

NEED FOR INFORMED CONSENT

It is obvious that every individual who participates in the patient's total care may have a stake in having every aspect of the procedure and/or treatment covered by the patient's informed consent. Courts have variously defined the language and extent that an informed consent should have in its construction. One court has stated that the patient deserves a full account of the anticipated dangers that pertain to the procedure he is asked to approve. Others indicate the belief that how much of a disclosure is required, or whether it is necessary at all, depends on the plaintiff's showing by expert testimony what reasonable medical practitioners in the community would say in similar circumstances.[5]

California decisional law is weighted heavily in favor of the layman, seemingly to equalize his chances by holding that "a physician subjects himself to liability if he withholds any facts which are necessary to form the basis of intelligent consent." Other courts have held that the type of procedure and its safety or risks should guide the practitioner in determining what constitutes sufficiently complete and informative disclosure. A so-called "middle ground rule" has been stated as follows: "The duty narrows then, on the average case, to disclosure of dangers of which it is likely that the patient is unaware. The doctor should have little difficulty in choosing the risks that are likely to be essential to an intelligent decision by his patient."[6]

Consents, informed or otherwise, are almost never stipulated in statutes or regulations. However, hospital bylaws, which reflect medical ethics and custom and the desire of the profession to protect itself, often require consents in enumerated procedures and circumstances. Likewise, common-law principles endow adult and mentally competent persons with the right to limit the use of their body or incursions upon its privacy. Consents, therefore, come into question only after the act and in those circumstances when the patient, or those who legally succeed him, feel he has been dealt with unjustly. It is not so much that a consent is mandatory, as that assault and battery upon another person is tortious. Therefore, the medical community seeks to prevent, in advance, a charge of assault and battery that is technical and circumstantial, rather than intentional. In obtaining the patient's informed consent, the information given him must generally include a description of the medical problem, the nature of the remedy to be tried, and the risks involved. In some cases, courts have suggested that the patient is entitled to know his chances for recovery and alternative methods for helping him.

In comparison, the holding of a Texas appellate court in a malpractice case illustrates the greater latitude given professional defendants in that jurisdiction. In *Anderson v. Hooker*,[7] the plaintiff, who had undergone an operation for removal of a servical disc, suffered a stroke in the recovery room. He alleged that consent to the operation was fraudulently obtained, inasmuch as the surgeon had never mentioned the possibility of stroke or that another of his patients two months earlier had had a stroke after the same operation. This evidence was excluded as improper. The court held that testimony of expert witnesses had borne out the doctor's contention that in obtaining an informal consent, he need not tell patients of specific adverse results. Further, the court was willing to accept the defendant's testimony that a stroke was not an anticipated risk of the operation.

UPDATING CONSENT FORMS

It is increasingly evident that standard hospital forms, where the incoming patient gives blanket authorization "to perform whatever operative procedures are found to be necessary," are legally inadequate and do not meet the criteria for an informed consent. In a Pennsylvania case,[8] a patient was admitted to a hospital under the care of an orthopedic surgeon who had been treating him and signed a blanket form. Subsequently, this doctor called in a neurosurgeon for consultation, and the latter decided an exploratory laminectomy was necessary. To this the orthopedist agreed. No one discussed it with the patient, asked his consent, or described the risks and alternatives. Following the operation, the patient was left paralyzed from the waist down.

The court found for him on the grounds that the initial consent could at best have been relevant only to the orthopedist's care. It would be hard to construe it as consent for the secondary surgeon.

A consultant called in for special service to the patient should not rely on the primary physician to obtain consent for him. This is especially true of dental specialists, to whom patients are often referred for elective or emergency procedures. While the doctor may delegate procuring the consent to his physician or nurse agents, he should personally undertake verbal confirmation unless his agent's ability and qualification to describe the procedure will stand up in court.

There is little doubt that traditional consent forms leave much to be desired. They are prepared in accordance with a standard medicolegalistic format, in the often technical language of the health care professional, and incorporate vague escape clauses for the hospital or doctor. As a result, the patient agrees to "whatever medical procedures are deemed advisable by the members of the medical staff." Further, the particulars are generally open-ended, and little attempt is made to qualify or interpret them even for patients whose general intelligence or sensory faculties are incapable of grasping the significance or warnings involved. On the other hand, writing out a detailed description in addition to the consent form for the patient or his guardian is a great task. It may place undue stress on the limitations that might inhibit corrective procedures during or immediately after the operation.

As a mean between the two extremes, some individuals and institutions use a broadly termed consent form that refers to and is predicated upon a thoroughly informative discussion between the physician and the patient. If the duty of procuring consent is delegated to the nurse, she should use a specific written consent form. She should have it signed by the patient and spouse, where necessary, or by the parents or guardian in the case of minors or incompetents. Needless to say, records should be available to show that consent was given before sedation.

The discussion and grant of consent by the patient should not consist simply of the physician's word or a chart notation. This could be considered self-serving evidence and therefore poor proof. Properly, such a discussion should be noted and charted, but in addition should be witnessed by a hospital employee and/or a member of the patient's family. The date, time, and length of discussion might prove to be important evidence. The names and addresses of those present should be on the written form, which should be signed by the patient or his guardian.

The more complete the information given before consent, and the more detailed the written consent, the easier it is for the physician to protect himself against future litigation. For example, when a minor comes of legal age, he or his parent or legal guardian can sue for damages that took place after consent was given during his minority. For this reason, adequate records must be kept on experimental and heroic measures taken in the diagnosis and therapy of children. Records which show that the defendant acted with the informed consent of the child's guardian, and that his action was approved by other competent parties after objective examination, would go far to thwart a later claim.

EXCEPTION: EMERGENCIES Consent may be unnecessary in an emergency. Also, some courts have felt that circumstances may create an emergency sufficient to dispense with full disclosure for an informed consent. When a minor unaccompanied by parents or a legal guardian must be treated immediately to preserve life and limb, the nursing supervisor is justified in taking whatever means are necessary. Otherwise, she should not proceed in the hope of getting signed permission later.

The Legal Position of Minors

While the probative force of a minor's consent is not fixed in every court, most often it is recognized and upheld where its terms are advantageous to the minor, or where its disavowal causes mischief or obvious inequity.

Marriage does not transform minors into adults. Many courts believe, however, that marriage may enable minors to undertake many adult responsibilities and be held to their performance. This would depend on their visible maturity and independence. A young couple, both employed, can marry, rent an apartment, buy furniture, for instance. A landlord or a creditor who is very careful would insist on having a parent cosign a lease or a chattel mortgage, but many persons having dealings with them and noting their apparent independence will be protected from their default in most instances. If minors are married but still obviously dependent upon parents, then in most instances the courts will continue to regard them as legally incompetent. Marriage is therefore sometimes (though not always) held to enfranchise or emancipate minors from the legal restrictions of their minority. That is, it gives them the legal rights of an adult or gives a strong impression that they are equipped to undertake adult responsibilities.

In a Western state an eighteen-year-old married couple with one child were living on their own. They agreed to have a physician perform a vasectomy on the husband that would render him sterile. The doctor received a written and informed consent from them. Later, domestic problems arose, and the husband sued the physician on the ground of lack of consent of his parents. The case included elements of a lost marriage and psychic damage. The judge instructed the jury that a minor who marries is often considered emancipated and is legally responsible for decisions that affect himself, his spouse, and his children, so long as he is not the victim of fraud. Further, any minor may be capable of consenting to medical care, depending on the factors of age, intelligence, training, experience, economic status, employment, general conduct as an adult, and freedom from parental control.[9]

Nurses in public health service, student nursing and occupational nursing services are often faced with legal problems in handling females who have not reached their majority or become emancipated. Such situations also create risk for physicians and other supervisors. One such danger zone is the prescription and dispensing of contraceptive pills or devices, and pelvic examinations for female high school and college students without parental knowledge or consent.

Often in camps, schools, and other institutional surroundings, parents waive in advance the need for their assent to medical decisions taken with regard to their children. The legal value of such blanket consents is somewhat greater than that of blanket hospital consent forms because the time and distance factors are recognized. If public officials feel that a public need is more important than the rights of an individual minor or guardian, then the public need supersedes those rights. This principle is illustrated by the military and by public health programs. Nurses and physicians generally find their guidelines in hospital bylaws and regulations; these are carried over into private office procedures as well. Telephone calls to parents and guardians are fairly simple in many instances, and doctors and nurses are often in a good position to make a judgment on their necessity. Obviously, emergency situations change the rules temporarily. But when the emergency is concluded, it shows good faith and good judgment to inform the parent or guardian in a frank and complete manner.

CONSENT AFFECTED BY DRUGS

Although the law presumes that an adult is fully competent and in possession of his faculties, unless conclusively proved otherwise, he may temporarily suffer the loss of his faculties under the influence of drugs and narcotics. In this case, a patient may claim that his consent, if given, was invalid since he did not comprehend the nature, terms, and effect of his consent. Therefore, he could allege that the operative or diagnostic procedure was an assault and battery or an invasion of his bodily right to privacy. His attorney may place in evidence the hospital chart, which shows he was heavily sedated and narcotized. The jury could then weigh such evidence against the presumption that an adult who consents is competent to do so. In one case where the patient had received, within the period consent was given, various doses of Librium, Carbital, Parnate, and morphine sulfate, the jury found from the testimony of credible witnesses that he was mentally competent at the time of consent.

WHEN USING X-RAY EQUIPMENT

The need for informed consents is especially acute in relation to radiological procedures, since the equipment and theory are complicated and difficult for the layman to understand.[10] If the radiological team members use such procedures as carotid angiography, myelography, discography, mammography, and others requiring great expertise, informed consent before proceeding is especially desirable. The more unusual, the more radical the departure from standard practice, the more likely this imposition of the ancient rule of *Carpenter v. Blake:* the doctor who innovates does so at his own risk.

WHEN USING ANESTHETICS

Before administering anesthetics, it is generally necessary to obtain consent from the patient, or from his legal guardian if the patient is not legally competent to give it. The competent patient is legally entitled to determine whether he wants it, and if he does, what form he wants used. If his consent is oral, it should be witnessed and charted as a voluntary and informed act.

UNORTHODOX PROCEDURES

English courts closely examine consents for what would be otherwise serious offenses of assault and battery. This is especially true in the area of homotransplants and homografts. In the United States, the physician is given much greater latitude, provided he secures informed consent.

It is basic law in all Anglo-American courts that before undertaking unorthodox surgery or procedures, the physician or dentist is obligated to give complete information to the patient and his spouse. Further, the physician or dentist must tell parents, when the patient is a minor, "that the procedure he proposes is novel and unorthodox and that there are risks incident to or possible in its use."

In one case violating this rule, the New York State Supreme Court found an orthopedic surgeon guilty of malpractice in the death of a fourteen-year-old boy following an operation.[11] The surgeon performed a spinal jack to correct scoliosis. Three weeks later, the patient suffered severe hemorrhage and died. The surgeon was the only doctor in America who used such a technique. He had been retained by the parents but had failed to get their informed consent. The hospital knew this, and knew also that his methods were legitimate. Therefore, the hospital had no responsibility, either originally or secondarily, to intercede.

There is another legal aspect to this case. The surgeon had performed the same operation at another hospital, and when the patient died, he was barred from practicing there again. However, the New York court held that the second hospital, the one in which the boy had died, was not derelict in allowing the surgeon to practice there. In Ontario, on the other hand, the hospital chiefs have legal authority to dismiss an attending physician from the roster and are required to do so if they feel his treatment endangers a hospital case. In decisional law this can be one part of the total care, including nursing service, for which a board of trustees through the hospital is responsible to patients. Generally, in American law, so long as a procedure is accepted by a respectable minority of the medical profession, it is not deemed experimental, but merely an exercise of the physician's professional choice and judgment. Nonetheless, the physician must fully inform the patient to assure a proper and valid consent.

ORGAN TRANSPLANTS AND SKIN GRAFTS

State laws may require contractual satisfaction for organ transplants or skin grafting between living persons. Such procedures are often fairly complicated even when the donor is a corpse. In either case, it may be as dangerous to exceed the consents as it is to move ahead without them. This is not yet a clear-cut area, and much presently depends on local ordinances and hospital committee bylaws. However, model acts are being circulated to state legislatures to formalize the donation and receipt of organ grafts for transplants. These seek to rule out having the same doctor medically advise, approve, and surgically remove the organ from one person and implant it in another. (See also Chapter 7.)

WITHDRAWAL OF CONSENT

In our earlier discussion we touched on the difficulties encountered by nurses and technicians in carrying out assigned duties that are protested against by minor or adult patients. What does the practitioner do if the patient orders him to stop? He discusses the matter with the patient's family or physician if reasoning with him proves unsuccessful.

What if he demands that the practitioner stop after he has begun? When a patient's reaction indicates that an injected needle has struck a major nerve, it becomes a question of fact as to whether this is a regrettable accident or an act of negligence. One patient with several complaints which had resulted from an automobile accident some months prior was treated by an orthopedist. In the course of treatment, he was injected with 5cc. of procaine. As the needle was inserted, he screamed with pain and begged the physician to stop. Instead, the physician injected two more times. The patient claimed permanent damage in pain and partial paralysis. The standards of care were examined by medical experts on both sides. To reinsert the needle over the patient's objections could be interpreted as negligence or as assault and battery, since consent was withdrawn and the doctor could terminate the act without endangering the patient.

In a 1964 verdict handed down in Georgia involving an x-ray technician, a supervising physician, and a referring physician, a patient charged violation of her consent.[12] She claimed that although she had agreed only to take barium by mouth, the physician directed that a barium enema be administered. The technician then inserted a Bardex catheter tube into her colostomy over her vigorous protest. She claimed he did it forcefully and violently, and perforated her colon. The court held that she had not withdrawn her consent in time; when a patient cries out in pain or anger, this does not signify that she has withdrawn consent. The Georgia court said:

> To constitute an effective withdrawal of consent, two distinct things are required; the burden of proving each being on the plaintiff:
>
> 1. The patient must act or use language which can be subject to no other inference and which must be unquestioned responses from a clear and rational mind.
> 2. When consent to bodily contact is revoked, it must be medically feasible for the doctor to desist.
>
> To permit a lesser standard would be to subject the medical profession to an endless possibility of harassment. This is something the profession should not be called upon to bear, dealing as it does with human life and human frailty.

False imprisonment, false arrest, malicious prosecution, and conversion all come within the general area of invasion of the right to privacy.

FALSE IMPRISONMENT

False imprisonment (or *illegal detention,* as it is sometimes called) means intentional confinement without authorization by one who physically constricts the plaintiff, using force, the threat of force, or confining clothing or structures. Although one need exert no force or have any malicious intent, to detain another without his consent in some circumscribed area is grounds for a charge of false imprisonment. Innocent error resulting in detention, mistaken belief that there is authorization, or lack of malice all may seem to be mitigating factors but are no defense against a charge of false imprisonment. In defending against this charge, one must be not only *reasonable* but also *right.*

False imprisonment must not be confused with statutory authority which permits hospitals to quarantine in a particular place for a limited time patients suffering from contagious diseases, such as active tuberculosis. Such patients are legally protected, since authority to quarantine is renewable on show of cause by the hospital. The patient, his family, or his guardian can dispute such action by disproving the contention.[13]

Nursing and medical staff and hospitals may be parties to illegal detention of patients. This sometimes happens in mental hospitals, where a protesting individual is detained under seemingly valid commitment procedures and documents. In one case, a hospital made no attempt to check into the truth of the patient's claims and instead held him, although their own recorded examination and observation raised grave doubts that he was mentally incompetent. The health officer who signed the commitment papers had never even examined the patient, and on the word of the physician, the hospital resisted release even on a court order. His attorney finally freed him by obtaining a writ of habeas corpus. The court ordered both the hospital and the committing parties to pay substantial damages.[14]

Compulsory confinement or hospital detention cannot be justified by a patient's failure to pay for service. Nor is one permitted, except with appropriate police intervention, to take an employee into a room and keep him there against his wishes while questioning him about some occurrence.

Exceptions

Various cases are on record, such as *Warner v. State of New York,* which hold that confinement will not be viewed as unauthorized if it is "necessary to prevent a crazed or insane party from doing some immediate injury to either himself or others." There are other exceptions to the charge of false imprisonment. One may not be charged with false imprisonment if he confines another to defend himself, other persons or property, or to effect a lawful arrest. Confinement is sometimes authorized by parents, guardian, or by the patient himself. If this consent is exceeded or fraudulently obtained, its limitations or revocation by the consentor, followed by failure to release the patient, does constitute false imprisonment.

FALSE ARREST

False arrest is defined in *Black's Legal Dictionary* as "any unlawful physical restraint by one of another's liberty, whether in person or elsewhere." When a civilian directs a police officer to arrest a person and the arrest is unlawful, the civilian can be liable for false arrest. If there is no arraignment, no institution of regular criminal procedure, then the peace officer becomes guilty of trespass on the person of the one he arrested; this is a separate tort.

A private person can make an arrest without a warrant for a crime committed or attempted in his presence. He can also make an arrest for a crime committed not in his presence, if it was felonious in nature. This is riskier, since innocent error is no excuse. Peace officers can arrest persons, without warrants, for crimes of any type attempted or committed in their presence. They can also make an arrest for a felony, whether witnessed by them or not. They can even make an arrest without a warant if they have *reasonable cause* to believe a felony was committed.

False arrest is not unlike false imprisonment and often follows in that fashion. They can both be grounded in innocent mistakes. However, in malicious prosecution, the defendant has instigated or prosecuted out of bad motive.

MALICIOUS PROSECUTION

Malicious prosecution is initiated out of a desire to harm or by inconveniencing another without probable cause to believe that the charge will hold. A prosecution for any motive other than to bring the accused to justice may be characterized as malicious prosecution. *Malice* itself has been described as the intentional doing of a wrongful act without just cause or excuse. An essential element of a cause of action for malicious prosecution is that the proceeding terminated in the plaintiff's favor. A discharge by a committing magistrate is prima facie evidence of "without probable cause." While an indictment creates a presumption of probable cause, the plaintiff can try to show that it was handed up because the defendant withheld information.

Associated with this tort is one called either *abuse of process* or *malicious use of process*. Here the tort-feasor properly secures legal process, such as a writ, for one purpose and seeks to use it for another. For example, courts have held that prosecution for issuance of a check without funds, if really used to collect a debt, constitutes an abuse of criminal process. On the other hand, serving the defendant with a summons so that he will stop ignoring or avoiding a valid legal issue is not abuse of process.

CONVERSION

This tort involves an unlawful exercise of ownership over property that belongs to someone else. Frequently only a thin line separates conversion from larceny and embezzlement, which are criminal offenses. For example, a hospital employee may, without authorization, lend a floor waxer owned by the hospital to a friend, with the understanding that it will be returned in a day or two. At the moment it changes hands, the employee is liable to civil or criminal prosecution.

CASE CITATIONS

1. *Al Raschid v. News Syndicate,* 265 N.Y. 1 (1934).
2. *Murphy v. Dyer,* 421 P. 2d 966 (1966).
3. *Croce v. Myers,* 29 S.E. 2d 553 (1944).
4. *Brown v. Wood,* 202 So. 2d 125 (1967).
5. *Smith v. Seibly,* 431 P. 2d 719 (1967).
6. North Carolina Supreme Court, No. 682.
7. *Anderson v. Hooker,* 420 S.W. 2d 235 (1967).
8. *Gray Case,* 223 A. 2d 663 (1966).
9. *Ditlow v. Kaplan,* 181 So. 2d 226 (1965).
10. *Hales v. Raines,* 162 Mo. A. 46 (1911).
11. App. Div. 20, 739, Fiorentino Case 227 N.E. 2d 296 (1967).
12. *Mims v. Boland,* Georgia Court of Appeals No. 40637 (1964).
13. Application of Halko, 54 Cal. Rptr. 661 (1966).
14. *Wood v. New York,* 280 N.Y.S. 2d 609 (1967).

CHAPTER 7

THE DEFAMATORY TORTS: LIBEL AND SLANDER

LIBEL AND SLANDER

Defamatory statements, whether oral, written, pictured, or otherwise communicated, are those which tend to expose a person to hatred, contempt, or aversion, or to lower the opinion of him held by the community. It need not project an image of immorality or ignorance. Defamation affects his reputation. While it may also disturb his peace of mind, the law is interested in the effect on reputation because this in turn influences his ability to enjoy normal social life, earn a livelihood, and bring up a family.

Slander is oral defamation. Because it is by nature more limited than libel, most slanders are not actionable without a showing of special damage. However, slander that indicates a person is guilty of an indictable offense involving moral turpitude; that he suffers from a loathsome disease such as syphilis, gonorrhea, or leprosy; that demeans him in his trade or profession; or that imputes inchastity to a woman is actionable without a show of special damages. *Libel* consists of defamatory statements or materials conveyed by written words, pictures, cartoons, recordings, broadcasts, or telecasts from a prepared source such as a script. Since libel can be broader in its publication, it is generally actionable without the plaintiff's need to show special damages.

Defamation, whether libel or slander, cannot legally be stopped before publication. Nor is it actionable unless it will have an effect. Therefore, it depends on communication of the defamatory statement or material to a third party.

Of Persons

A nursing supervisor, employer, or physician who, in speaking privately to a nurse or technician, calls him lazy, inefficient, dishonest, ignorant, unchaste, or anything equally derogatory, is not practicing defamation. However, when he makes such a statement in the presence of other persons or brings it to the attention of others by any means of communication, the charge may be raised. Every subsequent publication creates a new cause of action and liability, so that everyone who repeats a slander or a libel is responsible for the damage caused by the repetition, even though he indicates that it originated with someone else and even though he believes it to be truth.

In anger or emotional stress, a nurse may tell the patient that others, doctors or nurses, are at fault. Even when this is most obviously unjustified, it may mean (at least) the expense of a preliminary defense. But the expense is less important than the loss of professional reputation, confidence, and position. Therefore, even the unintentional instigator may have to defend himself in a court suit based on defamation or slander.

Sometimes a nurse is concerned about the treatment used by a physician. She must remember that a physician may use unorthodox techniques, experimental drugs, or therapy without danger to his professional status or reputation so long as he has the patient's consent to try new methods, or is using the methodology of a respectable minority of his peers.[1]

It is quite simple to prosecute libel and slander if the plaintiff has been belittled or maligned in connection with the conduct of a special duty, skill, trade, or profession. Therefore, every member of the health care team has a special stake in refraining from idle conversation, comment, gossip, and inaccurate reports. These may not only give rise to suits in negligence and malpractice, but may also find the unwary person vulnerable to suit in defamation.

Qualified Privilege

Practitioners should not volunteer adverse comment against coprofessionals and other members of the hospital staff unless ethics and duty require that the truths be expressed. In this situation, the practitioner may make a report in a proper manner that provides a defense against a charge of slander or libel. Such a safeguard is necessary. Otherwise, hospitals, business relationships, and professional services might become bogged down by dishonesty and incompetence. Such a truthful and nonmalicious report is known as *qualified privilege.* It provides some immunity against a charge of libel and slander.

Qualified privilege also protects a doctor or nurse who makes a professional report on a patient. However, they too lose this protection if indifference to truth, or malice, is obvious from their statement or their conduct. An example of the latter is seen in a case that might easily have occurred against a school nurse. A physician, by mistake or confusion of names or record cards, noted on a thirteen-year-old girl's record that she was pregnant and sent the record to the school authorities in a regular report. After being informed of the report's falsity, he refused to correct it.[2] A report of this type is libel per se, but the doctor was protected by a qualified privilege that extended to reports furnished by him. His stubborn refusal to rectify a seeming error caused the court to rule that he acted with malice, thus nullifying the privilege.

Nurses may use qualified privilege to report on inefficiency, negligence, or incompetence of coemployees, or to respond to a request for references. This is a privileged communication for the benefit of the nurse, her superiors, and hospital management. Hesitancy in giving accurate information about a former employee when one has been named by him as a reference is often mistakenly based on a fear of being sued. When one invites a reference inquiry in seeking employment, the inquirer is entitled to know all the facts, and his informant may give them without fear. The informant, however, must relate only the facts, and not offer opinion or hearsay.

For example, in a recent case a registered nurse failed in a libel suit against a hospital and director of nurses. The latter had stated in writing to a nurse's registry that the plaintiff's times of duty coincided with disappearance of narcotics. The court found no evidence to show malice, but rather a genuine concern to caution the nurse's employer and other potential employers.

A nurse caring for a person who has a claim against an employer or another person should be wary of opinionizing. It is difficult enough for physicians skilled in diagnosis to distinguish between true pain, injury, and malingering. A nurse's statement could involve slander, libel, and/or breach of the patient's privilege of confidential communication. However, if a patient files a suit in negligence against a nurse or physician, the patient thereby waives his privilege and the defendants may testify fully in their own defense.

A mistake in reporting or identifying chest plates which results in a patient's being a suspected or confirmed tubercular may be actionable as libel if the patient is damaged, deprived of employment, or put to the expense of other treatment. However, if a hospital employee or physician spreads this error by mouth, it is slander and possibly slander per se.

Members of the office or hospital staff should not make damaging remarks about patients they know or patients for whom they perform a service. Regardless of any privileges that may be involved, it is easy to make an apprehensive and ill person excited about statements that relate to his character, personality, and condition which might degrade him or hold him up to ridicule.

Defense Against Libel and Slander

The classic and complete defense against libel and slander is to prove the truth of the defamatory statement. A true statement, no matter how malicious, is not slander or libel. However, it must be a complete truth; courts deal severely with near-truths or half-truths.

If a plaintiff can prove libel and/or slander, and can demonstrate its monetary cost, the court will set reimbursement (damages) which the defendant must pay. Damages generally cover not only financial loss, but also whatever special or exemplary damages the court assesses.

INVASION OF PRIVACY

Invasion of privacy is a group of personal torts that deal with encroachments upon the right of another. They may be defined as trespasses upon his body and/or his personality. The Supreme Court of the United States has interpreted the right against invasion of privacy as inherent in the Constitution. As stated by Justice Louis Brandeis,[3] the First Amendment "sought to protect Americans in their beliefs, their thoughts, their emotions and their sensations." It conferred the right to be let alone.

Exposure of the Person

All members of the health team are required to give treatment or care with decency, respect, and the greatest degree of privacy possible. The patient has a right to be seen, examined, handled, or observed only by those persons essential to his care or treatment. Unnecessary exposure of his person or discussion of his case is actionable unless specifically authorized in detail by the patient. As the highest court in New York stated:

> Decent and respectful treatment is implied in the contract from the confidential relation of the parties and especially because of the necessary

exposure of the person required of the patient in connection with the services to be performed pursuant to the contract. This implication arises whenever one person is placed in the control or protection of another.[4]

Patients who are moved through hospital corridors or into examination or treatment rooms should be covered and not exposed unnecessarily to other hospital personnel, patients, or visitors. This right also exists in wards and shared rooms. Hospital personnel must respect the patient's right against invasion of his physical and mental privacy. In addition, while he is in their care they have a duty to protect him against such violation. Courts have held that the mere entry of a male patient into a female patient's room with malice or intent to do harm would entitle her to recover damages for mental anguish.[5] An innocent, inconsequential, and purely accidental intrusion is not compensable. There must be an immediate or imminent physical invasion of the person or his sense of security.

AFTER DEATH

Even after death, the patient's right to be unobserved, to exclude unwanted operations and unauthorized touching of his body, persists. It passes to his spouse or heirs, and they have the right to bring suit if these prerogatives are violated without their consent, as in performing an autopsy. (In the Philippines, the Civil Code notes that the ownership of the body reverts to the decedent's estate. However, if efforts to find the deceased person's kin prove fruitless, the hospital authority may authorize tissue or organ transplants.) Familial property rights in a dead body extend beyond humans. In an interesting Florida case, a court held that speedily willful cremation of a dog which had been under treatment by a veterinarian gave a proper cause of action for damages because it was done without consent of the owner.

While this is the understanding in most jurisdictions, it is a formal statute in some.[6] It has been argued that since the person's body is his or her possession in life and must be unviolated in almost every instance, this is the legal basis for freedom to authorize the use of his tissues or organs in transplants before or after his death. A special form is generally used to implement the donation. This document is helpful in the face of subsequent challenge, where the action is not positively prohibited by statute.

According to this form, the donee and the surgeon or other person effecting the donation should be specified in writing, as should the purpose of the donation. Donor and donee must be willing and competent to consent, and the surgeon must be properly qualified.

There must be no evidence of fraud and every evidence of free and informed will; witnesses should be able to attest to that.

Eavesdropping

Statutory and decisional laws on libel, slander, business and product defamation, and invasion of privacy are often examined within the context of the First Amendment, which states an American's rights to freedom of speech and press. In a rather famous case on this subject,[7] the Supreme Court of New Hampshire considered a situation in which a landlord hid an eavesdropping device in the bedroom of his tenants, a young married couple. The court held that an intrusion upon one's physical and mental solitude or seclusion constitutes invasion of privacy.

Publicity by the Mass Media

This decision extends to televising the actions of a person without his knowledge and consent. However, a closed-circuit television system used in a hospital for treatment, with the patient's understanding and approval, is legal, provided it is used only for the purpose originally agreed to.

Publishing someone's name or picture cannot be restricted if the one who does so is merely exercising a constitutional privilege granted by the First Amendment. For example, if one's name appears in the course of reporting a newsworthy event on television, film, or in a newspaper or magazine article, he cannot prevent this type of publicity. We know from the daily papers and television that in many instances the subjects would rather cover their faces or otherwise avoid notice. Yet we do see the pictures of men alleged to be criminals and women alleged to be homewreckers, with all the details. Such exposure can be challenged. The test is the one of true public interest being served by reporting as against lurid conjecture or repetition of an old story for special or self-serving motives. New York's state supreme court, in conforming to that state's civil rights law, confirmed a decision against a large magazine publisher by pointing out that "mere dissemination of news" is one thing, but handling it in a manner to advertise for a particular purpose or profit, or using it in a manner to induce a gain in circulation, affronts the law.

The civil rights laws reiterate these common-law safeguards by prohibiting the use of a photograph or the testimony or statements of another party to advertise or promote the sale of products, services, or reputation, without the individual's written permission. In a hospital, the patient's consent is required to photograph him, and again to publish such a photograph. Further, if the photographer is a stranger to the patient's treatment, the patient must agree to his admittance. This must be secured on the basis of normal and established principles of contract because unlike libel and slander, truth is no defense against a charge of invasion of privacy.

In Signing Documents

One may use the name of another in signing a document by two provisions only: (1) if a person is specially empowered by law, or (2) if the one who sees the signature knows it is written as an act of agency, and this fact is stated in writing adjacent to the signature. To write another's name may be construed as an act of deceit or negligent misrepresentation, and in many states as an invasion of privacy.

PRIVILEGED COMMUNICATION

Privileged communication statutes specifically prevent divulgence of information gained during or as a consequence of a patient's professional treatment. But beyond statutory protection, the patient has a right to privacy that is part of our common-law heritage. Such protections are especially guaranteed him in law when they cause him harm in reputation and loss of livelihood or profit, or where they are used by another to enhance that other party's reputation or to bring him profit or other economic advantage. Essentially, the civil rights acts protect the individual from the latter, the libel laws, from the former.

Tempering the concept of privileged communication is that of *greater public need.* According to this, privileged communication may be waived if the professional feels that the public's right to know outweighs the patient's right to privacy. Of course, this is not to be taken lightly. A few years ago, when a Communist conspiracy against the national interest was discovered and the principals fled to foreign countries, the psychiatrists who had attended them disclosed the subject matter of their sessions with these patients. Their action was considered by most to fit the concept of greater public need. Similarly, a physician is obligated, whether out of obedience to a local ordinance or out of a sense of responsibility, to warn authorities when he discovers a patient with a disease classed as dangerous and communicable, or narcotics addiction, or a gunshot wound.

Privileged communication is also qualified in some states by the legal principle that each spouse has a right during marriage to know the existence of any disease which might have a bearing on the marital relationship.

There are many kinds of privileged communications. Freedom from libel and slander exists for legislators when they are conducting government business. Judges and attorneys may also enjoy special immunities during trial. Statements made by witnesses in the regular course of a judicial proceeding are absolutely privileged, so long as they pertain to the subject of the inquiry. If these statements are volunteered, extraneous, and malicious, they are not considered privileged.

However, we are more concerned with a very special privilege of communication that has been held to exist between clergyman and penitent, between lawyer and client, between physician and patient, and sometimes between nurse and patient. Privileged communications as determined legislatively are held to promote and preserve certain selected relationships. These have social value and would be hampered or destroyed by fear of disclosure. Information acquired in the course of examining and treating the patient is a privileged communication. The physician-patient relationship bars the disclosure of a confidential communication before the grand jury to the same extent that it bars disclosure at trial in states where such a statute exists. Ethically, and in some jurisdictions legally as well, the nurse may not divulge information obtained during the performance of her professional services for a patient, unless the patient waives the privilege and authorizes her to disclose the information, or unless she is obligated by a higher duty or court order to do so. The nurse should share her knowledge with her nursing and physician superiors only insofar as this information is of importance to the care and well-being of the patient. They are qualified in ethics and law to receive this information, no matter how confidential.

Communications between patient and professional must remain a secret between them so long as such communications were made to aid treatment of the patient, and for as long as the patient requires secrecy. These communications remain privileged when made in the presence of a third person, such as a nurse or technician, who is assisting the major professional or who may give information to the professional in charge. The decision in *New York v. Goldwater* [8] upheld a statute which provided that a doctor, surgeon, or professional or registered nurse should not be allowed to disclose information acquired while attending a patient in a professional capacity.

This statute applied to investigations by city authorities, as well as to judicial proceedings, the decision held.

We have noted the passage of the right to privacy from the dead to their living heirs, which determines the right to perform autopsy. However, the right to make decisions as to release of privileged communications has also passed to the decedent's living legal heirs.

A physician disclosed to an insurance company that his patient, now deceased, had announced a suicide intent to him during treatment for a peripherovascular disorder. The court held that he had violated the principle of privileged communication. It noted that the statement was covered by the privilege since the modern physician treats the whole man, even where primary treatment is for varicose veins. The decision stated: "The physician-patient privilege exists for the benefit of the patient during his lifetime and for the prevention of his disgrace after his death, and cannot be taken away because the physician failed to treat an illness disclosed to him by his patient." The court in this statement indicated the physician's responsibility to order psychiatric consultation in light of the patient's disclosure. It further demonstrates that sometimes, in giving evidence to fight a patient's claim for damages, one may lay the basis for his own involvement in litigation. This frequently occurs in suits derived from hospital incidents.

The patient, dead or alive, has the right to enforce silence only where the communication was made as part of the cause of diagnosis and treatment. Both doctor and nurse may freely testify as to extraneous communications. Therefore, in one case where the patient's widow claimed that her husband had been fatally burned by a defective fuel system in his truck, an attending nurse was permitted to testify that the deceased told her the fuel system had backfired on him.[9]

Statutory restrictions vary as to privileged communications contained in a patient's hospital records. There is no doubt that the patient can waive the privilege and require an opportunity to examine and copy the records. In addition, in some states such as New York, the civil practice act and rules of civil practice provide that a physician or nurse must disclose information as to a deceased patient's physical or mental condition if his surviving spouse or parent waives the privilege and makes such a request.[10]

In a federal hospital case, where the question of government immunity or liability under the Federal Tort Claims Act was at issue, the patient brought suit because portions of his hospital record were made available to his former wife without his permission.[11] The court held that if his rights were violated this was a clear discretionary function of the staff member and therefore was excluded from suit under the federal act.

In some states a statute presupposes that if a patient is called as a witness in his behalf, his physician, who has treated him for a condition with reference to which he is claiming malpractice, then he should allow the defendant to examine such a physician before the trial and take a sworn deposition, or series of answers, from him. Whether this will be admissible during the trial will be determined by the judge's application of the pertinent rules of evidence.

Courts are loath, however, to find a professional defendant guilty where there is any indication that it is done in the public interest.

In *Schwartz v. Thiele*,[12] after an altercation in a parking lot with the plaintiff (a woman), the doctor learned her name and address and sent a petition to the Counselor on Mental Health of the county psychiatric department stating that though she was not his patient, he believed her to be mentally ill. On the basis of this letter, the counselor obtained a court order appointing a physician to examine the woman as to her mental health. The order was set aside on receipt of a report from the plaintiff's personal physician. The plaintiff sued, charging invasion of privacy.

In dismissing her suit for damages, the court pointed out that physicians filing such a petition are statutorily immune from civil or criminal liability. Since the plaintiff did not allege in her complaint that the physician *did not* act with probable cause, the presumption would be that he *did* have probable cause for writing the letter. To have proved the defendant guilty of invasion of privacy, the plaintiff would have had to show that his action was taken without cause, in a spirit of malice, unreasonableness, and caprice.

On the other hand, some jurisdictions statutorily allow research groups or hospitals to divulge information on the condition and treatment of patients being used in medical research so long as they do not disclose the exact identity of the patient. The statute limits this to circumstances when it will advance medical research, medical education, or the effectiveness of manpower and facilities.

Privileged communication has been thought to interfere with the physician's right to testify in his own defense. Some courts feel that the patient has waived the privilege by cross-examination of the physician on the stand. Others, as in Ohio, feel that within limits, the doctor can, at the court's discretion, testify in his own defense so long as he does not reveal communications made to him by his patient or his professional advice given to his patient. The same applies to nurses.

CASE CITATION

1. *Sherman v. Board of Regents of New York,* 266 N.Y. 2d 39 (1966). (1966).
2. *Virgil v. Rice,* 397 F. 2d 719 (1967).
3. *Olmstead v. United States,* 277 U. S. 438, 478 (1928).
4. *Stone v. Eisen,* 114 N. E. 44, 45 (1916).
5. Washington Supreme Court, March 25, 1965, Logan v. St. Luke's Hospital 65 Wash. 2d 915.
7. *Hamburger v. Eastman,* 206 A. 2d 239 (1966).
6. Act of Republic #349, 1056 (Philippine Republic) Philippines.
8. *N. Y. v. Goldwater,* 284 N. Y. 296 (1940).
9. *Taylor v. Reo,* 275 F. 2d 699 (1960).
10. As decided in New York, 269 N. Y. 2d 919 (1966).
11. *Varachek v. United States,* 337 F. 2d 797 (1964).
12. *Schwartz v. Thiele,* 51 Cal. Reptr., 767 (1966).

CHAPTER 8

CONTRACTS

CONTRACTUAL RESPONSIBILITY

Civil liability may arise from a tortious action directly or as a result of a relationship between employer and employee, as described elsewhere. Civil liability may also be created by contractual circumstances, in most instances through express agreement, that is, an oral or a written statement, and in some through implied agreement.

The nurse's fundamental responsibility is to care for the ill, the injured, and the infirm. The nurse, unlike a friend or a member of one's family, receives payment for fulfilling this responsibility. Her promise to nurse is by its nature contractual. The nurse acting as an independent contractor is responsible for performance of the contract, and her actions may result in a breach of contract. The nurse acting as an employee or agent is doing so on a contractual basis. She may or may not be authorized to make contracts for her employer or principal. Nonetheless, by establishing the legal basis for a contract sometimes unwittingly, she may cause contractual liability for the employer. In the event of a breach of contract, the third party would look to the employer for a remedy and the courts would probably uphold his claim, provided validity could be shown.

It often happens that the nurse as agent must judge whether or not her interests or her employer's interests are protected in a contract, and whether or not it is advisable to terminate the contract without penalty, that is, without having to pay for services or products as though the contract was consummated. Sometimes they are faced with the threat of actual breach of contract by one on whom they depend.

ELEMENTS OF THE CONTRACT

Some Terms Often Used

In a sales contract, the seller may be called the *vendor* and the buyer, the *vendee*. If the contract involves credit obligation, the party acknowledging the promise or obligation is the *promisor* or the *obligor* and the party receiving the promise is the *promissee* or *obligee*.

When contracts have a value in themselves, e.g., for exclusive privileges, or service contracts, or by their terms permit the transfer of the rights and duties of either party to a third party, they are *assignable*. The party who assigns his rights or duties is the *assignor* and the party who receives the transfer is the *assignee*.

Most contracts are assignable. Some, however, are nonassignable by reason of their terms or their nature. One may not, for example, assign personal injury claims, workmen's compensation awards, or wages for labor. Most leases, which are popular forms of real estate contracts, are assignable only at terms set by the landlord.

Definition of Contract

A contract has been defined as a promise or set of promises the performance of which is recognized as a duty in law. When that duty is not performed according to the terms of the contract, the law provides a remedy. Not every promise is contractual; social agreements, moral agreements, and agreements of conscience are not generally matters of contract, and a failure to carry out the agreement would not involve liability.

There are several components of the contract: consent of persons involved; consideration to every party to the contract; lawful object or purpose; competency of the parties; a form required by law.

Offer and Acceptance

In any contract there must be an offer and an acceptance of that offer. The offer may be positive, e.g., employment, or negative, e.g., a promise to refrain from doing something. The offer should be definite, and should be communicated by words or actions.

The acceptance by the offeree—the party to whom the offer has been made—should be unconditional and in accord with the contract terms as to price, amount, time of delivery, and other details.

Consideration

In general, money or the promise of money is a contractual consideration. Consideration may be positive in the sense that it involves the giving of something of value, or negative in that it involves a promise to refrain from bringing suit or to accept certain conditions such as providing uniforms.

Consideration is not a factor when it involves anything for which one is legally bound. For example, a contract between a father and his minor children, in which he agrees to provide shelter, would be invalid, since this is his legal duty.

Agreement

There must be real agreement between parties who are competent to make a legal contract, and the objectives of the contract may not be immoral or illegal.

Intent

One of the things that distinguish a contract from a promise is the actual intent to enter into a binding agreement. In this regard, the courts will consider the reasonable impression created in the mind of the offeree. It is possible for a statement that sounds like an offer to be made as a joke or in anger. Would a reasonably prudent man have accepted the offeror's statements as having contractual force?

The general rule is that a promise not expressly made will not be read into a contract unless it arises inevitably from the contract's terms.

Silence does not convey assent except in the unusual circumstance in which a previous transaction led to this understanding. On the other hand, the offeror may stipulate that silence signifies rejection of the offer.

Assent signifies full knowledge of the offer and the intention to accept the terms of the contract in full. In many states, including New York, an offer may be revoked before it is consummated by contract, if the foregoing provisions have not been met.

Certain conditions may attach to a contract. These may be concurrent in most instances. For example, in a sales contract, delivery and payment are presumably concurrent unless the parties agree otherwise. Conditions precedent and conditions subsequent to the contract are self-defined.

TYPES OF CONTRACTS

Unilateral Contracts

The contract initiator, or offeror, generally sets the conditions and the period of time for conveying acceptance by the other party. Contracts are said to be unilateral if the response to the offer is an act. Most express or implied contracts for sale or purchase which are completed at the moment are unilateral.

Bilateral Contracts

"I offer you, if you will do . . ." A contract is bilateral where a promise by the offeror begets a promise by the offeree. "I offer you, if you promise to do . . ." Most employment contracts and many contracts for sale or purchase of materials or services to be provided later are bilateral contracts.

Newspaper ads, circulars, and price quotations given over the telephone or quoted in a newspaper generally are not held to be legal offers, but rather preliminary invitations to bid.

INVALID AND UNENFORCEABLE CONTRACTS

Invalidity and Termination

Contracts can be invalidated by many of the same considerations that terminate offers. For example, contracts based on illicit relationships are invalid; so are usurious contracts.

The contract is invalid if at the time it is made intoxication or drug addiction of one of the parties is such as to preclude legal transactions. Emancipation resulting from marriage, military service, or contracts for necessities may make minors liable for the reasonable value of any items covered by contract.

Where an infant 18 years of age or older enters into a contract in connection with his business, the reasonableness and necessity of which may be demonstrated by a third party, then such a contract may be enforced.

TYPES OF CONTRACTS THAT MUST BE IN WRITING

Certain classes of contracts may not be enforceable even though valid in every detail, if the statute of frauds requires that they be in writing. These classes of contracts are regarded as offering unethical persons the possibility of profiting greatly through lying, distorting facts, or reporting the facts inaccurately and where carelessness in preparing the contract could make the innocent the prey of unscrupulous persons.

The statute of frauds handed down from earliest recorded times in the English Common Law has found its place in the substantive law of every United States and Canadian jurisdiction. The language may not be identical in these, but the legal principles that are set forth governing sales and transactions involving the transfer of property and services are standards. For this reason, it is commonly known as the "statute of frauds," whatever its official title and section number in the laws. It must be pleaded by the defendant as part of his defense, or in his request that the court summarily dismiss the action against him.

We shall next consider the usual requirements of this statute.

A promise to pay the debts of another person must be made in writing. For example, John Jones' child is treated by Dr. Smith; it is clear that John Jones is responsible for paying Dr. Smith's fee. If, however, John Jones asks Dr. Smith to treat Jack Black, a friend, John Jones must make a written promise to pay, or Dr. Smith's claim for payment will not be upheld. This precaution is unnecessary in the usual family relationships recognized by Canada and the United States. In Ontario and most other provinces of Canada, the patient is personally liable for nursing and medical charges, and this liability is transferred to his estate upon his demise. A husband is liable for services rendered his wife unless public and prior disclaiming of such liability has been given. A parent or legal guardian is liable for services rendered a child under the age of sixteen.

Contracts for the sale or rental of real property must be in writing, where the lease is for a period of more than one year.

Contracts for the sale of goods or other things of value above a fixed amount, e.g., $50, must be in writing.

Contracts that will not be carried out for a long time because of the nature of the underlying promise must be in writing. The usual statutory language describes these as contracts "not to be performed within one year," or "not to be completed before the end of a lifetime." Obviously employment contracts are affected by these provisions.

An example is that of a school nurse who is employed by a municipality for ten months annually, from September 1 through June 30. The contract she enters into on September 1 need not be in writing. She then arranges to accept employment at a camp during July and August for the next two years. Such agreement would have to be in writing.

OTHER REASONS FOR TERMINATION OR INVALIDATION

In addition to these recognized reasons for termination or invalidation of offers or contracts, others are common. Impossibility of performance may cause a contract to be unenforceable. For example, a hospital makes a contract to purchase certain surgical equipment manufactured in a foreign country. War breaks out, and it becomes impossible for the contractor to import the equipment. The contract cannot be enforced.

Where the promisor dies, becomes seriously ill, or is incapacitated, he cannot be held to the agreement.

A contract cannot be enforced if the subject matter is illegal of itself. This is, the contract must not contemplate violation of criminal statutes or antitrust laws. Parties to the contract may not agree to a violation of duties owed the public or in situations where they are responsible. Wagers or usurious transactions are likewise unenforceable.

Questions of legality of a contract may arise from the circumstances surrounding it. The use of fraud, deception, trickery, or duress in preparing the contract or having it accepted will make it illegal. Lying about licensure makes a contract voidable and unenforceable against the victim. However, where one knows of these factors and accepts the benefits of the contract and then fails to honor the contract, money damages may be in order. For example, a nurse falsely claims to hold state licensure and performs duties allowed under such authority. Unless the contract is immediately challenged at the time her employer finds out she lied, he would probably still be required to pay her as agreed. He could not possess such knowledge and then refuse to pay her when she completed her duties.

The possible validity of the contract must be measured in relation to its parties. A minor can disaffirm most contracts, even where he has misrepresented his age to induce the other party to agree to the terms. An infant or minor can also defend against a suit for breach of contract by posing infancy as the defense. Therefore, he can refuse to carry out his end of the contract whether it means he must perform a service or pay for value received. However, if an adult third party is involved, as his associate, the age of the minor cannot be used as a defense by the adult codefendant. Nor can an adult codefendant use it as an excuse to break the contract.

One whose insanity is legally established cannot be a party to a contract, but it frequently happens that questionable insanity is given as a reason for disaffirming the agreement. In such a case the law favors the party who has been misled, and may require the party claiming insanity to make full restitution before he can disaffirm the contract.

Where both parties to a contract are equally at fault, or have acted equally unreasonably or illegally, they are said to be *in pari delicto,* and the courts will not be available to either.

Where parties have done work for others without any contract or guidelines as to reimbursement or with an invalid contract, the one seeking payment may take the matter to court. The court will then order payment according to *quantum meruit*—what the work is worth. This is in accordance with simple social and legal theory against unjust enrichment at another's expense.

Damages arising from tort actions have been described. In contract actions damages are usually *compensatory.* That is, they are awarded in an amount that will apparently satify the loss. *Liquidated* damages are provided according to a formula set forth in the contract. Sometimes these damages are described in *penalty clauses.* *Consequential* damages are those limited to what supposedly was implicit in the understanding of the parties when the agreement was made. A plaintiff may bring suit for expenses he incurred in expectation that the contract would be fulfilled. The expectation covers monies paid or debts incurred in anticipation of, preparation for, and performance of the contract that he unilaterally honored. If there were portions of the contract that the plaintiff unilaterally dishonored, these would serve as the basis of a counterclaim by the defendant.

PROBLEMS IN CONTRACTS

Contract problems may arise because (1) one of the parties wishes to breach (or break) the contract, (2) one of the parties seeks to invalidate the contract in part or in entirety, (3) the parties dispute a promise agreed to but not written into the contract, (4) prices for materials or services have changed considerably between the making of the contract and its performance. The written contract is regarded as evidence of agreement, and any discussion held between the parties prior to executing the contract is considered as part of the written expression of agreement. Therefore, an oral agreement made between the parties affecting a written contract made before or at the time the written contract is entered into will not affect the terms of the latter.

A physician contended that he signed a contract to lease medical equipment because the true lendee was a lay person who could not do so. The physician claimed that he was told he would not have to pay the leasing charge. When the actual lendee failed to pay, the physician was held liable. The physician claimed that he was induced to sign the contract by fraud. Had he been able to prove the lessor's deception, and that he was defrauded by relying on the lessor's false representations, the contract would indeed have been considered void *ab initio*—from its inception. Parol or verbal evidence will not, as a rule, alter the terms of a written contract unless it too has been reduced to writing and signed by the party who is to be held financially accountable. A contract that does not with sufficient exactitude express the intention or describe the mechanism of execution agreed to should be supplemented by a signed memorandum between the parties, much like a codicil to a will, and attended by the same formality given the original document.

When a written contract must be interpreted by the court, the court will endeavor to determine the intent of the agreement between the parties at the time they signed the agreement. A catering service, for example, undertook to furnish food services for a period of 5 years to the patients of a nursing home, and to pay the nursing home 10 percent of the gross amount collected from the patients for the service. The nursing home agreed to give the catering service the exclusive food service privilege.

At some time after the service was installed, the nursing home experienced financial problems and went out of business. The owners renovated the facility and reopened it as an office building. The catering service then sued for breach of contract.

Was the nursing home thereby excused from further performance when it ceased to operate as a nursing home? The court stated that as a matter of law it was not excused. Rather, the jury was instructed that the basic issue was whether or not the nursing home had impliedly agreed to operate as a nursing home for the full period of five years. If the facts surrounding the case gave that implication to the written contract, then, notwithstanding the fact that the nursing home ceased its operations with good reason, it could be held liable for breach of contract.

Where a nurse has accepted an offer of employment, she would have a cause of action in the event the contract did not become effective at the time it should have. It is wise to have either a stated policy about terms and conditions of employment understood prior to the hiring, or to have proper terms of severance or firing stated in the contract.

Breach of contract action is available to both parties where the contract is valid. When a professional practitioner contracts to work for a given period which has been preceded by a training period, such as exists in the Veterans Administration Career Residency Training Contract, and leaves after the training period has been completed to take a better paying position, the employer is entitled to damages. The court will examine the contract to determine whether or not it is binding, that is, whether or not there is *agreement* supported by *real consideration*. Any condition that was precedent to the contract must have been properly fulfilled.[2]

Breach of contract for professional services may be examined as to quality and quantity promised and be either the plaintiff's sole complaint or associated with a cause of action in negligence or malpractice. The law imposes on persons of professional standing performing medical, nursing, and related services the duty to exercise a reasonable degree of care, skill, and ability, such as is ordinarily employed by others in the same or related professions. Since this duty exists apart from any express contractual obligation which the professional might have undertaken, a jury would examine the facts to determine whether or not the defendant had exercised the required degree of skill and care. Then, they may look further to additional criteria of performance the plaintiff claims.[3]

The *implied contract* has given rise to many problems in situations where the patient believes that the doctor or nurse has entered into an agreement to perform a particular service and bring about a particular result.

Doctors have been warned against stating, either verbally or in writing, that their techniques, therapies, or medications will bring about a particular result, because such statements are regarded as matters of contractual agreement which may give rise to damages. It allows the patient far more time in which to claim dissatisfaction than would otherwise be the case.

In certain instances, where the court seeks to save the patient's suit, the court may accept a complaint based on breach of contract, i.e., where the patient's right to sue for negligence has been extinguished by the passage of time.[4]

In one case, an attempt was made to overcome the statute of limitations, an action for malpractice being brought more than two years later. The complainant stated that the physician and hospital had breached their implied contract to perform their duties and render their services in accordance with the community's accepted standards of skill and care. In Virginia, where suit was brought, the statute of limitations in contracts is five years. The court defeated that attempt by holding that regardless of the language it *was* a suit for personal injury and care and therefore came strictly under the malpractice statute of limitations.[5]

As a general rule, a practitioner is not held to warrant that his diagnosis is correct or that his treatment will be a success, unless he expressly makes such a promise or establishes a special agreement to that effect. Frequently, the nurse acting as agent for the physician inadvertently creates such a situation. This might happen in the course of securing the patient's consent for the doctor to employ a new technique, device, or drug, or a certain surgical procedure. Or it might happen that in an effort to comfort an apprehensive patient or to create a climate of sympathy, the nurse may give inappropriate assurances and lead the patient and his family to believe that a favorable outcome is guaranteed. As an agent her statements can bind her principals.

Medicine, in the view of the medical profession and the courts, is not an exact science and no member of the health team is considered an insuror or guarantor of good results. But a patient who is misled by an avowal of a cure may have grounds for a breach of contract action.

When a former patient institutes an action for breach of implied or express contract which is not in writing, he must demonstrate by offering convincing evidence that such a contract existed. The court need not accept the plaintiff's word as to the terms of the implied contract. This is especially true when his version sounds "unique and unusual" (as where a patient alleged that a neurosurgeon promised that diversion of the patient's auditory artery would in no way impair his hearing).[5, 7]

ABANDONMENT

Abandonment means that the nurse has unilaterally severed her relationship with the patient, without giving reasonable notice, and at a time when there is still a need for continuing nursing attention. While many see abandonment as tortious conduct, it is fundamentally a breach of implied or express contract. Acceptance of a nursing assignment is regarded as a contractual matter, generally inferred from accepting the nursing assignment with respect to a particular patient. In the case of the private duty nurse who wishes to withdraw from the further care of a patient who still requires nursing care, the patient must be given adequate notice to allow him to obtain and instruct a replacement. Where possible the nurse should secure her replacement, or should give sufficient notice so that the patient may hire the replacement himself, if he so wishes. It is preferable that notice be given in writing to whoever engaged her. Where withdrawal is caused by the patient's unwillingness or inability to pay for nursing care, notice should be given in writing. There should be some attempt to substitute a nursing service provided for indigents.

In introducing evidence to establish abandonment by the nurse, the patient must show resultant inadequate nursing attention or inordinate expense for replacement if she can sustain her claim of breach of contract. To claim damage, there must be a causal relationship between the abandonment and the alleged injuries.[8]

Abandonment is frequently claimed to be the cause of the patient's harm, yet the facts may indicate that he, rather than his attendant, created the abandonment, in which case his contributory negligence may strike his claim.

Where it can be shown that the patient actually abandoned the physician, the dentist, or the nurse, the court may disallow his claim.[9] This situation is illustrated by the following case: A man had stepped on a fish bone and a piece of the bone lodged in the ball of his foot. The skin wound overlying the bone appeared to be healing, but the wound was painful and limited the patient's ability to walk. He was admitted to the emergency room of the hospital, where an intern attempted unsuccessfully to probe the wound. The patient was referred to a private physician for treatment of the wound, which had become infected. Antibiotics and compresses were prescribed. Following several visits to the physician, the patient was instructed to undergo x-ray examination. He delayed doing this for 4 months, and by the time he did appear for the examination, the infection had become so severe that surgery was necessary. The patient sued the intern and the private physician.

The court was influenced in the defendants' favor by consideration of the standard of care generally maintained by them, and by testimony that x-ray examination probably was not practical initially because of the translucency of the fish bone and the acute nature of the infection. In some similar cases, however, the courts have held that physicians and dentists are obligated to inform their patients of the risks involved in not keeping appointments for diagnostic procedures or treatments, when such risks should be evident to the average prudent practitioner.

While a charge of abandonment is not infrequently made against the private duty nurse, it is made against physicians and dentists far more often. The obstetrician, for example, has a responsibility to both mother and infant. The infant is his patient until the pediatrician or another doctor takes charge. Again, as a rule, the anesthesiologist is responsible for care of the patient while he is in the recovery room, but the surgeon retains overall responsibility from the time the patient is taken out of the operating room until he is released to the care of his referring physician.

CASE CITATIONS

1. *C.I.T. Corp v. Dr. Tyree* 151 S.E. 2d 42 (1966).
2. *U.S. v. Averich,* 249 F. Supp. 236 (1965).
3. *Mauldin v. Sheffer,* 150 S.E. 2d 150 (1966).
4. *Schwerman v. Public Util. Com.,* 227 N.E. 2d 220, 17 (1967).
5. *Greeson v. Sherman,* 265 F. Supp. 340 (1967).
6. *Shaw v. Scoville,* 369 F. 2d 909 (1966).
7. *Starr v. Fregosi,* 370 F. 2d 15 (1966).
8. *Lee v. Dewbre,* 362 S.W. 2d 900 (1967).
9. *Lindsey v. Mich. Mutual,* 156 So. 2d 313 (1963).

CHAPTER 9

AGREEMENTS OF GUARANTY, WARRANTY, AND SPECIAL PERFORMANCE

RIGHTS AND OBLIGATIONS OF BUYER AND SELLER

Sales transactions often give rise to contract actions, since the usual sale is contractual in nature. While a sale may be made immediately or consummated in a relatively short time, certain rights remain to both buyer and seller. Since the nurse is often a purchaser, she must be aware of some of the important issues that may arise. She must also realize that sale affords a basis for another type of breach-of-contract action termed a *breach of warranty*.

The seller has the right to expect that the payment given him or promised to him within a specified time will not be defective in any manner. For example, if the buyer pays by check, the seller has a right to expect that he has the authority to tender that check and that there are sufficient funds to back it. The purchaser has the right to expect that the articles purchased are as represented and that they are of satisfactory quality to do the job for which they are intended.

The seller may sometimes offer a specific or general guaranty, but in almost every case the sale is accompanied by some form of implied warranty. There is a basic difference between a guaranty and a warranty, as there is between an express warranty and an implied warranty.

GUARANTY AND WARRANTY

A *guaranty* is a written statement of the product's expected performance for a stated period of time and gives the buyer a remedy of refund or exchange on some stipulated basis if the product fails to live up to expectations. Government units that enforce business morality laws, such as the Federal Trade Commission, interpret the terms as a virtually unconditional promise. An *express warranty* is given orally or in writing and puts on record the seller's opinion of his product's safety, effectiveness, quality of construction, performance, and durability.

Product brochures and advertisements generally contain these statements. Often, they appear in the language of the sales invoice. Under ordinary contract rules dealing with oral or written evidence, any oral representations that are made before or at the time the contract or warranty agreement is constructed are excluded and inadmissible if they seek to alter the written contract, delete provisions, or add provisions. If the one who makes these is a dealer, he is giving an additional warranty. The same is true of oral warranties. An *implied warranty* is one derived "by implication or inference from the transaction." It has become traditional in the·sale of all commodities, although individual characteristics and customs may pose additional implications. The Uniform Commercial Code, a basic law that regulates sales in all states that have adopted it, formally includes implied warranties and defines their applicability. This code also defines express warranty.

Warranties can be qualified by clearly stated limitations or statements of disclaimer as long as these are not couched in vague language or hidden by print size or position in the sales contract. For example, there can be limitations on the time of accountability, on conditions of maintenance and handling, and on the place and manner of either purchase or return. An equipment manufacturer may state that he warrants his material only when he sells it directly or through franchised dealers. Since he has no way of knowing how old the machine is, or whether parts have been replaced with genuine replacements, he is well within his rights. Therefore, a buyer who does not subscribe to his terms of purchase and buys from another dealer could probably not enforce warranty rights against him. However, if the buyer can prove that an inherent defect in the equipment existed, independent of how many times the product changed hands before coming to him, he might be able to sue for negligence under the doctrine established by the case of *McPherson v. Buck.*

Most often there is no statement in the sales contract or in the warranty language that deals with giving the seller notice that the buyer wishes to invoke the warranty. In such a case, as where written notice is stipulated, the notice must be sent by registered mail, return receipt requested.

BREACH OF WARRANT: SUMMATION

When any product used directly in patient care or treatment does not live up to expectations or causes harm or loss, the supplier, manufacturer, and even the one who administers it may be liable. The plaintiff generally tries to make out a case on either of two theories, both of which can be pleaded at the same time:

1. The product was defective; any of the defendants involved in supplying it to him is liable for negligence in manufacturing it, storing it, administering it, diluting it, and similar negligence. This is a suit in tort, and the plaintiff must provide proof.

2. The product was defective, and the distributor or manufacturer breached his warranty. That is, the product normally carries an implied warranty of salability, wholesomeness, and fitness for the purpose sold. It was defective in that it was unsalable, unwholesome, and unfit. This is a suit in breach of contract, and the plaintiff need not prove that the manufacturer was negligent or careless, or at fault. He need only show that the product was defective or did not live up to its claims.

SUPPLYING BLOOD: SALE OR SERVICE?

Until 1966, courts viewed the supplying of blood as a service.[1] They did so because of charity implications and to conserve hospital funds and not curb the delivery of vitally needed blood. The theory was that it would be contrary to public policy to invoke strict warranty liability on nonbusiness organizations supplying an essential medical commodity. Following two lawsuits, in Florida [2] and New York,[3] most states, including New York, California, and Illinois, determined by statute that if the patient alleges harm came to him from a blood transfusion, he can sue the hospital and the persons administering the blood to him on the ground of negligence only. They ruled that supplying blood is a service, not a sale; therefore, the patient cannot sue in breach of warranty because that requires a sale to have taken place. The result was that patients who contracted serum hepatitis sued unsuccessfully in negligence, since there was almost no way they could prove their case.

By 1966, some state courts, feeling this to be an injustice, indicated that supplying blood by a hospital was a sale and not just a service. In these states (Florida, New Jersey), a plaintiff could bring a breach of warranty action. It should be noted in this context that commercial, nonprofit blood banks that supply blood to member hospitals were never protected against suit in breach of warranty. Legislatures did not wish to give them an unfair advantage over any other private enterprise. A New York hearing [3] described the gathering, processing, and distribution of blood as a worthy and humanitarian activity, but no more so than the manufacture of drugs and pharmaceuticals. Since blood banks donate blood only occasionally and generally sell it, they are not considered charitable institutions. Lately, then, the trend has been to examine very closely the nonprofit status of blood banks to see if they really fit the legal exemptions in those states (New York, California, and Illinois) that had provided them.

WARRANTY LIABILITY OF PHYSICIANS AND DENTISTS

Nurses employed in dental work often handle pricing and payments for the dentist. While they are not liable, they may create liability for the dentist by turning what could pass for a service into a sale. The nurse should therefore bear in mind that in discussing oral prostheses with patients, dentists should make it clear that they are not selling devices, either personally or as agents. The fee should not be broken down for the patient on the basis of the device as separate from the professional service. The patient might have a claim in breach of warranty if the device proved defective, without regard to the dentist's innocence or fault. So long as the plaintiff can establish that there was a separate sale, he can probably bring his action in breach of contract and enjoy the least crowded court calendar and the longest statute of limitations. The same theory applies to physicians [4] and nurses in such cases when they sell devices or drugs to patients in separate fashion. Breach of warranty is especially painful to physicians and nurses, since their insurance contracts rarely cover such liabilities.

LABELING OF MEDICAL PRODUCTS AND EQUIPMENT

In recent years, statutory and decisional law has required manufacturers of drugs and other products used by physicians, dentists, nurses, and technologists to disclose fully all claims for use, potential for doing harm, and contraindications. This has affected the labeling, promotion, and sale of such devices and equipment. In addition, individual practitioners and technologists may issue warnings concerning their use and administration. This alerts the manufacturer or distributor of the need to issue further advice or warning.

In 1967 the Electrical Council of Underwriters' Laboratories, a special advisory group of experts, cautioned manufacturers of the need to place warning markings on equipment designed only for ordinary locations and dangerous when used in certain hospital locations. For example, only equipment marked "Class 1 group C" or specifically labeled by the manufacturer is suitable for use in the operating room, where flammable anesthetic gases and antiseptic solutions may be in use. Included were incubators (in the delivery room), electroencephalographs, electrocardiographs, and cathode-ray oscilloscopes. Since they saw the warning letters, this may pose a standard of care both for the manufacturer and for hospital personnel. Similar potential liability situations may exist with regard to internally used devices, equipment, and prostheses.

For example, counsel for the American Medical Association discussed the medicolegal aspects of pacemaker battery replacements for patients who had returned for several years to the referring physician.[5] He pointed out that "medical ethics do not restrain a physician from giving to a patient, or a former patient, information that is necessary for his health." Thus the physician may warn a patient that batteries which had been expected to last five years actually last only from two to three years, and may have to be replaced earlier than expected if the pacemaker is to continue working.

Sometimes the quality of labeling medical products plays an important part in a physician's or nurse's defense. In one case, a patient sued a doctor for malpractice when, following injection of antivenin into two snakebitten fingers, he suffered from gangrene and partial loss of the fingers.[6] With each package of antivenin (a commercial antidote for rattlesnake poisoning) the manufacturer is required by law to provide accompanying labeling. Therefore, in addition to the label on the package, a leaflet or product brochure is enclosed. This is called the *manufacturer's labeling*. It contains instructions as to how, how much, when, and under what circumstance the product is to be used. In this case, the doctor used the drug differently from the manufacturer's recommendation and in fact against the latter's listed warning. When the plaintiff tried to show this by having the labeling admitted as evidence, the judge rejected it. He did allow the medical expert to describe its contents. The doctor's peers testified for him, stating that they used antivenin just as he had. The jury felt that the doctor and his peers were more competent to judge how the product should be used than the one who made it. They did not find the doctor guilty of malpractice.

If there had been an impurity in the antivenin, or if the advice given in the manufacturer's leaflet had been misleading or improper, the patient could have sued the drug company directly in breach of implied warranty. The responsibility would be held by the manufacturer, even if the patient received it from a doctor, bought it from a retailer, or received it as a sample in the mail. This is true too of all food products. In *Cornish v. Sterling Drug Company, Inc.,*[7] an antimalarial drug with retinopathologic side effects that were at first unknown by the manufacturer was the basis of a suit in breach of warranty. Here the manufacturer noted the side effect and changed his product labeling, notifying the doctors who used it. The court held that he had carried out his duty to warn and that the plaintiff could not collect damages from him. The court further indicated that there may have been grounds for negligence against the practitioner involved.

Since there were such indications of possible professional negligence, the court declared that a prescriber who writes too long and too frequently may be abrogating standards and therefore possibly liable. Similarly, the pharmacist who refills without authorization is often found to be the proximate cause of injury, and, having breached a statute, he is especially vulnerable. This is equally true of the private or hospital nurse. On the other hand, the pharmacist and nurse who perform their duties *with* authorization, using a drug supposedly pure but actually harmful to the patient, have been held by the Florida Supreme Court and others as *not* liable to a charge of breach of implied warranty.[8]

CASE CITATIONS

1. *Peilmutter v. Beth Israel Hospital,* 308 N.Y. 100 (1954).
2. *Russell v. Community Blood Bank,* 185 So. 2d 749 (1966).
3. *Mt. Sinai Hospital v. Community Blood Bank,* 190 N.Y.S. 2d 870 (1967).
4. *Cheshire v. Southampton Hospital,* 278 N.Y. 2d 531 (1967).
5. R. P. Bergen, *Journal of the American Medical Association,* **201**(5), p. 412 (1968).
6. *Crouch v. Most,* 432 P. 2d 250 (1967).
7. *Cornish v. Sterling Drug Co., Inc.,* 370 F. 2d 82 (1967).
8. *McLeod v. William S. Merrill Company,* Florida Supreme Court (1965).

CHAPTER 10

THE NURSE AND
CRIMINAL LAW

DEFINITION OF CRIME

In Chapter 5 we differentiated crimes from torts and indicated that the nurse has many reasons to be aware of danger areas that may involve criminality. She may meet these through her functional status as a nurse or an employee, through her association with other persons, or through her individual actions as a member of society. Criminal liability may arise from assault, conspiracy, larceny, narcotics violations, manslaughter, and even homicide.

The terms *crime, public offense,* and *criminal offense* are all synonymous and are ordinarily used interchangeably. They include the breach of any law established for protection of the public for which a penalty is imposed or punishment inflicted in any judicial proceeding. Crimes are acts or omissions forbidden and punishable by the force of common law (common-law crimes) or as defined in penal statutes and procedurally regulated by criminal codes. Crimes are described according to degrees, which are based on conditions that categorize the crime and the penalty. They are punishable upon conviction by some form of penal discipline, i.e., fine, imprisonment, or both. In most jurisdictions today, criminal law is purely statutory. In New York, for example, there are no common-law crimes. Crimes are divided into misdemeanors and felonies. There is a group of crimes which are technically misdemeanors but sometimes regarded as *quasicrimes.* These include traffic violations and other infractions of ordinances and relatively minor regulations.

FELONIES AND MISDEMEANORS

Felonies are crimes punishable by death or imprisonment in a state or federal penitentiary. *Misdemeanors* are any crimes less serious than felonies. Parties to a felony are either principals or accessories after the fact. The statute of limitations for a felony or conspiracy to commit a felony is generally five years from the time of commission. Any party to a misdemeanor is a principal and punished as such. The statute of limitations for a misdemeanor is two years in the criminal codes of many states.

SPECIFIC CRIMES

Homicide

Homicide is defined by Section 179 of the Penal Law of New York as the "killing of one human being by the act, procurement or omission of another." It is classified in the following ways: *Justifiable homicide* is the intentional taking of another's life as an act of either justice or self-defense. The sheriff commits justifiable homicide in the line of duty, as does the executioner. *Excusable homicide* has been described as "the killing of a human being, either by misadventure or by self-defense." One who, while doing a lawful act, unintentionally and unfortunately kills another commits excusable homicide. The law does not classify it as a felony but may determine some degree of punishment for it. *Felonious homicide* is the wrongful killing of a human being and may be called either murder or manslaughter. A fetus, if viable and capable of life separated from the mother, can be the victim of felonious homicide.

We noted earlier that tort law and civil responsibility for harm parallel criminal liability in cases of gross negligence. In such cases, the defendant is alleged guilty of harm ensuing from reckless or wanton acts that show disregard or indifference to human life or suffering. If the defendant knew the wrongfulness of the act and its harm and did it anyway, the case is termed *criminal negligence*.

If a death results and if the criminal act contributed significantly to it, the defendant is held fully responsible, even if there is another intervening and contributing cause. For example, a man is shot in the course of an armed robbery and is brought to the emergency room of a hospital, and there bleeds to death because of the negligence of the attending physician or nurse. The robber who fired the shot will be held responsible for his death and will be charged with the felony of murder. On the other hand, if death is attributed to the secondary or intervening causes and not at all induced by the primary one, the defendant will not be held responsible for homicide.

In an interesting case in California that created considerable publicity, a chiropractor was alleged to have fraudulently misrepresented to a patient his ability to cure a particular form of cancer. From this cure the patient subsequently died, without having the chance of survival that surgery would have offered. The chiropractor was charged with the felony of murder as well as the felony of grand theft.[1] When he appealed, the higher court held, however, that in order to be translated into felony murder, the felony must itself be inherently dangerous to life, and indicated that such was not the nature of grand theft; therefore the patient's death could not be classed as homicide.

A corporation cannot be held guilty of homicide and other crimes requiring intent; its agents can. They can be tried criminally, along with their corporate employer, and receive prison sentences; the corporation itself pays fines for penalties.

New York's penal law defines *manslaughter in the first degree* as where the victim is killed while the defendant was engaged in the commission or attempt to "commit a misdemeanor affecting the person or property either of the person killed or another." This includes cases where there is willful killing of a viable fetus by injury inflicted on the mother, as in abortion deaths. *Manslaughter in the second degree* involves culpable negligence of a drunken doctor or nurse. It also applies to a woman who submits to an abortion which kills the fetus.

Assault

Just as the tort of negligence is related to the crime of gross negligence, so is the tort of assault related to the crime of assault. Felonies of assault are statutorily defined as those which involve intentional injury, bodily harm to another by administration of poison, anesthetics, or narcotics, or willful and wrongful blows with weapons or other instruments. *Justifiable assault* may be very close to the felony of assault. It is defined as the use of reasonable force in defense of one's home, property, or person against one who is about to commit a felony against any of these. The law indicates key words that may save an innocent person from indictment for assault such as that the action was done *with no more force than necessary.* Also, there should be a show of reasonable regard for the assaultee's safety. In some hospital circumstances, a little foresight will clarify the issue of possessing authority, either actual or consigned by parent or legal guardian, in handling of lunatics, would-be suicides, or turning over criminals to the police.

Attempt

The crime of *attempt* is an act or acts done with the intent to commit a crime, but short of its actual perpetration. Like homicide, it has several degrees depending on the quality, the means, and the time of arrest. An attempt to commit a felony is itself a felony in New York. In practice this means that a wrongdoer may be tried for the crime indictable, for a lesser degree of the crime, for the attempt to commit it, or in a lesser degree for attempt. This gives the prosecutor the opportunity to secure the conviction his evidence will support.

Extortion and Blackmail

Extortion is the crime of obtaining money or property by means of fear, threat, or oral coercion. If a written document is involved, the crime is termed *blackmail.*

Larceny

Larceny involves taking the property of another with the intent to keep it for one's own use or to deprive the owner of its use permanently. It may be called *grand larceny* or *petty larceny,* depending on the value of the article. Taking such expensive articles of hospital equipment as instruments, medicines, and antibiotics results in a charge of grand larceny. When materials come into one's hands in a legal and ordinary manner, as when drugs are sent from the pharmacy to the nursing station, and are then taken away for personal use or are sold, the crime is called *embezzlement.* It is close to larceny in nature and penalty. Although there is no excuse for taking the possessions of others, showing the intent to return them alters the larceny to conversion (see Chapter 7). This carries considerably lesser penalty and stigma in the laws of all states. One who is charged with larceny cannot defend himself by claiming the consent of the victim if it was falsely obtained or if property was parted with for an immoral or unworthy purpose. A "joyride"—the unauthorized taking of a car or ambulance—is larceny according to New York state law. The intent to return the car is no defense, but the actual return of it may be mitigating. One who receives the fruits of a larceny is a felon, as is any accomplice to a larcenous act. Larceny carried out against a member of one's own family is still larceny. In fact, where a husband steals from his wife, he can be tried for larceny and she can testify against him.

Where a fellow employee asks another to take an article that is not his property and give it to the former for his use, it amounts to an invitation to join a conspiracy to perform a larceny. This applies to instances where one hospital employee asks another to turn over an unclaimed article left by a former patient, or drugs or hospital materials. Other examples of such wrongdoing which may support criminal charges both for conspiracy and for the actual crime are enticing or assisting inmates of hospitals, institutions, or sanitariums to escape and willfully advising, encouraging, or abetting suicide. A person who even appears to go along with another in a plan to do something criminal is classed as a conspirator. Conspiracy has a continuing nature, even if the would-be conspirator withdraws from the conspiracy, unless he gives complete information to the authorities long before the act is consummated.

Mishandling of Valuables

Taking valuables from a dead, inebriated, or unconscious patient is considered larceny and assault but not robbery, because the valuables are not taken by force or fear. Hospitals generally establish a regular procedure for handling the valuables and clothing of dead patients; the nurse should acquaint herself with them. As a general rule, if these things belong to a minor, they are turned over to the parent or guardian who has assumed responsibility for the patient's burial. In the case of a spouse, remainders go to the surviving husband or wife. Where state law requires, the hospital turns over the deceased patient's personal property to the public administrator or retains it until an authorized demand for it is made.

A hospital that asks a patient to surrender valuables for safekeeping will not be liable for loss by theft if he refuses. If a hospital does not offer to safeguard valuables, it can be held liable if, for example, a ring is stolen from the finger of a patient by a nurse while the patient is unconscious. To prevent mistaken imputations, employees should be careful to ask for and acknowledge receipts when they are involved in the storage, handling, or transfer of all hospital equipment. They should not take hospital materials, such as uniforms, home to use or launder. On severance especially, they should make sure that all returnable items are receipted.

Abortion

Section 80 of the Penal Law of the State of New York defines and prescribes the punishment for *abortion*. It states that a person who "with intent thereby to procure the miscarriage of a woman, unless the same is necessary to preserve the life of the woman, or of the child with which she is pregnant" prescribes a drug or other substance or uses an instrument is guilty of abortion. Despite a spate of legislative attempts to liberalize abortion laws presently in the criminal statutes, most U.S. states and Canadian provinces deal harshly with abortion. In New York, testimony of the woman is enough to convict the abortionist and his or her accomplice, even without corroboration by another witness. The woman is *not* considered an accomplice, even though she arranged for the abortion, authorized it, and cooperated. An abortion committed on a nonpregnant woman is not classified as merely an attempt under New York state law, but as the full crime of abortion.

Criminal abortion and *illegal abortion* are usually synonymous, because only therapeutic abortions are legal in all states. The nurse who is involved as a principal or an accessory in a criminal abortion knows the nature of her crime. Where a nurse innocently abets the commission of a criminal abortion, she will probably be found innocent of blame, provided her innocence is demonstrable and shows ordinary prudence. As a matter of ordinary prudence, she should not withdraw in the midst of a procedure where to do so would increase the patient's jeopardy. However, where she knows, or ought to know beforehand, the nature of the act, she may then bear the same penalty as the actual perpetrator.

In criminal law the hand can be considered a weapon or instrument. In one landmark case in Pennsylvania, the fist of a former world champion prizefighter was held to be a deadly weapon. In a recent abortion case, the hand and fingers of a physician were considered an instrument within the statutory definition of abortion.[2]

The normal defense to a charge of illegal abortion is that there was a therapeutic need for it. Most hospitals require that in every case of abortion a signed statement from the patient, properly witnessed as to the cause, is to be secured at the time of admission. If the abortion has been induced by any means whatsoever, the hospital authorities must report any statement obtained from the patient or physician to the district attorney's office and record this statement on the patient's clinical record. Suicide and voluntary submission to an illegal abortion both nullify the beneficiary's right under an insurance contract in New York.

In some states, a nurse who participates in a procedure to sterilize a person for contraceptive purposes without medical or eugenic requirement is liable according to criminal statute, as well as (probably) civilly liable to a nonconsenting marital partner.

Needless to say, there is no coverage from hospital or malpractice insurance for crimes. Intoxication and narcosis also nullify insurance. These are standard exclusions, since no insurance contract can promise, plan, or agree to an illegal performance or excuse a criminal act.

Kidnapping and Illegal Adoption

Kidnapping can be either a felony or a misdemeanor. A nurse can find herself in either situation by intent or by accident of circumstances. Any unlawful detention that is willful and intentional may be considered to be a felony kidnapping. There is no statute of limitations in kidnapping or homicide. Intent in kidnapping may equal proceeding "without legal authority" in civil cases. Therefore, helping parents in broken marriages to retrieve or keep children illegally can be hazardous.

The nurse is frequently collaterally involved in adoptions. To avoid becoming entangled in illegal adoption procedures, she should have some general idea of the adoption law in the state where she practices. She must be sure that informed consent and a properly signed release exist in private adoptions. As a general rule, she should try never to be the one who delivers the child from one person to another. Also, she should not handle money between the parties unless assigned to do this by an authorized agency that is honestly attempting to conceal parental identities for the child's future welfare. Since selling a baby is illegal, money paid to the natural mother should represent only the amount actually expended for medical care and placement of her child. This is controlled by statute in New York (Domestic Relations Law, Section 110 et seq.) and most other states.

Violation of the Nursing Practice Act

Some years ago the American Nurses' Association, in reporting results of a questionnaire survey made with the cooperation of state nurses' associations, listed some of the most common ways in which nurses violate their professional code. These include the following:

1.   Practicing medicine without a license, diagnosing, prescribing, or giving unauthorized treatments. These are violations of the medical practice act.

2.   Practing nursing while under the influence of drugs or alcohol.

3.   Negligent assignment and employment of unqualified persons, such as students, aides, and attendants, to duties that require professional competence.

4.   Theft of hospital or office supplies or drugs.

5.   Improper and/or slanderous communications.

6.   Improper acceptance of tasks for which one's training is inadequate, or assignment of tasks which are legally nondelegable.

Essentially, any violation of the professional nursing code provides a basis for civil, and frequently even criminal, liability. This is true not only for the professional nurse, but also for all other members of the nursing team.

In most state nursing acts (e.g., New York), disciplinary proceedings may be initiated which involve the possibility of suspension, revocation of license, or fine against any nurse proven guilty of a crime, gross immorality, or conviction of a felony. Such proceedings may also be based on proof of negligence and incompetence; drunkenness or drug addiction; unprofessional, fraudulent or deceitful practice; or willful disregard of the provisions of the nursing practice act.

Violation of the Medical Practice Act

Violations of the medical practice act are generally misdemeanors. In some states, however, they are felonies.[3] In an Arizona case a doctor, in the mistaken belief that he could practice without a license in that state's hospitals, was ultimately refused a license on grounds of felonious and therefore unprofessional conduct. A nurse who practices medicine without a license violates both the nursing and the medical practice acts. She may be criminally charged and lose her license. The same result may occur if she performs an exclusively medical or surgical act, even if the act has been delegated to her by a licensed physician. In *Fowler v. Norways Sanitarium*,[4] a chief nurse had directed that an x-ray film be taken of the plaintiff's decedent. The court found that she had *not* violated the medical practice act. The court always scrutinizes the circumstances in making such a decision, keeping in mind that the purpose of the medical practice act is to prevent the public from being victimized by fraud or misrepresentation.

Often the surrounding circumstances and the action taken determine whether the nurse has practiced medicine. For example, a school nurse may observe that a child is flushed with fever, verify this by a temperature reading, and make the child comfortable while awaiting treatment. But if she institutes treatment by administering antibiotics, she is practicing medicine. It is questionable whether she could administer drugs or other treatment to the patient by the direction of a physician she contacted by telephone in an emergency. She could follow his directions only if he was the child's physician and was actually present. A nurse cannot follow a doctor's orders unless they grow out of an actual patient-doctor relationship. Such a relationship is of a continuing nature or grows out of an examination of the patient.

While nurses are not qualified to diagnose, they can observe signs and state their findings, so long as they do not try to treat on the basis of what they have seen or found.[5] The term *diagnose* here is not to be confused with *nursing diagnosis,* which is a proper and expected function of the nurse.

Since a statute which prohibits the practice of medicine and surgery without a license may be violated by an unauthorized person who dispenses a drug or a remedy, the nurse may also be criminally charged and lose her license if she assists anyone in a practice for which he is unauthorized in law.[6] Therefore, a nurse may not assist a chiropractor in x-ray diagnosis of a patient if, under state law, the chiropractor is forbidden to use x-ray equipment.

An unlicensed person (or corporation) that practices medicine by employing licensed practitioners is guilty of practicing without a license.[7] But a hospital that employs nurses is not considered practicing nursing without a license. A licensed person who aids and abets another in practicing either medicine or nursing without a license is himself subject to prosecution. The existence of criminal intent, so important in characterizing most crimes, is not necessary to support conviction of the crime of practicing medicine without a license.

CRIMINAL LAW

Having discussed the kinds of crimes with which the nurse may become involved, we now turn to the assumptions and provisions of criminal law and society's method of dealing with criminal defendants.

While criminal statutes are generally subject to restrictive interpretation, in keeping with our American concept of justice, those criminal statutes that have been created by health legislation enjoy greater latitude. Here even traditional safeguards such as the Fifth Amendment may not aid the accused.[8] Supreme Court Justice Douglas noted in his dissent to the liberal construction given to such laws by the courts: "It is a fundamental principle of Anglo-Saxon jurisprudence that guilt is personal and that it ought not lightly to be imputed to a citizen who has no evil intention or consciousness of wrongdoing." He continued: "I do not think we should take such liberties in expanding criminal statutes in which the sovereign once was considered under a duty to be explicit, and the subject entitled to the doubt."

In civil law, victory depends on bringing to the court a mere preponderance of proof according to regular court rules of evidence. It differs from board hearings, which permit hearsay evidence (administrative law) and may be decided on what the board thinks is "substantial" evidence. Criminal law, by contrast, has very strict rules for admission of evidence and requires proof of guilt beyond a reasonable doubt for conviction. In our legal system, one is presumed innocent until proven guilty. This is opposite to those jurisdictions influenced by the Roman Code. In criminal law one is presumed responsible for his acts, however, and the burden of proof is on the accused to refute this. So if it is clear that X committed the crime, it is X who must show he was insane or senseless at the time.

Implicit in the normal legal analysis of a crime is the element of intent, which is composed of *mens rea*—the criminal state of mind —and malice, as evidenced by the criminal act. However, there are numerous statutory crimes, as we indicated previously, that need not contain the element of intent.

One who participates in a crime under threat or duress, or who is in reasonable apprehension of instant death or grievous bodily harm, may be excused. When he is under the effect of drugs, alcohol, or any other forces that might influence him to commit a crime without his intent, the crime may not be excused, but his punishment may be lessened. The degree of guilt must be established by the jury and if they feel the defendant was not in complete possession of his faculties, they may convict him of the crime in a lesser degree, and such a decision will be upheld as being within their right of judgment. Although temporary insanity brought on by intoxication is no defense, anyone suffering from permanent insanity, even if *initially* brought about by drunkenness, cannot be held responsible for a crime.[9]

Most jurisdictions based on English common law follow the M'Naghten Rule to determine whether insanity is a defense in a criminal proceeding. This rule states that the accused will not be held responsible if his mental condition precludes his knowing the difference between right and wrong, that is, the quality and nature of his criminal act. Other states also recognize a defense of "acting under irresistible impulse" as an expansion of the M'Naghten Rule.

Irresistible impulse replaces reason and conscience by its force on an individual.

Two other principles given some weight in criminal defense are the federal Durham Rule and that of the American Law Institute, both of which are more liberal for the accused. The Durham Rule has been statutorily adopted by Maine and is stated as follows: "An accused is not criminally responsible if his unlawful act was the product of mental disease or mental defect." [10]

A person accused of a crime who pleads not guilty by reason of insanity cannot be ordered by a court to submit to psychiatric examination. He may do so voluntarily where state law does not prohibit court-ordered psychiatric examinations or where state law specifically authorizes it (about thirty states). In no state, however, may psychiatrists be ordered to override the objections of the accused. Such a move would violate constitutional safeguards against self-incrimination.[11]

There are many safeguards for one who is criminally charged. *Due process*, a constitutional guarantee, requires the criminal statute to denote clearly the prohibited act that will be punishable. It may not be vague and indeterminate or it will not be a guide for ascertaining the standard of guilt required. If the statute is vague, it may be found unconstitutional. However, some criminal statutes which have as their objective public health and safety, e.g., food and drug laws,[12] are permitted to be couched in language that is more flexible.

Due process requires as minimal protection that a person be advised that a charge is being made against him; that the charge accuses him of certain punishable offenses, whether civil or criminal; and that he has an opportunity to defend himself by counsel chosen by himself or provided for him or even, in rare cases, by acting as his own counsel. In the cases of *Escobedo v. Illinois* [13] and *Miranda v. Arizona* [14] the United States Supreme Court defined and interpreted the defendant's right to remain silent and to engage an attorney. The court also defined circumstances that disqualify confessions in criminal cases, such as failure to warn the defendant about the weight of the confession or any other abdication of constitutional right by unawareness. In the criminal law of many states as well as under the Federal Rules of Criminal Procedure, the judge may not accept a plea of guilty unless it is first determined that such plea is made voluntarily and with understanding of the nature of the charge. If the plea is not made on these terms, the conviction following it is reversible.[15] Essentially the same is true of a confession and an admission against oneself.[16]

On the other hand, the California Supreme Court has held that statements made by pharmacists later charged with forging narcotics prescriptions to narcotics officers were admissible as evidence, even though the defendants were not advised of their right to obtain counsel or to remain silent. The court felt that this was in the preliminary stages of investigation and questioning of the licensees and that they were not in custody, therefore not inferentially under police pressure. The same would have been true of a nurse questioned at the hospital or in her own home.

In a recent case that bore on the voluntary nature of a confession, a convicted criminal sought to reverse the judgment of conviction on the grounds that he was drunk when he contacted the police and confessed his crime.[17] In upholding the validity of the confession, the appellate court differentiated between voluntary intoxication under which the defendant divulged his criminal action and another hypothetical case where the intoxication was police-induced, thus leading to the confession.

In an Arkansas case, the defendant voluntarily confessed, gave additional evidence, and rejected the right to counsel and the right to remain silent, in an attempt to "get a fix" he sorely needed in exchange for his cooperation.[18] The court of appeals, noting that the issue of voluntariness might depend in part on the strength and resilience of a particular defendant, felt that since the defendant's condition was voluntarily induced, the admissions were unaffected. In general, where a statement is taken when the defendant is under the influence of alcohol or drugs, he must prove that his condition rendered him unable to understand the meaning of his statement. The burden is always on the defendant when he maintains he was not responsible for the criminal act.

The right to due process applies only to judicial proceedings, although it has often been construed by courts to apply to quasi-judicial proceedings, such as before boards or agencies.[19] Due process requires a full hearing before a competent tribunal.

In many cases the United States Supreme Court has dismissed actions against defendants who were not accorded the constitutional safeguard of the Sixth Amendment, which states that the defendant in a criminal proceeding has a right to a speedy trial.[20] Speaking of one defendant in such a case, the Court said: "The pendency of the indictment may subject him to public scorn and deprive him of employment, and certainly will force curtailment of his speech, associations and participation in unpopular causes." It then reemphasized the right of dissent and stated that the rights defined by the Sixth Amendment are made applicable to the state by the Fourteenth Amendment. The Fourth Amendment gives the defendant the right to know who has accused him, and the right to confront the accuser and cross-examine him. The effect of these amendments has been limited somewhat by the Supreme Court's interpretation in special circumstances attending the detection of traffickers in narcotics.[21] However, their general impact is clear.[22]

The Fourth Amendment protects Americans from unreasonable search and seizure "in their persons, houses, papers and effects." Recently, the right to refuse city health inspectors permission to enter a home without a warrant, and the right to refuse entry of a fire inspector into a warehouse without a warrant, were upheld by the Supreme Court. These rights were upheld despite specific ordinances that permitted inspection without a warrant. Apparently the Court held such ordinances to be fundamentally unconstitutional.[23] This does not preclude voluntary admission, however. Evidence seized without a warrant or involuntarily given is not admissible in court. The basis for this refusal must be that the purpose of the inspection connotes a criminal infraction. Thus, the Fourth Amendment is associated with the right against self-incrimination afforded by the Fifth Amendment. Previously the Court had held that the Fourteenth Amendment brings the protection of the Fourth and Fifth Amendments to citizens in acts performed by the states and their delagees. However, the Supreme Court has indicated that premises which require a license might in some circumstances have to allow inspection by state officials even without a warrant. Therefore, a hospital licensed by the state authorities must stand inspection at a reasonable time and in a reasonable manner.

A police officer can make an arrest without a warrant when he has probable cause to believe the person he takes into custody has committed a crime. He can then search the defendant and even direct the taking of a blood sample without violating the defendant's constitutional right to be free from *unreasonable* search and seizure. The constitutional right to due process and against self-incrimination protects the individual only against compulsion in testimony or communications. It does not impair the admission of such test results. A California court in a criminal action stated: "Records that are required by law to be kept are not protected by the privilege against self-incrimination." [24]

The nurse, both as an independent contractor who frequently resides at the patient's home for the greater part of the week and as a hospital staff member living in, must understand the constitutional rights of homeowners and tenants as guaranteed by the Fourth Amendment. These rights are to some extent determined by the express or implied contract provisions agreed upon by the parties at the assumption of the assignment. The nurse who undertakes a position in exchange for a specified fee, plus board and lodging, is essentially not a tenant but a lodger. Hence her right to privacy in those lodgings may depend on the same body of law within that jurisdiction which applies to hotels and their guests, innkeepers, and boarding house operators. In theory, then, in most instances, her room and her personal belongings are not immune to inspection, unless it is of an unreasonable, arbitrary, and capricious nature. The rights of the individual under the Constitution are clear and expansive; they are known as *whole-citizen immunity*. They are often narrowed voluntarily when the person assumes a specific work assignment, either expressly or implicitly. While the nurse can revert to whole-citizen immunity from search and seizure by quitting the assignment or the premises, she probably enjoys less freedom from invasion of privacy and search than the average citizen at this time.

A nurse, like every other citizen, should know her rights if charged with a crime. We can set them out in general terms, but local laws may vary substantially and the facts of each individual case may differ. The nurse's best protection is to secure the aid of a lawyer.

Since crimes are wrongs against society for which the public requires the punishment of the offender, they are most often initiated as police actions on the basis of a complaint or a special or routine inspection. If a hospital employee makes such a complaint, he should be very certain of the facts on the basis of firsthand observation and knowledge and be prepared to come forward with proof to substantiate his accusation. To cause the arrest of another unjustly is to place himself in jeopardy for charges of false arrest or malicious prosecution. A well-founded suspicion which is not motivated by malice can and should be reported to the nurse's superior in safety. Indeed, this is an agent's duty to a principal. But to reiterate, open accusations and the preparation of warrants should be surrounded by the same certainty that the state will have to demonstrate to convict.

DETENTION AND SEARCH

The police have a right to detain the individual long enough to verify his name, address, and an explanation of his actions, without arresting him. The person can refuse to answer, thus requiring police either to arrest him or to release him. They cannot force him to answer or sign a statement, or promise to "make a deal" in exchange for a confession or information.

If a person is detained for questioning, the policeman may search him to determine if he is carrying a dangerous and concealed weapon. If, while he looks for a weapon, he finds barbiturates, narcotics, or anything else which it is a crime to possess, he can take it and make an arrest for possession. (This has been challenged in the courts.) On the other hand, if he finds something the individual has a right to possess, he must return it.

It is a crime to resist a lawful arrest, and police can use force against it. Arrest or detention may be lawful even if the person is innocent. When the police make a lawful arrest, they can search the person arrested as well as the immediate area where the arrest is made. In all other situations a *search warrant* is needed. This is an order in writing, signed by a judge, directing a police officer to search a certain place for personal property and to bring the property to court. The warrant must describe with particularity the place to be searched and the personal property to be searched for. The policeman is generally required to show the warrant and give notice of his authority or purpose before making a search. A policeman having a warrant may break open a door or window if he is refused admittance after giving notice. However, if the property sought may be easily and quickly destroyed (for example, drugs or policy slips), or if the policeman is endangered by identifying himself, the judge issuing the search warrant may direct in writing that notice is not required. The policeman may then break into the premises unannounced. Anything unlawfully seized by the police may not be used as evidence against the person later. If personal property or money is taken, the owner must be given a receipt specifying the amount of money or the kind of property.

ARREST AND PRETRIAL PROCEEDINGS

When an individual is arrested, a permanent record is made of this fact. The record stands even if he is later acquitted. In some cases, he may also be fingerprinted and photographed. But if he is acquitted, he may demand the return of the fingerprints and photograph.

The person arrested has a right to obtain counsel or to have one provided for him before he answers questions or decides to remain silent. He also has the right to telephone his lawyer, family, employer, or a friend.

Once arrested and booked, the person must be taken to court without unnecessary delay. If the court is not then open, he can be held in the police station until it is open. However, if he is a first offender arrested for a misdemeanor or disorderly conduct, he must be allowed (with certain exceptions) to obtain bail at the station house. *Bail* consists of money or other security deposited with the proper official to assure the appearance of the defendant in court; it permits him to be released from jail. If the person is not a first offender and is booked for a more serious crime, he is not automatically entitled to bail.

At the defendant's first appearance before the judge, he must be told the charge against him. If he is not accompanied by counsel, the judge must also inform him of his right to have a lawyer and to have one assigned by the court if he cannot afford one. However, if he wishes, the defendant is entitled to proceed without counsel and handle the case himself.

If the defendant is charged with a more serious crime which entitles him to a preliminary hearing, the judge will then ask whether he wishes to waive the hearing. No one may compel him to waive it; he has a right to insist that it be held. If he waives it, he will be held over for the grand jury or for trial, depending on the crime of which he is charged. If he is charged with a minor offense or other crime not entitling him to a preliminary hearing, he will be asked at this stage to plead guilty or not guilty. If he pleads not guilty, the case will be set down for trial or the trial may take place immediately. If he pleads guilty, he will stand sentencing.

The defendant may apply to the court for bail. This may be done prior to the adjournment, which is allowed to give him an opportunity to obtain a lawyer, or at the preliminary hearing. In some cases the judge may release the defendant without bail on the understanding that he will voluntarily appear in court at a later time to answer for the crime. The defendant not released on bail will be jailed.

CASE CITATIONS

1. *People v. People,* 51 Cal. Rptr. 225 (1966).
2. *Palmer v. People,* 424 P. 2d 766 (1967).
3. *Fitzpatrick v. Board,* 394 P. 2d 423 (1964).
4. *Fowler v. Norways Sanitarium,* 42 N.E. 2d 415 (1942).
5. *Burt v. People,* 421 P. 2d 480 (1967).
6. *State v. Henning,* 78 N.E. 2d 588 (1948).
7. 298 Mass. 363, 70 Corpus Junis Sec. 833.
8. *United States v. Dotterveich,* 320 U.S. 277, 286 (1943).
9. *Cook v. Georgia,* 151 S.E. 2d 155 (1966).
10. Maine Revised Statutes Ann., ch. 149, sec. 17B (1964).
11. Minnesota Supreme Court 40301 (1966).

12. Federal Food, Drug, and Cosmetic Act, 191 So. 2d 33 *(State v. Buchanan)* (1966).
13. *Escobedo v. Illinois,* 378 U.S. 478 (1964).
14. *Miranda v. Arizona,* 384 U.S. 431 (1966).
15. *United States v. Kincaid,* 362 F. 2d 939 (1966).
16. *People v. Baksys,* 272 N.Y. 2d 488 (1966).
17. *People v. Schomfert,* 19 N.Y. 2d 300 (1967).
18. *State v. McFall,* 428 P. 2d 1013 (1967).
19. *Koelling v. Board of Trustees of Mary F. Skiff Memorial Hospital,* 146 N.W. 2d 284 (1966).
20. *Lewis v. United States,* 385 U.S. 213 (1966).
21. *McCrary v. Illinois,* 386 U.S. 300 Supreme Court (1967).
22. *Gecht v. Patterson,* 386 U.S. 605 Tenth Circuit Court of Appeals (1967).
23. *Camara v. Muncipal Court of San Francisco,* 387 U.S. 527 (1967).
24. California Supreme Court 9272 (1966).

CHAPTER 11

DRUG AND NARCOTICS VIOLATIONS

STIMULANT AND DEPRESSANT DRUGS: THE FEDERAL LAW

Narcotic drug controls which affect public and professional members of the health care team originally developed federally from the right to tax. For this reason the Harrison Narcotic Act (26 USC 4701 et seq.) is incorporated in the Internal Revenue Code. For this reason also, until 1968 the Federal Bureau of Narcotics, which acted as the federal enforcement agency, was a subdivision of the Treasury Department. However, with current proliferation of non-narcotic drugs whose use tends to be abused, new laws were passed to effectively prevent the illicit manufacture, distribution, and use of these drugs. Since they were not narcotics and subject to a stamp tax, responsibility for their control fell to the Bureau of Drug Abuse Control, Food and Drug Administration, which is part of the Department of Health, Education, and Welfare. In 1968, in the course of reorganization within the executive branch of government, President Lyndon B. Johnson removed both bureau enforcement agencies involved and combined them under the Department of Justice into the Bureau of Narcotics and Dangerous Drugs. This new bureau administers all the federal narcotics laws and the Drug Abuse Control Amendment of 1965.

None of these laws has specific sections that relate to the art of nursing. If one wishes to manufacture or distribute these drugs, he must be registered under both laws. Registration is available for wholesalers who want to sell narcotic drugs. The doctor who wishes to prescribe, order, or keep a stock of these drugs must also be a registrant. The pharmacist in retail practice must be a registrant to order, stock, and dispense narcotics. The hospital pharmacy must also be registered to carry out these activities. Each of these is a registrant for a special class. There is no class or registration for nurses. Therefore, a nurse may possess a narcotic drug only as a patient or as the doctor's agent administering the drug.

STIMULANT AND DEPRESSANT DRUGS: THE STATE LAWS

While we have been examining federal law, the Uniform Narcotic Drug Act or similarly acceptable legislation is in effect in every state. In some instances, state and local regulations are more stringent, and this should be known and respected by members of the health professions.

The thrust of both the federal and the state acts can be summarized by noting that they prohibit any person from manufacturing, holding, selling, buying, prescribing, administering, or giving away any narcotic drug except as authorized. Further, provisions are made for licensure of manufacturers and wholesalers as well as for the establishment of categories of drugs affected and the classes of persons who may buy and sell, prescribe, and dispense them. The laws soften the language of licensing by calling it "registration" and making it optional. However, outside of certain federal and official exemptions, there is really no means for those who seek to provide the narcotics to those who will prescribe or dispense them.

Finally, the federal and state laws restrict the legitimate traffic in narcotics to qualified manufacturers, wholesalers, pharmacists, medical and dental practitioners, and researchers. Narcotics may be purchased only pursuant to official narcotics order forms or prescriptions. Pharmacists may fill prescriptions issued by doctors legally qualified to do so in furtherance of a bona fide physician-patient relationship.

The nurse, in the absence of law and regulations to the contrary, may take the dispensed narcotic to the patient for whom it is prescribed and administer it to him if such an order has been given by the physician. Under certain circumstances, authorities will allow her to hold the patient's narcotics prescription for him as a matter of safekeeping and administrative assistance. She is not, however, in possession of the drug at any time, and that is why she may not keep the remainder of the drug after the patient has died or left the hospital.

Since all parties who handle narcotics as registrants must maintain records which are subject to inspection, the nurse plays a part in maintaining these records in keeping with her responsibility to carry out medical orders in supplying or administering the drug to the patient and in requisitioning it from the source of supply.

The nurse is expected by law to administer drugs according to her limitations of legal status, training and experience, and according to the order of a licensed practitioner. A patient may obtain these drugs only with an oral or written prescription issued by an authorized practitioner in a physician-patient relationship. That is the extent of their legal entitlement under the Drug Abuse Control Act, as under the federal and state narcotics laws.

Nurses, pharmacists, and others in control of drugs at authorized institutions prepared an inventory of the drugs on February 1, 1966. They were required to keep their invoices and prescriptions for amphetamines, barbiturates, and the other drugs on the list for a three-year period. Certain state laws (e.g., in New York) required the inventory also to be submitted.

The recording requirements apply to physicians and their nurses when they regularly dispense such drugs to their patients and make either a separate charge or combine it with charges for other professional services. Authorized practitioners and hospitals may maintain separate files on these drugs, as is now done for narcotics. However, the law permits them to keep prescriptions for stimulant and depressant drugs in the regular file of prescriptions if they wish. To clarify the point, physicians, pharmacists, and any other authorized persons who dispense these drugs are required to keep records and make them available to government inspectors.

To comply with record requirements, prescription orders must contain the name and address of the patient and the date of issuance. State law may require the name and address of the prescriber as well. Federal law states that stimulant or depressant drugs may be dispensed by telephoned or oral instructions of the physician. However, no prescription order for these specially controlled drugs can be renewed more than five times or dispensed or renewed more than six months after the date of issue. After the five renewals or six months, the physician may give additional authorization for refilling. In some states, such as Pennsylvania, pharmacists have been especially cautioned that the order authorizing a refill for a dangerous drug must come directly from the physician.

The following acts are specially prohibited by the new amendments (note that 1, 2, 3, and 6 apply to the nurse's handling of all prescription drugs): [1]

1. Compounding or dispensing the designated drugs, except by authorized parties, for legal distribution and administration.

2. Distributing the drugs to any persons who are not licensed or authorized by federal or state law to receive them, such as persons outside the physician-patient relationship. Penalties for selling or giving the drugs to minors without a prescription are especially severe.

3. Possession of stimulant or depressant drugs except as authorized by law, that is, as a patient, or incidental to the legal dispensing or administration of the drugs.

4. Refilling of prescriptions for these drugs more than five times or more than six months after they were initially prescribed.

5. Failure to prepare, obtain, or keep the required records and to permit inspection of and copying of such records, and refusal to permit entry or inspection as authorized.

6. Making, selling, keeping, or concealing any counterfeit drug equipment, and the doing of any act which causes the sale of a counterfeit drug. This includes buying amphetamine derivatives, such as desoxyephedrine, and labeling and dispensing them as trademarked (brand-named) product to patients inside or outside the hospital.

Many state laws have been enacted to restrict the use of amphetamines, barbiturates, and other drugs by stating that they must be dispensed by prescription for their proper medical uses. The new federal law specifically provides that it shall not be construed to weaken in any way the drug laws of the various states.

Most states have enacted strict and effective administrative rules and regulations that affect nurses, among others. For example, in New York state, control of narcotics, as well as depressant and stimulant drugs, is administered by the Bureau of Narcotic Control of the New York State Department of Health. In effect, the nurse's requirements are similar to those for handling narcotics:

1. No hospital, maternity home, laboratory, nursing home, convalescent home, or home for the aged may possess, use, distribute or dispense any depressant or stimulant drug without having first obtained a certificate of approval from the State Department of Health. These institutions must have twenty-four hour staffing by registered, professional nurses or licensed practical nurses in order to qualify for this certificate.

2. Nursing homes, convalescent homes, and homes for the aged cannot keep a stock of these drugs on hand or build a stock from leftovers. They may obtain custody of stimulant or depressant drugs

prescribed for patients in their care only by prescriptions issued by an authorized prescriber in the name of an individual patient and dispensed by an authorized pharmacy.

3. A prescription, to be effective in legalizing the possession of depressant or stimulant drugs, must be issued for legitimate medical purposes only. The responsibility for the proper *prescribing* of these drugs is on the physician, dentist, podiatrist, veterinarian, or other authorized practitioner. A corresponding responsibility for proper *dispensing* of such drugs rests with the pharmacist who fills the prescription, as well as with the nurse who administers it. All prescriptions for depressant and stimulant drugs must be *dated as of, and signed on, the day when issued* and bear the full name and address of the patient and the practitioner.

4. In New York and some other jurisdictions, a prescription for a depressant or stimulant drug may be filled only by a licensed pharmacist, a pharmacy school graduate, or a senior or junior pharmacy school student under the supervision of a licensed pharmacist. The statute excludes mention of a nurse's right to do this but does not interfere with the physician's prerogative to dispense drugs. If a nurse does more than administer any prescription drug, as well as narcotics and drugs whose use may be abused, she can be excused only if she acts as an agent for a physician or dentist.

5. In hospitals, laboratories, nursing homes, convalescent homes, and homes for the aged, depressant and stimulant drugs designated as inventory-required drugs must be kept in a locked, secure place, just like narcotics: "Ward, floor, station, or working stocks should be kept in double cabinets under locked protection of suitable locks and keys. Spring locks or combination dial locks are not acceptable. Both cabinets, inner and outer, shall be stationary."

In hospitals, written orders for depressant and stimulant drugs for hospitalized patients must be signed by an intern, resident, attending physician, dentist or podiatrist, or by a veterinarian in a veterinary hospital. Interns may prescribe depressant and stimulant drugs for any patient in connection with their hospital duties. Whoever the prescriber, his full signature is required on the patient's drug order sheet. The intern is acting as an agent for the prescribing privilege of the physician, as the nurse is permitted to be his agent for the administering privilege.

PRN (provide whenever necessary) orders for depressant and stimulant drugs are permissible but are not valid beyond seventy two hours, regardless of the type of case treated. Such orders must thereafter be rewritten.

Orders for depressant and stimulant drugs should be given immediately before they are to be administered. Routine orders for these drugs are not permissible. Each order must be specified for the individual patient and signed by the prescriber.

6. Nursing homes, convalescent homes, homes for the aged, and other facilities authorized by the state to possess and distribute depressant or stimulant drugs to patients in their care must keep a record of all such drugs received in custody and dispensed. A separate daily running record should be kept of each prescribed drug received. It should include the date, name, and quantity of the drug; names of the prescriber, patient, and pharmacy; and serial number of the prescription. A separate record must be maintained of such drugs administered, with the date and hour, name and quantity of the drug, prescriber, patient's name, signature of person administering, and balance of such drug remaining. This is clearly a nursing responsibility.

7. Depressant or stimulant drugs must be prescribed for individual patient use only and may not be administered to any other patient. A nurse may not count out, or measure out, the dose to be administered according to a charted order from a bulk container of these drugs.

Patients leaving any nursing home, convalescent home, or home for the aged may take depressant or stimulant drugs prescribed for them if the practitioner does not direct otherwise. The nurse or physician must obtain receipt for these drugs. If these drugs are no longer required by the patient, they must be surrendered to the Bureau of Narcotic Control. They are not to be returned to the nurse, practitioner, or dispensing pharmacist. An inventory should be prepared on the prescribed form in triplicate and forwarded by prepaid express to the Bureau. Narcotics and stimulant or depressant drugs dispensed by practitioners from their own stock may be returned to the practitioner if no longer required. If the practitioner refuses them, they should be returned as specified previously.

Nurses should clarify for themselves the requirements of their state, as well as institutional policy, which govern their handling of drugs. The nurse who is employed outside the hospital must, as a physician's or dentist's agent, keep a record of his initial inventory of dangerous drugs. She should also be ready to assist him in keeping a record of all such drugs received gratuitously or purchased for office use. By procuring duplicate invoices for the latter, she can establish a sufficient record of purchase. The doctor's records for purchase of narcotics remain in his order book. In addition, the nurse must help maintain a record of all such drugs adminstered or dispensed by the physician from his own stock. In dispensing these, the physician must prepare instructive and required labeling, as well as record their disposition.

Since members of the nursing team are respected and appreciated as educated and ethical individuals, their responsibilities respecting narcotics and abuse of drugs go farther than meeting legal requirements in practice.

By their example and their educational force they can be very influential in reducing and preventing abuse, pointing out both its sociopathic character and the actual physical harm and mental disorder it engenders.

CASE CITATION

1. Sidney J. Willig, "Drugs, Dispensing/Administering," p. 126, *American Journal of Nursing* (June, 1964).

CHAPTER 12

STATUTES OF LIMITATIONS

*S*tatutes of limitations are legislatively determined to prescribe the period of time in which claims can be tried or rights enforced. Statutes of limitations have as their objective the curtailment of unwarranted or stale claims—claims, in short, that may gain advantages in time through loss of witnesses, changes in the social and political climate, and statutory changes. The period during which a suit may be filed in contract, tort, or slander is governed by the statute of limitations imposed by the state. The times vary from action to action, from state to state. Connecticut, for instance, has a one-year statute of limitations for malpractice, while New York has a three-year statute of limitations. As a general rule, the statute for torts is a few years and for contracts about two or three times as long; that for serious crimes is much longer or endless. For example, there is no statute of limitations for homicide. A minor has time until he reaches his majority and, in some cases, some time after that to sue in tort or contract

Law generally provides that a potential plaintiff in a malpractice or negligence case who is insane when his cause of action ordinarily accrues receives the statutory time benefit from the time he is declared sane once again.[1]

Where the plaintiff's case is jeopardized by the closeness of the end of the allowable time period, the court in its discretion may accept less complete and less formal pleadings if it feels that the plaintiff's cause may be valid.[2]

Often, states differentiate between time allowed to commence a suit based on negligence, and that based on professional negligence or malpractice. It is advantageous at times from the defendant's point of view to have the court consider negligent nursing acts as malpractice. Frequently the malpractice statute has a far shorter time limitation in which suit can be initiated. Conversely, the terms of malpractice and negligence are interchanged when the plaintiff needs a longer time before commencing suit. In fact, even where both statutes of limitation apply, plaintiffs may still choose to resort to a claim that the malpractice was in the form of a breach of contract, express or implied, between the patient and the defendant.[3] Sometimes circumstances allow a person who brings suit for professional negligence to elect suit in tort or for breach of contract. The form in which the suit is brought determines the statute of limitations that applies. Since a cause of action in breach of contract starts at the time of the breach, it differs from a tort case. In the latter, the statute of limitations starts from the time of damage, or from the time of discovery of the damage in some jurisdictions.[4] Preparing the case in terms of breach of contract rather than the tort of negligence or malpractice has the second advantage of bringing the suit more quickly to trial, because the tort calendar in every jurisdiction is very crowded. The one disadvantage for the plaintiff is that in most jurisdictions juries grant higher awards for tort liability than for breach of contract.

A single transaction may cause injuries to one person and property damage to another. The fact that both forms of damage arise from the same occurrence does not change the statute with respect to each. In one case where a couple tried to sue for the failure of an operation to sterilize the husband, they were frustrated by a two-year statute of limitations in that state. However, the wife could still bring suit for damages to herself from the results of the childbirth which occurred because the operation failed.[5] Her allegation was that the physician had not exerted proper skill and care in performing the operation and therefore failed to accomplish the results he had promised. This, she insisted, constituted a breach of warranty and a cause of action in contract, so that she might recover damages for the medical expenses of the unexpected pregnancy and for special care and attention that the child would need.

However, in every state the effect of the statute can be decreased where the plaintiff can show that some legal disability prevented prior action.[6]

The courts react to what they consider outrageous or inequitable conditions resulting from strict interpretation of the statute of limitations for negligence or malpractice. This has resulted in their finding and applying numerous rules that broaden the period of discovery on the basis of fraudulent concealment, contract violation, or continuing negligence in those jurisdictions where the statute has not been legislatively rewritten to protect against unjust loss of suitability. For example, Tennessee has a one-year statute of limitations for malpractice. In one case,[7] the plaintiff alleged that the doctor had never probed a nonhealing wound for ten years, and that a substitute physician had done so and had removed pieces of surgical sponge from the site of the operation. The court felt that if these allegations were true, the case should not be barred because the statute of limitations had run out. They therefore held that even though the original negligent act had occurred ten years previously, the continuance of the physician-patient relationship for the enusing ten years kept the negligence alive. Every time the doctor told the patient that the wound was not healing because she was a diabetic, the negligence was being renewed. Permission to sue the doctor in spite of the one-year statute was allowed only because of the "continued treatment–continuing negligence" theory. However, a concomitant suit against the hospital for negligence in failing to provide sponges with radiopaque threads at the time of the operation was held not to survive the statute of limitations for negligence.

The statute of limitations may not preclude a claim as a result of an earlier transaction between the patient and the doctor. This decision was stated in *Borgia v. City of New York*[8] and is held by many states in cases where treatment by the physician can be considered continuous in the absence of legislative action bearing on the discovery rule. Massachusetts follows the same premise.[9] Most states, in suits for medical malpractice, now follow the rule that the statute does not begin to run out until the patient discovers, or with reasonable diligence would have discovered, the practitioner's alleged negligence.[10] However, where an excessively long period elapses, even courts that follow the discovery doctrine may not choose to apply it.[11] The length of time they allow to elapse takes into account the fact that the defendant finds it increasingly difficult to locate witnesses as the case drags on.

In *Flannery v. Estate of Mengel,* a patient discovered, sixteen years after the doctor's death, that he had left a sponge in her abdomen while operating on her a few years prior to his death. The court held that she had a valid action against his estate, despite the long passage of time.[12] While the reported cases deal with medical malpractice, there is no reason to believe that the courts would view nursing or dental malpractice in any other way.

In some states, such as Texas, the rule is that action for damages caused by a foreign object's being left in the patient's body arises at the exact time the malpractice occurs, even though its presence may not be discovered for some time.[13] However, this will not hold if fraud is exerted to prevent discovery by the patient. As we have indicated, the more general rule, and one growing in acceptance, is that the statute of limitations does not begin until discovery, since this is when the patient first knows that a cause of action exists.

In Virginia, where the statute is effective when the act is done, both time of discovery and the continued-treatment theory are for the most part ignored.

Even those states which specifically deny application of the discovery rule will consider whether the treatment that is the subject of the action had been continued long enough past the initial act of harm to come within the statutory time allowance.

The foregoing discussions demonstate that decisional law varies greatly in interpreting statutes of limitations. Some jurisdictions are flexible. Others refuse to reinterpret them on the ground that this is strictly a legislative responsibility.

Most states have a one-year statute of limitations with regard to workmen's compensation claims. Here, too, some jurisdictions use a liberal approach that calculates the years as starting when an ordinary prudent person should have been aware that he had a compensable injury. Since a nurse is supposed to have a superior knowledge of health and physical conditions, the statute has on some occasions been construed less liberally for nurses.[14] In one case, a nurse strained her back in caring for a bed patient. She applied heat therapy to herself and kept working until eventually she asked for a transfer to a less strenuous ward assignment because of her pain. She made a claim after more than a year had elapsed, and was refused by the agency. The court rejected her appeal in view of her training and experience, which supposedly should have led her to file a claim earlier.

CASE CITATIONS

1. *Lacy v. Ference,* 151 S.E. 2d 763 (1966).
2. *Burger v. Burnett,* 265 N.Y. 2d 499 (1965).
3. *Manning v. Serrano,* 97 So. 2d 688 (1957).
4. *Fradley v. Dade County,* 187 So. 2d 48 (1966).
5. *Doerr v. Villate,* 220 N.E. 2d 767 (1966).
6. *Lacy v. Ference,* 151 S.E. 2d 763 (1966).

7. *Frazor v. Osborne,* Tennessee Court of Appeals (Nashville) 414 S.W. 2d 118 (1966).
8. *Borgia v. City of New York,* 216 N.Y.S. 2d 897.
9. *Pasquale v. Lentino,* N.W. 13, 385 Massachusetts Superior Judiciary Court (1967).
10. *Bishop v. Byrne,* 265 F. Supp. 460 (1967).
11. *Grey v. Silver Bow County,* 425 P. 2d 819 (1967).
12. *Flannery v. Estate of Mengel,* Pennsylvania Court of Common Pleas, Tuglire County No. 208 (1967).
13. *Gaddis v. Smith,* Texas 407 S.W. 2d 873 (1966).
14. *Watkins v. Home Indemn.,* 409 S.W. 2d 359 (1966).

CHAPTER 13

FIDUCIARY RESPONSIBILITY OF THE NURSE

IMPORTANCE OF A WILL

"Do I need a will? is a question asked frequently by nurses and others. Most people should have a will, regardless of whether they are salaried or self-employed and regardless of their annual wages. A properly executed will assures the individual that all his property will be disposed of in accordance with his wishes. The average hospital employee today has insurance and pension benefits on a personal as well as an employment basis, furnishings, perhaps a home and a car. Having a will generally saves the estate time and money and allows the assets to be distributed by a person chosen by the testator, in the manner chosen. Taxes can be considered and minimized, and provision can be made to cover the expenses of the funeral and the immediate needs of the defendants before probate. A will with a common-disaster clause (e.g., where a husband and wife lose their lives at the same time) often saves one set of estate taxes for the heirs.

Depending on age requirements in a particular state, any person may make a will, subject to certain safeguards. Generally the will-maker, or *testator*, must be 18 or older to will personal property, such as money or jewelry, and at least 21 to will real, or land, property. Whether the will is typed on a standard form or handwritten (holographic), it will be valid only if executed properly, with the testator's signature at the physical end of the will and witnesses as required.

The *probate* (proving) of a will by an executor is generally less expensive than the administration of an estate and generally saves time. When a will is not in existence, the court will appoint such *administrators* and guardians as may be necessary; this will cost the estate service and bonding fees. The administrators may be completely unacquainted with the deceased. The property will be distributed according to the law of the particular state, regardless of even the known wishes of the deceased. In some states, divorces or annulments, since they conclude the marital relationship, automatically exclude the former spouse from any role in a will made previously. In other states, where there is no will the former spouse is automatically included.

Since life insurance benefits can be a source of immediate cash for the family, a record of the policy numbers, insurance companies, and beneficiaries should be given to the executor, with a copy placed in a safe deposit box. The executor should also have a list of stocks and bonds owned, and of any banks where an account is held.

THE NURSE'S RESPONSIBILITY

We have examined legal considerations that affect nursing activities from numerous aspects. As an independant contractor, the nurse often undertakes fiduciary responsibilities other than those of agency. Because of her close relationship with the patient and the members of his family, she often assists them in problems not truly related to her immediate duties. There is nothing wrong with this if she recognizes her limitations in law and in fact. A nurse should inspire confidence and reliance.

Many states have *conservatorship laws* which permit the appointment of a person to protect the property and estate of someone whose impaired mental or physical capacity makes it difficult for him to manage his own affairs. If the person is completely incompetent, a committee is formed. However, this high degree of incapacity is not necessary for the appointment of a conservator. Also, the persons involved generally try to avoid proving incompetency (which is essential for committee appointments) because of the stigma involved.

A nurse is eligible to be appointed a conservator of the property of a person who has not been declared incompetent judicially, yet who is unable to care for his property by reason of advanced age, illness, infirmity, mental weakness, intemperance, addiction to drugs, or other causes. However, this can become a full-time job. It also requires a great deal of legal information for which the assistance of an attorney is required.

Very often while attending aged or terminal patients, the nurse becomes involved with the preparation and execution of a will.

Under proper circumstances, a nurse may be a beneficiary of a will. However, she should avoid being a witness and should not undertake the duties of an executrix. This involves more than forty separate duties and responsibilities. The active nurse cannot afford to accept the position unless she has the time and freedom to undertake it.

Because most nurses have come to realize the problems in signing as a witness to a will, many hospitals have clerks or volunteers who will accommodate bedridden patients. For the nurse, it poses the danger that she will lose time in a surrogate court later on if the will is challenged. Further, if she is fortunate enough to have a bequest made to her by the deceased, she may not legally be a witness to the will.

Generally, a promise to make a gift is legally unenforceable, while an executed gift is irrevocable. However, a promise of a gift inserted in a will may be legally enforceable, depending on *availability* and the clarity of the disposition in the view of the surrogate. Since a nurse caring for an ill person has considerable influence and evokes gratitude for her services, she must be careful not to disqualify herself from the testator's final act of kindness by lack of understanding. Any promise made to her in the will should be witnessed and should have been made at a time when the patient was in possession of his faculties and not under the influence of drugs or coerced by fear. The testator's *testamentary capacity* (soundness of mind), without prompting, to comprehend the nature of the act he is about to perform, the limits and character of his property, and the natural objects of his bounty are of prime importance, especially if the will is later challenged. He may be an eccentric, even a monomaniac, yet have testamentary capacity.

The right to make valid oral and handwritten wills has recently been reinstated for civilian and military personnel engaged in extraterritorial actions which are technically not wars, such as the Vietnam action. These wills are valid for one year after discharge. When recognized for seamen on the high seas, the will is valid for three years from the time it is made.

THE PHYSICAL FORM OF THE WILL

As previously stated, the testator or testatrix must sign at the physical end of the will. This is intended to protect the deceased from fraudulent additions. Where there are no probabilities of distortion or wrongdoing, and the testator failed to sign the will, the provisions in the will still remain valid and will be carried out, provided they can be understood in terms of the testator's desires and purpose. The will need not be held defective if witnesses sign before the testator, or if the latter acknowledges his signature to each of two or three witnesses at different times. In any case, the time and circumstances of the signing and witnessing of the will can be entered in the nursing chart to provide a further validating record for the future.

TERMINAL-CARE PATIENTS

Private nursing care involves a transaction with the patient. Therefore, nurses providing terminal care should state the conditions of the employment relationship, such as rate of pay, in writing, to be signed by the patient or his legal guardian or agent. Physicians and hospitals are affected in the same manner by these circumstances.

In private-duty nursing, when attending a terminal patient where death is expected, responsibility for payment is best stated in writing by a healthy responsible adult. This assures that the nurse's payment will not be delayed by the patient's death.

In most states a nurse may not testify to a personal transaction with the deceased.[1] Therefore, she cannot effectuate a claim against an executor, an administrator or survivor of a deceased person, or against the committee of a lunatic. She cannot testify as to the value of the services, the number of visits made, the care administered— nor as to statements of account given and unpaid prior to the patient's death.

Many states have statutes that limit the time during which a nurse may file her claim. They are relatively short—six months to one year in most states. One has to be prompt about pressing a claim. Therefore, pay in terminal cases is best established on a bimonthly basis. Bearing the above in mind, the nurse should seek not to fall behind more than two weeks in payment for services in terminal-care situations. In fact, foreseeable terminal care is best covered by a written agreement that is kept up-to-date and witnessed like a will in the event additional duties are undertaken and/or additional promises made or consideration offered or pledged. On proof by other parties that care was given over a certain period of time, a claim based on *quantum meruit* can be exercised. This is the actual worth of the claim, based on the time spent and the average pay for such an effort. However, the problems can be avoided if tardiness in payment is discouraged while the care is still going on.

If the nurse has enjoyed a close relationship with a patient in terminal care and has been named in the will, she should not accept such benefit in place of her regular salary or be a witness to the will. She must keep in mind that any business arrangement made by her with a terminal patient is suspect and may be voided if it profits her. Sale or barter of personal property and real property would be included.

If the person cared for is solely responsible and dies, a claim should be made immediately against the estate. Such a claim enjoys many priorities according to law, and promptness may further it still more. Where the person dies *intestate* (without having made a valid will), the administrator should be presented with the bill. Where the person dies having made a valid will, the executor should receive the bill. In most jurisdictions, the bill must be presented during the probate proceedings. If the nurse cannot deal directly with the family, she should send the itemized bill to the executor or administrator of the estate. If she cannot find out who he is, she should hire a lawyer who can. He can also advise her whether formal affidavits in support of her claim must be submitted.

CASE CITATION

1. New York Civil Practice Act, Section 347.

CHAPTER 14

THE TRIAL

As we pointed out in our earlier discussion on the growth and development of private law, liability law as it affects the nursing and medical professions began by trying to protect the public against what were then criminal violations by members of these professions. Today this motive still underlies some professional criminal liability, but its penal rather than remedial character has set it apart from professional civil liability as we know it. However, every compilation of the criminal statutes or codes has certain sections which deal directly with the problem.

There has been a noticeable departure from the evidentiary requirements and punishment implied in the approach on the basis of criminality. Today's professional and others with skills in the health sciences are more often subjected to examination for liability in tort, or civil wrong, and for breach of contract. In these actions, as mentioned previously, the plaintiff must prove the validity of his case by only a preponderance of the evidence. Further, tort and breach-of-contract actions may be remedied by payment reflecting the damage suffered by the plaintiff. In criminal liability, if the people reacting to the complaint of a member of the public, or their official agents, seek to prove criminal liability of the defendant, they must assume a far greater burden of proof and demonstrate the defendant's guilt beyond a reasonable doubt. Since the ultimate goal is to protect the public as well as the individual, a finding of guilty results in a fine, a prison term, or both. The same circumstances that give rise to a criminal charge may form the basis for a civil case in the torts of assault and battery.

For example, a nurse is criminally assaulted. She identifies the man and charges him. He is indicted on a charge of rape and assault. The state prosecutes him and must sustain the burden of the proof to the degree required in criminal cases. At the same time, she may bring a civil suit against him for damages, medical expenses, and pain and suffering. In her suit, *she* rather than the state is the plaintiff; she has to prove her case by only a preponderance of the evidence.

Privity is a legal connection between the parties before the suit. Privity has no application in tort cases, but in contract cases it was traditionally of great importance. It has now been generally eliminated as to breach-of-warranty (contract) actions, first involving food and drugs, and then other commodities. In many jurisdictions its application has gone beyond ingested products to other categories of consumer goods. In one case, a man fired a shotgun, but the shell was defective and a bystander was injured. A Michigan court held that privity was not required by the injured plaintiff, who could recover under common-law implied warranty from the manufacturer.[1] This does away with the need for multiple lawsuits along the chain of distribution. It is also more realistic in terms of advertising and merchandising techniques, which are aimed directly at the consumer.

At some point the nurse may find herself a plaintiff in an action, a defendant, or a *witness* (person giving testimony in a court hearing). The nurse appears in court more frequently as a witness than as a sole defendant. In recent years, however, she has been cited with growing frequency as a codefendant.

This is approximately the situation that exists in Canada. A check of the Court Clerk's Office in the Queen's Bench, high court in Manitoba, for example, showed that nursing personnel are more likely to be witnesses than defendants. Yet in the Canadian provinces also, nurses are now being called as codefendants. This is done not only to seek contribution but to facilitate the plaintiff's counsel's examination and for discovery of essential information. Thus, in a Manitoba case, two registered nurses and a student nurse, along with the hospital, physicians, and instrument manufacturers, were named defendants when an infant suffered loss of his penis, allegedly due to an imperfect piece of electrical equipment used for nonmanual circumcision. They were charged with negligent use of an unsafe and dangerous instrument and with failure to pretest it, thereby negligently providing the instrumentality by which the patient was harmed.

SUMMONS AND COMPLAINT

The usual civil litigation starts when the defendant is served with a *summons,* which is usually accompanied by a verified *complaint.* This gives the nurse or physician an opportunity to file an answer in a stated period of time—about two weeks in most jurisdictions and at various court levels. Should the defendant ignore the summons and complaint, the plaintiff can apply to the court for a default judgment. The plaintiff my have gained some advantage because of the defendant's reasonable delay or unawareness. A defense attorney can employ various measures at this point to nullify such an advantage.

Occasionally the attorney for either side may subpoena a nurse. A *subpoena* is a court order commanding the person on whom it is served to appear at a given time and place to testify. Refusal to honor the demand renders the nurse subject to contempt-of-court proceedings, which are unpleasant and may involve fine and imprisonment.

CONDUCT AS A WITNESS

A nurse who ministered to the patient may testify for him voluntarily or involuntarily, as a so-called *hostile witness.* By contrast to the physician defendant's evidence, hers may be either objective or subjective. In either case, so long as it was arrived at during the patient's treatment, it is legally admissible. Before appearing in court, she should determine whether she is allowed to testify concerning confidential or privileged communications made to her by the patient. If this is not obvious, she should obtain expert advice.

Once having taken the oath, the nurse should reflect the ethical objectivity and dignity of her profession. As a witness, she is obligated to speak the truth based on facts known to her. This is far more preferable to impressions, assumptions, or hearsay, which may be disallowed by the judge. She should never allow personal loyalties or prejudices to color her statements, thus avoiding harm to an innocent person or protection to a guilty or negligent person. The witness should answer as concisely as possible and only in response to questions and after an opportunity to weigh her answer. She should use language that laymen, in this case the judge and jury, can understand. Not only can she speak from her actual recollections, but she will be allowed to refresh her memory by recourse to notes. If for any reason she feels harassed by an attorney, she should feel free to appeal to the court to stop at once this wrongful practice. She will certainly feel more at ease if she thoroughly prepares herself for the testimony she will be called to give. When a case is concluded, it is reasonable to assume that either side may appeal it. Therefore, she should prepare a brief personal memorandum of her testimony for possible future use.

THE MEDICAL RECORD AND THE NURSE'S CHART

The patient's *medical record* is a written account of his illness and treatment by all members of the health team during his stay in a hospital or other institution, or by a doctor in private practice. This record can be important evidence in a legal proceeding.

While the form of a medical record may vary, in hospital practice it usually has two parts. The first is a preface, which is static and contains the information necessary to identify the patient. The second is dynamic and historic, since it gives the clinical history of the patient's treatment. As such, it includes the nurse's charts and notes. The notes are admissible in evidence to establish an issue of fact which would entitle plaintiff to take his case before a jury.[2] The charts are part of the patient's medical record. They can be used when the plaintiff is trying to show that consent was fraudulently obtained by either party to the suit.[3] The medical record also contains an exact record of the treatment given the patient by all other members of the health team, and the rationale for the treatment. In it are signed consent forms or records of the patient's refusal of recommended procedures, x-ray, laboratory, and consultation reports, and the physician's order. This is why, when an order is unclear or definitely in error as to limb identification, it is mandatory to correct it and add the appropriate signature. In this way, the record shows that an error was caught and corrected. Ethics and law require that where an error is found belatedly after its execution, it should be entered also.

The record also contains the results of physical examinations and progress reports. Since the nurse's recorded observations are in the same record for the same patient, it is obvious that the observations should be of the same general tone, otherwise someone has been careless in observing, examining, or reporting. The nurse's chart is an important guide for the doctor in diagnosing and prescribing for the patient. Therefore, it must be legible and concise, and must employ explicit and standard terminology. Any errors in this record must be corrected and initialed.

Before hospital records are admitted as evidence in the trial proceedings, the attorney must prepare the foundation for their admission. Sufficient foundation exists if both parties seek to use them extensively.

THE NURSE AND PHYSICIAN AS EXPERT WITNESSES

When the nurse is summoned to testify as a witness, she must realize that the court, through the judge, may exert considerably more authority than she has ever experienced. The time of testifying may be varied. It is difficult to be certain when a case will be tried, let alone when a specific witness will be called to the stand. The rules as to what testimony will be allowable are complicated; sometimes testimony is excluded on technical grounds. The witness must answer all questions put to her. She can refuse only if she does not know the answer or if the question impinges on privileged communication. This is equally true of the physician.

A physician or dentist who will testify for the plaintiff and who examines the plaintiff for that purpose may present (preferably) objective evidence, such as electroencephalograms, x-ray fiindings, fluoroscopic findings, biopsy results, and direct visual observation. He can also present subjective assertions, but they must have some support in objective findings or they will not be accepted by the court.[4] Pennsylvania law requires that where medical witnesses testify against a party, the latter has a right to exclude the testimony if he has not received their report thirty days before the trial. This refers to the medical report of any physician who has treated or examined him, or has been consulted about the injuries complained of.[5]

While a physician is generally regarded as a competent expert where the issue is nursing malpractice, the nurse is rarely considered to be an expert on malpractice. However, the increasingly professional status of nursing is beginning to change this view. A nurse or medical technician often has been deemed to posses sufficient training and experience to qualify her to testify. An Illinois appellate court, for example, stated that the lower court made an error in excluding a technician's testimony and opinion as to proper practice in applying dressings while treating a postappendectomy abscess. The technician was found competent to testify as to whether an externally applied gauze dressing could work its way into the body.[6]

A physician or dentist may be competent to testify as an expert even in a field in which he is not a specialist. Training, board status, or other proof of special expertise bears on the weight, not the admissibility, of his testimony. A general practitioner is therefore held competent to testify as to the accepted practice of specialists.[7] However, the physician should have had some experience in the field in which he testifies. For example, in a case involving orthopedic surgery, the view of a specialist in internal medicine as to how to set a fracture and apply a cast might either be disallowed or given very little weight as evidence.

In a personal-injury case, a medical expert testifying for the plaintiff may hypothesize. That is, he can be asked by the latter's attorney whether a given condition of the plaintiff may or could be caused by the accident involved. Further, any expert, medical or nursing, does not have to be familiar with the local medical or nursing standards. So long as he knows the standards of care that generally constitute reasonable care and skill, the court will accept his testimony.[8] Therefore, the plaintiff may offer the testimony of his own medical or dental expert even if he cannot testify on the standards of care in a specific hospital or locality. Such an expert is permitted to give an opinion on what he consider to be the standard of medical or dental care in the community where the treatment was given.[9]

In every suit against a nurse, doctor, or dentist for professional negligence, the knowledge and skill of the defendant are properly at issue. He will testify that his treatment or care of the patient was proper and necessary. His credibility becomes a matter for the jury to weigh. Therefore, both in pretrial examination or discovery procedures and in cross-examination during the trial, the nurse, technician, or doctor may be questioned as to his education, licensure, training, experience, professional affiliations, and the like.[10]

In almost every jurisdiction, there is statutory authorization of pretrial discovery. Its substance varies significantly between jurisdictions and courts. Generally it permits discovery of all matters relevant to the case. Before the trial, the plaintiff can utilize discovery procedures to examine nurses, aides, and technicians, as well as physicians, who were present or participated in the patient's treatment, as to what was done from the time the patient was admitted. This covers all areas from preliminary diagnostic procedures to treatment or surgery to subsequent care. Information is elicited in the form of sworn testimony.

If a professional is to be a defendant, the plaintiff's attorney can question him about elements of his experience and education that would bear on his credibility and professional skill. He can be asked about his professional affiliations, his writings, or books he has available to him on the subject of the complaint. This will enable the plaintiff's attorney to examine him on his knowledge and expertise. He may also be required to answer questions as to the titles, board certification, degrees, and professional society memberships of all expert witnesses he expects to call in his defense, as well as texts or articles they will cite. He may not be asked any information that would represent legal conclusion. He may be asked if he has insurance and what its limits are (depending on state rules) [11] but he may not be required to supply the name of his insurer or a copy of his insurance policy.

A defendant nurse, doctor, or dentist often exonerates himself by testifying as an expert in his own behalf, especially when the plaintiff fails to refute or rebut his testimony with his own expert. In one case where a mental patient jumped out a window, the doctor testified that he had followed the open-door policy of the institution and had acted in accord with accepted medical standards. Since no expert appeared to qualify that policy and question the medical standards, the court accepted his testimony as the only yardstick available.[12]

Expert Testimony Based on Opinion

Expert testimony based on opinion is admissible, but may bear small weight with a jury. In a 1963 trial for first-degree murder, a number of psychiatrists testified that in their opinion the accused demonstrated a lack of criminal intent and premeditation. The jury returned a verdict of first-degree murder, which was upheld on appeal. The appellate court stated: "It must be kept in mind that an opinion is only an opinion. It creates no fact. Because of this, opinion evidence is considered of low grade and not entitled to much weight against positive testimony of actual facts such as statements by the defendant and observations of his actions." [13]

Medical experts may opinionize, but they may not speculate as to unproven "facts" and then postulate from that point. Relevance therefore is of great importance in developing convincing evidence as to proximate cause. In one case where physicians were sued in negligence for the loss of an eye,[14] the plaintiff set forth a theory that the eye drops administered had been contaminated with infective organisms. An appellate court held that the plaintiff's medical experts should not have been allowed, without basis in proven evidence, to speculate that the eye drops were contaminated and then deduce from that they were the source of infection.

These holdings often depend upon the jurisdiction. In 1967 the Ohio Court of Appeals held that a defendant physician cannot be compelled to provide the sole expert testimony through cross-examination.[15] The objection must however be asserted and the doctor thereafter must not nullify it by voluntary admissions. For example, in a Texas case, a plaintiff had failed to establish by expert evidence what the accepted medical standard in the community was as to disclosure of risks to a patient prior to a stapedectomy. Thereafter, the defendent testified that he had warned the patient of possible total loss of hearing, as was the standard practice.[16]

Hypothetical questions have relatively the same status as testimony based on opinion. They must be based on facts that pertain to the issue, and not on one party's view of the facts; otherwise, they are inadmissible on the ground of leading the witness. Also, if substantial error is caused when hypothetical situations are put to an expert witness, a new trial may be requested and granted.

Reimbursing Expert Witnesses

When a plaintiff's attorney agrees to pay an expert who will testify in the plaintiff's behalf and indicates that this is done with the plaintiff's affirmation, the fee is payable as a lien on the eventual judgment. A New York court has gone so far as to rule that the attorney is responsible for its payment. He will be liable to a third person for money collected by him for his client if the attorney, with notice of the third party's claim, pays it to his client.[17] Today, a plaintiff's attorney who does not, or cannot, provide expert testimony in refutation, may try to use the defendant as the expert, even though he is a hostile witness. From this witness he seeks to elicit the contradicting elements that will defeat him.

ADMISSION AGAINST INTEREST

Sometimes, especially in the immediate circumstances of the injury, a defendant admits errors, which is against his own interest. Such admissions constitute important evidence. In some cases, even where the plaintiff lacks expert medical testimony, these admissions have been enough to carry the case to the jury. They are even more damaging when made in pretrial deposition.

In several Eastern states, courts have ruled that physician defendants in malpractice suits can be required to answer as experts during pretrial discovery proceedings.[18] The plaintiff's questioning may extend to the physician's opinion and judgment as exercised in the course of treating the patient. The plaintiff may properly question why he did or did not do certain things, as well as his theory and diagnostic basis for the course of treatment.

During trial, many courts now allow the plaintiff to call the defendant nurse, physician, or dentist to the stand as hostile witness and require him to answer questions as one who can give an expert opinion concerning the local standard of practice and the extent of any deviation from it.[19] However, courts have reacted differently to the use of defendant specialists as experts. In a Midwestern case the plaintiff sought to question the defendant on matters involving his judgment, knowledge, and opinion as an expert.[20] The court refused to permit this because the plaintiff had not called other medical witnesses.

The plaintiff's attorney tried to justify calling him as a witness on the ground of surprise, claiming that the physician had made an admission to the patient damaging to himself. Since this was not documented by a pretrial deposition, the trial court exercised its discretion and refused to admit his testimony.

SUMMARY JUDGMENT

Among the legal maneuvers that take place before, during, or after the adversaries have set forth their cases is a motion by the defendant for *summary judgment*. This is supported by affidavits purporting to show critical inadequacy of the plaintiff's case. In a negligence or malpractice action, for example, the defense would try to show that the action complained of was not proved to be the proximate cause of the patient's alleged injury. The defense must prove, however, that no issue of material fact exists; otherwise, the motion would be denied.[21] Courts have held that the plaintiff's right to trial of issue of fact precludes granting a summary judgment to the defendant on the grounds that the plaintiff failed to establish proximate cause.[22] However, the existence of a genuine issue of fact must be supported by affidavits, depositions, admissions, or other similar evidence.[23] It cannot be shown by mere allegations.

In cross-examination the credibility of the adverse party's witness or medical expert can be questioned. In some instances, attorneys have been able to demonstrate a witness's bias by forcing him to expose his political and economic theories. In other cases, attorneys can discredit the "expert" status of the witness by proving that he spent more time at other activities than at those in which he professed to be an expert. Trial courts have sometimes ruled a doctor's testimony inadmissible on the ground that he does not have specialist rating or experience. Appellate courts, on the other hand, have held that such rulings usurp the prerogative of the jury, which has a right to listen and decide, by comparison or otherwise, what weight they will accord such testimony.

A physician or dentist cannot be cross-examined on the basis of a text or article with which he is not familiar, even though written by an authority on such injuries. The same would apply to nurses and technicians. This depends much on the ingenuity of the plaintiff's attorney. For example, the latter can show that the text was used by the defendant while pursuing his professional education or training.[24]

When experts in a particular field form conclusions in an area in which they are not considered experts, they can expect to be challenged. So, for example, when an orthopedist testified in an accident case to his belief that the other party had lapsed into a diabetic coma at the time of collision, he was challenged by the adversary attorney, who could show that he had no special knowledge in diabetes.[25]

In some states, including Pennsylvania, court rules permit the appointment of an impartial expert where a medical witness who has testified for the other party has stated highly questionable and possibly unreasonable medical opinions.

Improper exclusion of medical testimony is also ground for granting a new trial.

In Minnesota, in medical malpractice actions, a plaintiff will not be permitted to compel expert testimony from the physician defendant without properly calling other medical witnesses. This is not in conflict with the court rule in numerous states that expert testimony is not absolutely necessary to establish a case for professional negligence.

While an attorney has wide latitude in his summation to the jury, he may never represent as a fact to the jury any information not supported by evidence introduced at the trial. He may hypothesize and he may conjecture, but he may not misrepresent.[26]

INSTRUCTING THE JURY

The attorneys may ask the court to *instruct* the jury in order to clarify issues that they must consider and to separate vital testimony from irrelevant details. Courts are not required to give every instruction requested. However, the judge need not give the instruction in the particular form set out by either party, even if such instruction does cite a recognized and accurate legal principle. So long as the subject matter is covered sufficiently and substantially in the instruction as given, the court has a right to rephrase it in whatever manner seems appropriate.[27] The judgment of the court cannot be ordered. If, however, the claimant or defendant feels that an instruction was improperly given or omitted, he can use this as the basis for an appeal.

The judge in the trial court, on application of the trial attorney, can direct a verdict in favor of the defendant. This is part of the judicial prerogative. He can do this when the plaintiff fails to make out a prima facie case, when the act complained of is obviously not chargeable as the proximate cause of the harm, or when the harm was accidental and unforeseeable. Either party may ask the trial court to direct a verdict in his favor. However, when this is done, the appellate court can examine the sufficiency of the evidence to see if the trial court erred in doing so. If error is found, the appellate court will order a new trial.[28]

The trial judge may reduce the jury's award of damages if he feels it to be unreasonable. This reduction is reviewable by the victorious plaintiff, just as the verdict upon which it is based may be reviewable by the defeated defendant. For example, suppose Nurse Jones is struck by a car while crossing a street on her day off duty. The driver is negligent. Nurse Jones is taken to the hospital and is off duty for many months. However, she is helped by any or all of three favorable possibilities.

1.   Among the fringe benefits of her employment is coverage of medical and hospital expenses for her injury.

2.   She receives partial or complete professional courtesy from physicians who treat her and the hospital that cares for her.

3.   She has a personal insurance policy that pays her costs and reimburses her a certain amount per week while she is disabled.

When she is granted an award at the trial, the question arises, Should these circumstances benefit the tort-feasor by lessening the sum he is to pay in damages?

Most states hold, in what is called the *collateral source doctrine*, that a tort-feasor has no interest in, or right to benefit from, reimbursement that the plaintiff secures from sources that have no connection with or responsibility to him. Therefore, the fact that the jury's award to Nurse Jones of $20,000 includes her medical care, loss of income, and award for pain and suffering does not mean that the tort-feasor should benefit by deductions to which she is entitled. On the other hand, if the tort-feasor has paid any preaward damages personally, through loans from friends, or through insurance coverage, a credit against the final judgment for damages will be allowed.[29]

In seeking an award of damages for personal injury caused by negligence, a long period may elapse between the harmful act and the final court verdict. Therefore, in dealing with substantial settlements, interest on the amount awarded is a serious consideration. In New York State the rule generally is that the award itself represents the extent of the defendant's financial responsibility to the plaintiff. Interest, therefore, accrues from the date when the verdict is rendered, rather than from the date of the negligent act.

In a suit in tort or product liability based on breach of warranty, the plaintiff may be entitled to punitive or exemplary damages in addition to simple or compensatory damages. Such special damages are awarded when intentional tort, such as fraud or libel, has been proved. A judgment to award special damages is generally discretionary with the jury but is reviewable by an appellate court where the action seems patently unjust or based on passion and prejudice.[30]

In Canada, most malpractice cases tend to be tried without a jury; smaller damages are awarded than in the United States. Damage awards in Vermont, Maine, and New Hampshire are apt to be smaller than those in Massachusetts or New York. As a rule, urban juries and courts seem to compensate more substantially than those in predominantly rural areas.

LITIGATION EXPENDITURES

Professional persons frequently incur sizable expenses in defense of suits. Often this defense is undertaken and paid for by their insurance carrier. Under the Federal Internal Revenue Code, litigation expenses are business expenses and are deductible if the legal fees arise in connection with the taxpayer's business, practice, or source of income. The litigation expense must have a business origin, not a personal one. Therefore, if a doctor is sued by a nurse's husband for seducing her and causing her to become a narcotic addict, he cannot deduct such legal expense.[31]

CASE CITATIONS

1. *Piercefiels v. Remington Arms, Inc.,* 133 N.W. 2d 129 (1965).
2. *Michaels v. Spiers,* 144 So. 2d 835 (1962).
3. *Geddes v. Daughters of Charity,* 348 F. 2d 144 (1965).
4. *Jensen v. Elgin, Joliet and Eastern Railroad Company,* 182 N.E. 2d 211 (1962).
5. *Coffrey v. Faix,* 233 A. 2d 229 (1967).
6. *Placentino v. Bonnefil,* 217 N.E. 2d 507 (1966).
7. *Brerman v. Reesinger,* 363 F. 2d 309 (1966).
8. *Bank of Sardis v. Sanders,* 145 S.E. 2d 59, 60 (1965).
9. *Lyon v. Wood,* 407 S.W. 2d 693 (1966).
10. *Myers v. St. Francis Hospital,* 220 A. 2d 693 (1965).

11. *Ibid.*
12. *Williams v. Morton,* 225 N.E. 2d 671 (1967).
13. *Commonwealth of Pennsylvania v. Carroll,* 194 A. 2d 911 (1963).
14. *Filanowicz v. Guarino,* 276 N.Y. 2d 656 (1967).
15. *Oleksiw v. Weidener* 2 Ohio St. 147 (1967).
16. *Texas Supreme Court, No. A-11180* N.P.N. (1967).
17. *Arello v. Levine,* 255 N.Y. 2d 921 (1965).
18. *Alterman v. Maimonides Hospital,* 270 N.Y. 2d 134, 219 (1966).
19. *McDermott v. New York Eye, Ear, and Throat Hospital,* 203 N.E. 2d 469 (1964).
20. *Hoffman v. Naslund,* 144 N.W. 2d 580 (1966).
21. *Scanlon v. Litt,* 191 So. 2d 553 (1966).
22. *Vigingardi v. Tirone,* 193 So. 2d 601 (1966).
23. *Dillon v. Greenville Hospital Authority,* 404 S.W. 2d 956 (1966).
24. *Ward v. Lamb,* 402 S.W. 2d 675 (1966).
25. *Arnold v. Loose,* 352 F. 2d 959 (1965).
26. *Koepel v. St. Joseph Hospital and Medical Center,* 155 N.W. 2d 199 (1967).
27. *Fleming v. Michigan Mutual Liability Co.* 363 F. 2d 186 (1966).
28. *Lyon v. Wood,* 407 S.W. 2d 693 (1966).
29. *Yarrington v. Thornburg,* 205 A. 2d 1 (1964).
30. *Roginsky v. Richardson-Merrell,* 254 F. Supp. 430 (1966).
31. *Finger v. United States,* 257 F. Supp. 312 (1966).
32. *Greenberg v. Commissioner of Internal Revenue,* 367 F. 2d 663 (1966).

GLOSSARY

ABANDONMENT unilateral severance of a contractual agreement which is implied or written

AB INITIO from inception

ABORTION (CRIMINAL ABORTION, ILLEGAL ABORTION) prescribing a drug or other substance or using an instrument "with intent thereby to procure the miscarriage of a woman, or of the child with which she is pregnant

ABUSE OF PROCESS (MALICIOUS USE OF PROCESS) securing legal process (such as a writ) for one purpose and using it for another

ADMINISTRATOR person chosen by the state to dispose of property in accordance with state law if the deceased has not left a will

ADMINISTRATIVE LAW (AGENCY LAW) regulates such agencies as those dealing with food, drugs, and utilities. It is similar in many ways to Roman law

ADVISORY COUNCIL aids the board of nursing on all matters that affect the rules and regulations to effectuate the nursing practice act, its interpretation, and recommendations as to its amendment or change that are to go to the legislature

AGENT person hired to act on behalf of a principal and subject to the latter's control. Generally (though not always) an agent is an employee

APPELLANT person who appeals a decision of a lower court to a higher court

APPELLATE COURT the court to which a judgment of the trial court is appealed

APPELLEE (RESPONDENT) the opponent of the appellant. The appellee claims that the decision of the lower court should stand

ASSAULT performing or threatening to perform intentional injury, bodily harm to another by administration of poison, anesthetics or narcotics, or willful and wrongful blows with weapons or other instruments

ASSIGNABLE CONTRACT a contract possessing value in itself, as a contract for exclusive privileges or provision of services; or one which by its terms permits the transfer of the rights and duties of either party to a third party

ATTEMPT an act or acts done with the intent to commit a crime, but short of its actual perpetration

ATTRACTIVE NUISANCE availability of an object that might attract children onto or into it or to use internally or externally. Examples are dumbwaiters or discarded medical equipment

AUXILIARY PERSONNEL unlicensed persons employed and trained to perform tasks which involve specialized services for patients under direct supervision of professional and practical nurses

BAIL money or other security deposited with the proper official to assure the defendant's appearance in court; it permits him to be released from jail

BATTERY intentional harmful or offensive bodily contact with another person without consent or with consent exceeded or fraudulently obtained

BLACKMAIL obtaining money or property by means of a written document used to coerce

BOARD OF NURSING the government agency that issues nursing licenses and regulations following the precepts of legislated nursing practice acts. The board of nursing then sets up the machinery to enforce compliance and to punish violations of the act and the regulations

BORROWED SERVANT transferral of a hospital nurse or other employee to the exclusive control of an attending physician

CHARITABLE IMMUNITY the doctrine that charity hospitals, acting as employers, are immune to suit. With the availability of insurance to hospitals, this concept is gradually being discarded

CONSERVATORSHIP LAWS permit the appointment of a person to protect the property and estate of someone whose impaired mental or physical condition makes it difficult for him to manage his own affairs

CONSIDERATION something of value as viewed by the law. It may consist of some right, interest, profit, monetary award, benefit to one party, or some forbearance, detriment, loss, or responsibility given, or undertaken by the other party

CONSPIRACY joining together of two or more persons for the purpose of committing a crime

CONTRACT an agreement, legally enforceable, between two or more persons to do or forbear doing something

CONTRIBUTORY NEGLIGENCE conduct by the plaintiff that causes unreasonable harm or risk to himself and/or his property. It may negate a negligence suit

CONVERSION unlawful exercise of ownership over property that belongs to someone else

CIVIL LAW regulates private wrongs and involves monetary reward for damages

CODES statutes published cumulatively

COLLATERAL SOURCE DOCTRINE states that a tort-feasor's payment of damages cannot be affected by the fact that the plaintiff received reimbursement from insurance or other sources. The tort-feasor has no right to benefit from such a circumstance

COMMON LAW derived, like Roman law, from the absolute power of the monarch. Its most important principle is precedent

COMPARATIVE NEGLIGENCE doctrine that bears on the damages paid to one who has been contributorily negligent. It states that even though the plaintiff has contributed in part to his own injury, he should not be prevented from recovering some of the damages from the party mainly responsible for the harm

COMPENSATORY DAMAGES determined on the basis of what financial loss the plaintiff has had and will have from his injury to person or property

COMPLAINANT generally, one who brings a criminal action, such as the state, on behalf of the alleged victim

CONSEQUENTIAL DAMAGES defined by *Black's Legal Dictionary* as "Such damage, loss or injury as does not flow directly and immediately from the act of the party, but only from some of the consequences or results of that act." In short, it may be remote yet actionable; may turn up later in time than the act that provoked the suit

CRIME (PUBLIC OFFENSE, CRIMINAL OFFENSE) the breach of any law established for protection of the public, as distinguished from an infringement of the private rights of the individual, for which a penalty is imposed or punishment inflicted in any judicial proceeding

CRIMINAL LAW regulates unlawful acts that threaten the welfare of society as well as that of the individual. Penalties include fine, imprisonment, and death

DAMAGES monetary compensation for one who has sustained loss, detriment, or injury to his person or property through the unlawful act, omission, or negligence of another

DANGEROUS DRUGS   drugs which are stimulants, depressants, or combinations of both; drugs which are hallucinogenic or psychotomimetics. In many state drug laws, all potent drugs such as those which require a physician's prescription are also classed as dangerous drugs

DECISIONAL LAW   determined by reference to precedent-setting court decisions. Decisional law is the source of many private laws

DEFAMATORY STATEMENT   one which exposes a person to hatred, contempt, or aversion, or lowers the opinion of him in the community. Such a statement may be oral, written, pictured, etc.

DEFENDANT   person against whom a lawsuit is initiated

DELEGATION   assignment of tasks to one who is lower in professional rank and theoretically less qualified. Delegation of physician tasks to a professional nurse and corresponding delegation of her responsibilities to other members of the nursing team have caused legal and ethical problems resulting in a need to redefine nursing functions

DIAGNOSIS   examination of a person for the purpose of determining the source or nature of a disease or other abnormal physical or mental condition. Medical diagnosis is statutorily a function of the physician

DIVISION OF POWERS   constitutional division of responsibility between federal and state governments

DOCTRINE OF FORESEEABILITY   obligation of the principal or agent to remove conditions or objects that can be expected to involve risk or danger, or to warn persons of their existence or take other precautions

DUE PROCESS   includes many safeguards for one who is criminally charged. Due process requires, for example, that criminal statutes must be couched in clear language and that the accused be informed of the nature of the charge against him and of his right to remain silent and obtain counsel

EMPLOYEE   one who is hired to perform a duty or service for an employer, subject to the latter's control. Unlike an agent, an employee's authority to act on his employer's behalf has not been formalized

ENTRAPMENT   the creative activity of law-enforcement officers for the purpose of proving an offense

EXECUTOR   person chosen by the testator to carry out the provisions of his will

EXEMPLARY (PUNITIVE) DAMAGES   separate from an award for loss or costs. They are intended to penalize the defendant for having acted in a malicious, fraudulent, or wanton manner

EXEMPT NARCOTICS (CLASS X) those which may be sold over the counter or which contain a stimulant or depressant drug in combination with another drug in such amounts as to make the combination drug non-habit-forming. These drugs are not regulated by the Drug Abuse Control Act

EXPRESS WARRANTY oral or written promise to make amends in the event of a product's failure. Unlike a guaranty, it may contain conditions on which amends will be made

EXTORTION obtaining money or property by means of fear, threat, or oral coercion

FALSE ARREST any unlawful physical restraint by one of another's liberty, whether in person or elsewhere

FALSE IMPRISONMENT (ILLEGAL DETENTION) intentional confinement without authorization by one who physically constricts the plaintiff, using force, threat of force, or confining clothing or structures

FEDERAL COURT SYSTEM one of the three main U.S. court systems. It is headed by the U.S. Supreme Court and involves lawsuits between citizens of different states and between citizens and government units

FELONIOUS HOMICIDE the wrongful killing of a human being. It may be classified as either murder or manslaughter

FELONY a crime punishable by death or imprisonment

FORESEEABILITY ability to predict possible results when duty is not performed, and to prevent these consequences when possible

FRAUD AND DECEIT misrepresentation of a fact known to be false with the intention of having another rely on it, to his detriment

FRAUDULENT CONCEALMENT (DISCOVERY RULE) the physician's, hospital's, or nurse's concealment of the patient's cause of injury. It gives the plaintiff the right to sue in the period starting from the time of his discovery

GOOD SAMARITAN LAWS limit liability when injury is incurred while giving emergency aid

GOVERNMENT IMMUNITY the rule of law that the government cannot be sued. This applies to federal and state governments. The latter have often delegated immunity to municipalties. On the other hand, immunity has been abrogated in special instances by the federal government

GRAND LARCENY, PETTY LARCENY degrees of the same crime depending on the value of the property taken

GREATER PUBLIC NEED doctrine that privileged communication

may be waived if the professional feels that the public's right to know outweighs the patient's right to privacy

GROSS NEGLIGENCE   characterized by a willful and reckless disregard for the person and/or property of another

GUARANTY   written statement of the product's expected performance and a virtually unconditional promise to exchange the product or give a refund if it does not live up to expectations

HOLOGRAPHIC WILL   a handwritten will. It is valid as long as it is properly executed, with the testator's and witness's signatures at the end of it

HOMICIDE   defined by New York's Penal Code as the "killing of one human being by the act, procurement or omission of another"

HOSTILE WITNESS   a witness who testifies for someone against his will

IMPLIED WARRANTY   derived "by implication or inference from the transaction." It is traditional in the sale of all commodities

INDEPENDENT CONTRACTOR   one who is hired to perform a service or job without supervision

INSTRUCTION   the judge's statement to the jury in which he clarifies the legal weight of issues they must consider and separates valid testimony from irrelevant detail and often crystallizes the contentions of the adverse parties

INTENTIONAL TORT   one in which a person "does damage to another willfully and intentionally, and without just cause or excuse"

INTESTATE   without having made a valid will

INVASION OF PRIVACY   trespasses upon the body and/or personality of another without his consent

INVITEE   one whose presence on the premises is essential to its operation or for whom the premises have a purpose, such as a patient in a hospital room

JOINT STATEMENTS   statements formulated collectively by associations in the health services. Purposes: (1) to state the limits of dependent and independent nursing functions, (2) to lessen the possibility of violation of medical practice acts and subsequent prosecution, and (3) to act as a basis on which a nurse can refuse to perform an act clearly outside of her scope

JOINT TORT–FEASOR   two or more persons responsible for a tort

JUDGE   one who hears cases brought before the court. His duties include examining the legal processes that precede the trial and the complaints, answers, and counterclaims. He may decide whether a jury is needed and during the trial conducts the proceedings in the courtroom. After the trial he hands down a judgment based either on his own authority (if he acts as trier in a nonjury trial) or on the jury's verdict

JUDGMENT   final order of the court, based either on the jury's verdict or on the judge's deliberations in a nonjury trial

JUSTIFIABLE ASSAULT   the use of reasonable force to repel someone who is threatening oneself or another, where there is a duty or social obligation to protect and defend or an immediate need to forestall grievous bodily harm

JUSTIFIABLE HOMICIDE   one class of homicide

KIDNAPPING   any unlawful detention that is willful and intentional. It can be either a misdemeanor or a felony

LARCENY   taking the property of another with the intent to keep it for one's own use or to deprive the owner of its use permanently

LAST CLEAR CHANCE   doctrine that the person who had the last opportunity to prevent the tortious act and did not do so may be considered negligent

LAW   a system of societal restraint and prerogatives which governs interpersonal relationships between the members of that society and certain extrapersonal relationships between the individual and society

LAWSUIT   an issue or case in court where one party has challenged another to a trial on the issue between them

LAWYER   one who undergoes professional training and is licensed to try cases before courts and to advise the public about their rights and liabilities under all forms of law

LIBEL   defamatory statement conveyed by written words, pictures, recordings, broadcasts, etc.

LICENSE   a legal document that permits a person to offer the public skills and knowledge whose practice would otherwise be unlawful

LICENSEE   a person on the premises because he has a legal right of entry or is a guest. Fire and building inspectors fall into this category

LIQUIDATED DAMAGES   the amount of damages to be paid if the contract or some part of it is not or cannot be performed. It can either be ascertained by court judgment or as an agreed-upon preestimate. It is not punitive like a penalty clause, which may call for excess over actual damages

LITIGANT   either party to a lawsuit

LOCAL COURT SYSTEM   one of the three main U.S. court systems. Its structure differs from state to state, depending on the custom or political subdivisions of the state and on the community's needs

234 THE NURSE'S GUIDE TO THE LAW

MALICE   the intentional doing of a wrongful act without just cause
or excuse

MALICIOUS PROSECUTION   initiated out of a desire to harm or
inconvenience another without probable cause to believe that the
charge will hold

MALPRACTICE   the form of negligence that occurs when a professional, in treating or caring for a patient, does not conduct
himself with responsible prudence and skill

MANSLAUGHTER IN THE FIRST DEGREE   defined by New York's
Penal Code as the commission or attempt "to commit a misdemeanor affecting the person or property either of the person killed
or another"

MANSLAUGHTER IN THE SECOND DEGREE   culpable negligence,
such as that of a drunken doctor or woman who submits to an
abortion

"MASTER OF THE SHIP" THEORY   generally applied to surgical
situations. It holds that the surgeon is in charge of the operation
much as the captain is in charge of the ship

MEDICAL RECORD   a written account of a patient's illness and
treatment by all members of the health team during his stay in
a hospital or other institution, or by a doctor in private practice

MENS REA   the criminal state of mind, specific intent, which separates crimes from torts

MISDEMEANOR   any crime less serious than a felony

NARCOTIC DRUGS   a group of substances including opium and its
alkaloids (codeine, morphine, and heroin) and derivatives; the coca
leaf and its principal derivative cocaine; the plant Cannabis sativa L.,
otherwise known as marihuana; and a class of synthetics called
opiates, such as meperidine, methadone, and anileridine.

NEGLIGENCE   the failure of a nonprofessional, in treating or caring
for a patient, to conduct himself with responsible prudence and
skill

NEGLIGENCE PER SE   literally, "negligence in itself." An inference
of such negligence may arise if standards of conduct set forth in
statutes are violated

NOMINAL DAMAGES   symbolic in nature

NURSING   care of the ill, injured, or infirm for compensation

NURSING ASSOCIATIONS   established for such purposes as (1)
promoting high standards of nursing education and practice, (2)
interpreting nursing to the public, (3) promoting the social and
economic welfare of its members, and (4) encouraging the participation of nurses in local, national, and international activities

PENALTY CLAUSE   describes a detriment that will be assumed or a sum of money which the party will undertake to pay, in the event he fails to perform or carry out the contract as promised. It may also be regarded as a prearranged-for feature

PLAINTIFF   person who initiates a lawsuit

POLICE POWER   the power delegated by the Constitution to the states to regulate an occupation, a profession, or a business when it affects the public health, morals, and welfare. This is further delegated by the state to local units that carry out the same functions

PRACTICAL NURSE   a nurse licensed to care for the physical health of a patient under the direct supervision of a physician or professional nurse

PRINCIPAL (EMPLOYER)   one who engages an agent to assist him or act on his behalf. The principal controls the agent

PRIVATE LAW   generally concerned with maintaining rights, duties, and other relations of private individuals or organizations. These relations include the law of contracts and the law of negligence. Private law is often based on decisional law

PRIVILEGED COMMUNICATION   doctrine that prevents a professional from divulging information gained during or as a consequence of a patient's treatment

PRIVITY   a legal connection between the parties before the suit

PROBATE   proving the validity of a will

PROFESSIONAL NURSE   a nurse licensed by the state to perform, for pay, services to the patient. Services include giving treatment and medication under a physician's orders, supervising the patient's physical and mental health and well-being, observing, recording, and interpreting symptoms and reactions, and supervising and delegating authority to subordinate personnel

PROXIMATE CAUSE   one in which natural and continuous sequence, unbroken by an efficient intervening cause, produces the harm and without which the harm would not have occurred

PUBLIC LAW   generally conceived in response to a public need for expansion of legal principles. Public laws are specific, dealing, for example, with taxation and conscription

QUALIFIED PRIVILEGE   a truthful, nonmalicious report by a health care practitioner about a professional person or situation

RES   subject matter of the dispute

RES IPSA LOQUITUR   literally, "The thing speaks for itself." It is the doctrine of implied negligence

RES JUDICATA   an adjudicated decision that will stand

RESPONDEAT SUPERIOR   literally, "Let the master answer." It means that the principal or employer is responsible when his agent or employee causes harm to the person or property of another party

ROMAN LAW derived from the absolute power of the monarch. It is characterized as a system of codes. It became known as civil law and later as the Napoleonic code

SEARCH WARRANT an order in writing, signed by a judge, directing a police officer to search a certain place for personal property and to bring the property to court

SEPARATION OF POWERS a doctrine of the Constitution by which the powers of federal government are delegated to three bodies: the executive, legislature, and the judiciary

SLANDER oral defamation

SPECIAL DAMAGES based on the actual and natural, but not the necessary, result of the injury

STARE DECISIS literally, "The previous decision stands." It is the concept of precedent, primary to common law

STATE COURT SYSTEM one of the three main U.S. court systems

STATUTE OF FRAUDS provides that no person shall be held to answer to the debt, default, or failure of another except by his signed acknowledgment; that a memorandum concerning an agreement to buy or sell must be complete and in writing and signed by the one expected to pay, when it exceeds certain limits set in time and money under the statute

STATUTE OF LIMITATIONS the time during which a case can be brought to trial or a right enforced. The objective is to curtail unwarranted claims or those which benefit from the passage of time (loss of witnesses, changes in social and political climate, statutory changes). Statutes of limitations differ between courts and jurisdictions and for different kinds of suits

STATUTORY LAW a law enacted by Congress or state legislatures under powers delegated by the Constitution. Statutory law is synonymous with public law

SUBAGENT agent of the agent. Where he has the authority or sanction of the principal or where subagency is necessary, the subagent can bind the principal just as the agent can

SUBPOENA a court order commanding the person on whom it is served to appear at a given time and place to testify

SUMMARY JUDGMENT a motion by the defendant's attorney to dismiss the case because of the plaintiff's failure to establish a prima facie case

SUMMONS AND COMPLAINT official notification of the nature of the suit and the fact of its commencement, served on the defendant

SURVIVAL STATUTES modify the common-law rule that tort actions do not survive the death of either the tort-feasor or the injured party

TESTAMENTARY CAPACITY   testator's soundness of mind. It is of prime importance to establish this, in case the will is challenged later

TESTATOR   person who makes a will

TORT   a civil wrong arising from a person's failure to use care in his contact with other persons, or his failure to refrain from injuring the person or property of another

TORT–FEASOR   one judged to be a wrongdoer in a civil suit for damages

TRESPASSER   an unwelcome and unauthorized presence on the premises

TRIAL COURT   in any of the three court systems, the first court to try a suit

UBERRIMA FIDES   "utmost faith," owed by professional people to those they serve

WILL   a legal document in which the individual bequeaths his property after death. It assures him that the property will be disposed of in accordance with his wishes. Anyone over eighteen may make a will for personal property such as money or jewelry; anyone over twenty-one may will land

WITNESS   person giving testimony in a court of hearing

WORKMEN'S COMPENSATION LAWS   laws covering remuneration to an employee for injury directly connected to employment

APPENDIX 2

TEN GOLDEN RULES OF NURSING

1. Your performance may readily reflect physical or mental fatigue; therefore, when you know you are insufficiently rested or you are nervous and upset, don't undertake a nursing responsibility disproportionate to the amount of effort, energy, and mindpower you have available.

2. Be honest with yourself and your associates as to your training and experience and don't let a false sense of pride cause you to undertake a procedure or duty you know you are unqualified for.

3. If you are reasonable and feel that your immediate associate or your patient presents an incompatibility problem, discuss it quickly and frankly with your immediate superior and be re-assigned.

4. Be careful not to let a sympathetic nature cause a tongue to utter indiscretions. You should be courteous, understanding, and cheering, but be careful not to stimulate dissatisfaction.

5. You have the right to question. You also have the duty to do so. That means that where you doubt the propriety of a procedure, equipment, or dosage of medication, it behooves you to have that doubt set aside to your satisfaction—with careful notes and written orders for record documentation.

6. Carefully maintain your records, written neatly and permanently, and make sure they go to the proper custodian.

7. Studiously develop your understanding of the interrelationships of your co-professionals at the hospital and join with them, as you join with the nursing service, in scrutiny of the care and treatment of patients and equipment.

8. Think affirmatively and constructively about the protective procedures your hospital or your association proposes. Not all of these are perfect, but they represent the best chance to keep you all free from suit—until a better set of regulations is promulgated. In

the interim, abide by the rules, and help others abide by them also.

9. If you make an error or come across an error, don't conceal it. Take steps to correct it. Most authorities on malpractice agree that the judge and jury are more sympathetic to health care personnel as defendants than others—but that the juror and judge will not countenance evidence of concealment or of disregard for patients' personal rights.

10. Not only need you be sure of yourself and your capabilities, your associates and their capabilities—you must be sure of the basic facts of hospital geography and drug and patient identification.

CODE OF ETHICS FOR THE LICENSED PRACTICAL NURSE

The following Code of Ethics has been adopted by The National Federation of Licensed Practical Nurses as a principle of conduct by which and through which its members, all licensed practical nurses, shall govern their private lives and nursing careers.

This digest of principles is designed to guide the nurse in and out of her profession—as an individual and as a nurse. It shall serve to guide her relationships—to the patient, to the doctor, to the patient's family, to the employer, to fellow nurses and as a member of the community.

1. The licensed practical nurse shall practice her profession with integrity.

2. The licensed practical nurse shall be loyal—to the physician, to the patient, and to her employer.

3. The licensed practical nurse strives to know her limitations and to stay within the bounds of these limitations.

4. The licensed practical nurse is sincere in the performance of her duties and generous in rendering service.

5. The licensed practical nurse considers no duty too menial if it contributes to the welfare and comfort of her patient.

6. The licensed practical nurse accepts only that monetary compensation which is provided for in the contract under which she is employed, and she does not solicit gifts.

7. The licensed practical nurse holds in confidence all information entrusted to her.

8. The licensed practical nurse shall be a good citizen.

9. The licensed practical nurse participates in and shares responsibility of meeting health needs.

10. The licensed practical nurse faithfully carries out the orders of the physician or registered nurse under whom she serves.

11. The licensed practical nurse refrains from entering into conversation with the patient about personal experiences, personal problems, and personal ailments.

12.   The licensed practical nurse abstains from administering self-medication, and in event of personal illness, takes only those medications prescribed by a licensed physician.

13.   The licensed practical nurse respects the dignity of the uniform by never wearing it in a public place.

14.   The licensed practical nurse respects the religious beliefs of all patients.

15.   The licensed practical nurse abides by the Golden Rule in her daily relationship with people in all walks of life.

16.   The licensed practical nurse is a member of The National Federation of Licensed Practical Nurses, Inc., and the state and local membership associations.

17.   The licensed practical nurse may give credit to a commercial product or service, but does not identify herself with advertising, sales or promotion.

SOURCE: *Bedside Nurse*, March 4, 1968.

THE CODE FOR NURSES

The nursing profession works with other health care groups to promote health, alleviate suffering, and attain therapeutic goals based upon human need.

Each nurse has a responsibility to individuals, sick or well, their families and the public. Such responsibility requires ethical practices and adherence to the laws relevant to nursing.

1.   The nurse provides services with respect for the dignity of man, unrestricted by considerations of nationality, race, creed, color, or status.

2.   The nurse safeguards the individual's right to privacy by judiciously protecting information of a confidential nature, sharing only what is relevant to his care.

3.   The nurse maintains individual competence in nursing practice, recognizing and accepting responsibility for individual actions and judgments.

4.   The nurse acts to safeguard the patient when his care and safety are affected by incompetent, unethical, or illegal conduct of any person.

5.   The nurse uses individual competence as a criterion in accepting delegated responsibilities and assigning nursing activities to others.

6.   The nurse participates in research activities when assured that the rights of individual subjects are protected.

7.   The nurse participates in the efforts of the profession to define and upgrade standards of nursing practice and education.

8.   The nurse, acting through the professional organization,

participates in establishing and maintaining conditions of employment conducive to high-quality nursing care.

9. The nurse works with members of health professions and other citizens in promoting efforts to meet health needs of the public.

10. The nurse refuses to give or imply endorsement to advertising, promotion, or sales for commercial products, services, or enterprises.

SOURCE: American Nurses Association.

RECOMMENDATIONS ON MEDICAL–NURSING PROCEDURES *

The Registered Nurses' Association of British Columbia and the British Columbia Hospitals' Association established a Joint Committee in 1962. The terms of reference for the Committee have been defined as follows:

1. To establish closer liaison between the two Associations through cooperative action, and to avoid duplication of effort.

2. To advise the Associations in education and counselling relating to nursing, medical and administrative aspects of hospitals.

3. To study and review nursing staffing patterns in hospitals, giving particular reference to the responsibilities, duties and hours of care spent by nurses in the various duties they perform.

4. To make recommendations to the Registered Nurses' Association of British Columbia and the British Columbia Hospitals' Association judged necessary as a result of the studies carried out by the Joint Committee.

Introduction

Realizing that some medical procedures are being carried out by nurses in hospitals in British Columbia, the RNABC/BCHA Joint Committee herein set out certain recommendations for the guidance of hospital management and the medical and nursing professions.

The recommendations were drawn up by a Task Sub-Committee of the Joint Committee and are intended as guides to indicate procedures that should or should not be performed by the graduate nurse.

Medical-Nursing Procedures

I. PACKING AND DRAINS

On written order of the doctor, it should be acceptable for graduate nurses to remove surface packing, packing inserted to promote drainage, and packing following removal of pilonidal cysts.

* Issued in 1965 by approval of The British Columbia Hospitals' Association and The Registered Nurses' Association of British Columbia.

The following should be performed by a doctor:

1. Removal of packing inserted to prevent or control hemorrhage.
2. Removal of packing which was inserted during plastic surgery.
3. Removal of packing and drains from scrotal or rectal areas.
4. Removal or shortening of drains.
5. Instillation into and irrigation of T-tubes and other tubes into such organs as kidney and gall bladder.

II. SUTURES AND DRESSING

With certain exceptions, on written orders of the doctor, it should be acceptable for graduate nurses to remove skin sutures, to change uncomplicated dressings, to remove colostomy rod, and to cleanse decubitus ulcers.

The following should be performed by a doctor:

1. All suturing in the emergency department.
2. Removal of sutures from inside the mouth, near the eye and following plastic surgery.
3. Removal of stay sutures.
4. Removal of sutures from a tracheotomy incision while the tracheotomy tube is still in position.
5. Changing of burn dressings (should be done in the OR).
6. Cleansing and debridement of burn areas and plastic surgery areas (should be done in the OR).
7. Debridement of any wound including decubitus or other ulcers.

III. INTRAVENOUS THERAPY

No nurse should administer intravenous therapy or blood transfusions unless there is evidence that she has had adequate special training in the procedure. Very few graduate nurses have received this training while students. Before this procedure can be safely entrusted to nursing staff in all hospitals, provision will need to be made for the necessary finance and personnel to set up training programmes at strategic centres in the Province.

It should be recognized also that the nursing staffs of hospitals should be increased to provide time for carrying out this procedure, if it is to be added to the present duties of nursing staffs.

It should be acceptable for nurses who have had adequate special training to administer intravenous therapy if this policy has been approved in writing by the appropriate hospital authority.

Only drugs approved by the Pharmacy Committee of the hospital should be added by a nurse, and then only into the bottle.

Only a doctor should administer ergot-type drugs intravenously. Only a doctor should inject a drug directly into the vein or the tubing.

There should be a signed order for every intravenous.

IV. OBSTETRICS

There should be signed orders for all treatments and medications for each patient.

It should be acceptable for a graduate nurse to perform rectal examinations.

The following should be performed by a doctor:

1. Vaginal examinations.
2. Initiation and administration of pitocin drip.
3. Determination of the feeding for the newborn baby.

V. ORTHOPAEDICS

On written orders of the doctor it should be acceptable for a graduate nurse (or other nursing personnel under the direction of a graduate nurse) to:

1. Remove a cast used for manipulation or following uncomplicated fracture.
2. Remove or replace traction not used in conjunction with a fracture.

The following should be performed by a doctor:

1. Application of a cast.
2. Application of traction for a fracture.
3. Application of a splint other than for first aid.

VI. MISCELLANEOUS PROCEDURES

The following should be performed by a doctor:

1. Serve as scrubbed assistant for major surgery.
2. Administer all anaesthetics. This includes the administration of anaesthetics such as tribromethanol (avertin) or thiopental sodium (sodium pentothal) by rectum before going to the OR.
3. Change a tracheotomy tube in the acute stage.
4. Pass urethral sounds.
5. Break up barium impaction with vulsellum forceps and proctoscope.
6. Carry out haemostasis with bladder tamponade.
7. Use a catheter guide.
8. Use filiform and follower.

9.   Pass a levine tube:
   (a)   for an unconscious patient.
   (b)   for a patient who has just had gastric surgery.
   (c)   for a paediatric patient.
   (d)   initial passing for an immature newborn.
10.   Prescribe feedings for sick babies.
11.   See every patient coming to the Emergency Department.
12.   Write the requisitions for laboratory and x-ray whenever medical information is required.
13.   Decide whether a patient is dead.
14.   Notify relatives of serious condition or death of patient.
15.   Obtain signed consent for abortion or for post mortem.
16.   Give patient or relative sufficient information to ensure that any consent form signed for procedures is an informed consent.

VII. DOCTORS' ORDERS

1.   All patients should have individual orders signed by the doctor. If given over the telephone the order should be signed by the nurse and countersigned by the doctor on his next visit.
2.   Orders for medications:

> there should be signed orders for all medications, including laxatives and sedatives

> only a doctor should compute dosage for any sedation.

JOINT STATEMENT ON NON–NURSING ACTIVITIES CARRIED OUT BY NURSING PERSONNEL IN SOME HOSPITALS *

Foreword

The BCHA/RNABC Committee began its study of the utilization of nursing personnel by investigating the question of medical procedures which are being carried out by nurses in certain hospitals in B.C. The booklet issued jointly by the two Associations, entitled "Recommendations on Medical-Nursing Procedures," was the result. This study was undertaken primarily to ensure the safety of the patient.

Another area of concern is the matter of non-nursing duties performed by nursing staff. In determining the actual number of hours of nursing care per patient day, many hospitals do not exclude the time spent by nursing staff performing duties that are more correctly the function of other departments.

The Committee has completed an investigation of the following areas where nurses assist. It is not our intent to recommend practice

---

* Issued in 1966 by approval of The British Columbia Hospitals' Association and The Registered Nurses' Association of British Columbia.

but to arrive at a common basis to determine actual hours of nursing care:

        A.   Dietary
        B.   Housekeeping
        C.   Pharmacy
        D.   Laboratory
        E.   X-ray
        F.   Social Service

In each case there has been consultation with representatives of the particular area of service and in certain cases the hospitals were surveyed to ascertain the extent of the problem. This booklet represents the official opinion of the two Associations with respect to the six areas studied. It is realized that there remain other problem areas such as clerical, portering, messenger and so on. These areas will be investigated in due course.

In the meantime it is recommended that:

1.   Each hospital give serious consideration to the question of whether nursing personnel are being utilized to the best advantage, and

2.   When nursing personnel must be assigned non-nursing duties, the time so spent be subtracted when computing the actual nursing time being spent on nursing care.

Non-Nursing Duties

A. DIETARY

Directors of Hospital Dietary Departments, selected by the B.C. Dietetic Association, met with the Joint Committee and it was agreed that the following are dietary duties, not nursing duties:

1.   Carrying trays to and from patients.

2.   Checking to see that the patients receive the correct diet. (Nursing should be responsible for preparing the patients to receive the trays, giving patients necessary help in feeding, checking as to whether patients eat their meals.)

3.   Preparing and carrying between-meal routine nourishments to and from patients.

4.   Preparing infant feedings.

5.   Collecting, washing, filling and returning jugs of drinking water.

6.   Preparing and delivering therapeutic diets.

7.   Formal teaching of the patient and/or relative while in hospital and prior to discharge on matters relating to therapeutic diet.

8.   Purchasing of foods and menu planning.

9.   Supervising and training of dietary personnel.

It was agreed further that the BCHA, the RNABC and the B.C. Dietetic Association should urge that:

1. Further efforts be made to obtain full or part-time dietitians for small hospitals.

2. Consultative service be provided for hospital dietary departments, preferably under the auspices of the B.C. Hospitals' Association.

B. HOUSEKEEPING

The heads of the Housekeeping Departments of selected hospitals met with the Joint Committee and it was agreed that the following are housekeeping duties, not nursing duties:

1. Mopping and cleaning floors, washing walls and dusting beds, tables, lamps, chairs, etc., in patient areas, including isolation.

2. Mopping and cleaning floors, washing walls and furnishings, including sterilizers, in the Operating Room, Case Room and Nursery. This includes mopping and cleaning between cases in the Operating Room and Case Room (under the supervision of nursing personnel).

3. Cleaning lavatories, washrooms, refilling soap and paper towel dispensers.

4. Terminal cleaning after discharge of patient: stripping, cleaning and remaking bed, removing and cleaning wash-basin, kidney basin, bed pan, etc.

5. Changing bedside curtains and draperies.

6. Caring for flowers.

7. Cleaning cupboards. (Cleaning inside medicine and other specially designated cupboards was considered a nursing responsibility.)

C. PHARMACY

Representatives of the B.C. Pharmaceutical Association met with the Joint Committee and the following definitions were agreed to:

Drug dispensing involves (1) the issuance of one or more doses of a medication in containers other than the original, such new containers being properly labelled by the dispenser as to contents and/or directions for use as indicated by the prescriber, or (2) the issuance of a medication in its original container with a pharmacy prepared label that carries to the patient the name of the prescriber as well as other vital information or a label prepared for nursing station use in a hospital. The contents of the container may be for one patient (such as an individual prescription) or for several patients (such as nursing station medication container).

Drug administration involves the administration of a single dose to a patient as a result of an order by a physician or dentist. The removal from the pharmacy or drug cupboard to the nursing station of a single dose of a drug from the storage container for immediate use falls under drug administration.

The following points were also agreed to:

1. Purchasing and dispensing drugs are pharmacy functions. In the absence of a pharmacist the administrator is legally responsible for purchasing drugs and the medical staff for dispensing.

2. Diluting intravenous solutions is a pharmacy function.

3. Administering a drug to a patient is a nursing or medical function. (See Joint Committee booklet on "Medical-Nursing Procedures" for statement on drugs which should be administered only by a physician.)

4. Ensuring that the proper mechanics are set up to maintain rigid control of narcotics is an administrative responsibility. By legislation either the pharmacist or a doctor must accept full responsibility for both the requisition for purchase and the distribution of narcotic and controlled drugs.

5. Every hospital should have a Pharmacy and Therapeutic Committee even if it is a one-man committee and even if there is no pharmacist. Evaluating new drugs is a medical responsibility.

6. If the employment of a full-time pharmacist is not justified every effort should be made to obtain the part-time services of a local pharmacist or else to arrange for a regional pharmacist to work part-time in a number of hospitals in an area. A less desirable alternative is to have consultation services from a pharmacist.

7. When in doubt the Hospital Pharmacy Manual published by the B.C. Pharmaceutical Association should be consulted.

D. LABORATORY

Representatives of the Canadian Society of Laboratory Technologists met with the Joint Committee and it was agreed that:

1. The volume of laboratory work is such that almost every hospital could and should fully utilize the services of at least one full-time registered laboratory technologist.

2. Even routine tests should be performed by qualified technologists.

3. Taking specimens of blood and gastric contents is a laboratory function. Preparing and supporting the patient is a nursing function.

4. Morgue attendant duties are a laboratory function and if carried out by an orderly the time should be charged to laboratory service, not nursing service.

E. X-RAY

Representatives of the X-ray Advisory Council met with the Joint Committee. It was agreed that taking and developing x-rays is the function of the x-ray Department. It was pointed out that:

1.   There is no shortage of trained x-ray technicians.

2.   Care by a nurse may be necessary in the case of a seriously ill patient or a baby.

3.   Every person taking x-rays or assisting should wear a "film badge" which will measure the amount of exposure encountered by the operator.

F. SOCIAL SERVICE

Representatives of the B.C. Association of Social Workers met with the Joint Committee. The present shortage of social workers is such that it is unlikely there will be enough to fulfill the requirements of hospitals in the immediate future. A social worker could be employed jointly by three or four hospitals.

Under the present circumstances nurses, and other hospital personnel, are performing a tremendous amount of social work. Examples include tracing the nearest relative when necessary and making suitable arrangements for placement on discharge. This time should not be charged to nursing services.

[   ] STATE NURSES' ASSOCIATION

The Interprofessional Agreement Concerning Administration and Dispensing of Drugs

The [   ] State Nurses' Association and the [   ] Hospital Association in their concern for ensuring safe patient care are acutely aware of the important role of policies and procedures relative to the handling of drugs and medications in hospitals and other health facilities.

A clear understanding of the legal role of the licensed nurse and the licensed pharmacist are basic to the establishing of such policies and procedures.

According to the [   ] State Pharmacy Act: "Licentiate in pharmacy" means a person licensed by the board of pharmacy of this state to *prepare, compound* and *dispense* physician's prescriptions, and to *sell* drugs, medications and poisons at retail."

According to the Nurse Practice Act #5: "The 'practice of professional nursing' means . . . : (c) the administration of medications and treatments as prescribed by a person licensed in this state to prescribe such medications and treatments."

Dispensing is defined as the issuing of one or more doses in a suitable container, such container being properly labeled by the dispenser as to contents and directions for use. Dispensing affects one or more patients.

Administration is defined as the giving of a unit dose of medication to a patient as a result of a physician's order. Administration affects only one patient.

The attached publication "Dispensing of Drugs and Prevention of Medication Errors" was developed by the Nursing Standards Committee of the [   ] State Hospital Association. It has been endorsed by the Board of Directors of the [   ] State Nurses' Association and has been accepted and published by the [   ] Hospital Association as a Standard of Care.

Both associations believe that implementation of the recommendations can reduce medication errors and provide safer care for patients.

Standards of Care

SUBJECT

Dispensing of drugs and prevention of medication errors

PURPOSE

The purpose of this Standard of Care is intended to reduce medication errors and to prevent such errors and provide safer care for the patients.

RECOMMENDATION

The Committee on Nursing Standards suggests the following:

1. All patients must be identified by a wristband which carries at least the patient's name and hospital number.

2. All orders must be written by the Physician. *Verbal orders must not be accepted* and telephone orders are accepted in emergency only and must be counter-signed by the Physician on his first visit.

3. A copy of the Physician's order sheet should be sent to the Pharmacy for the dispensing of drugs ordered.

4. All Physician's orders which are not clear or are illegible must not be carried out until the Physician is contacted for further clarification.

5. Allergies should be clearly identified on the patient's chart as well as on the nursing care plan.

6. All compounding of medications must be done by a Registered Pharmacist.

7. All medications issued through the Pharmacy must be clearly labeled with at least the patient's name, hospital number, name of drug, and dosage accurately defined.

8. Single unit dosages are available and we strongly recommend moving to this method of dispensing:

    a.   Oral medications—single unit dosage to be instituted.

    b.   Other medications, including subcutaneous, intra-muscular and I.V.—multiple-dose vials should be eliminated.

    c.   *Narcotics and barbiturates should be dispensed from narcotic counters.*

9. A medicine room should be at the nursing station, but separate. It should be constructed to provide privacy, should be well ventilated and lighted, and have hand washing facilities in close proximity.

10. Current Physician's Desk Reference should be kept at each individual nursing unit for reference.

11. Only licensed nursing personnel (Registered Nurses and Licensed Practical Nurses) may administer and record the administration of medications. To insure accuracy and patient safety, licensed nursing personnel must prepare and administer their own medications.

12. The nurse must check the medication three times while pouring.

13. Before administering the medication, the nurse must check the name and hospital number on the patient's wristband to insure the proper identification of drug with patient. *Do not rely on patient to acknowledge by name.*

14. Only those medications so ordered by the attending Physician for self administration, may be left at the patient's bedside.

15. To insure that the medication will not be given after it has been discontinued by the attending Physician, a red line is to be drawn completely through it on the Kardex with the word "discontinued" written over it and initialed by the nurse.

IT IS FURTHER RECOMMENDED:

As in all other areas of concern for patient safety, an Incident Report should be filed setting forth in detail *any* and *all* irregular happenings occurring relative to the administration of medications. Employees should be encouraged to report fully, knowing for certain that such revelations will not be used in a punitive manner against them. Incident reports are necessary for the protection of the patient, the employee and the hospital and should be used in a constructive manner to improve system and prevent further errors.

INDEX

Abandonment, 171–173
Abortion, 185–186
Abuse of process, 150
Administration, 249
  drug, 247
Administrative (agency) law, 8–9,
  11
Administrators of wills, 210
Admission against interest, 221–222
Adoption, 186
Advisory council for state board of
  nursing, 21
Affidavits, 222
Agents:
  definition of, 40
  nurses as, 39–64
Agreements:
  in contracts, 164
  of guaranty, 174–179
  and real consideration, 170
  of special performance, 174–179
  of warranty, 174–179
Alberta Registered Nurse Act, 22
Alcohol, 189
Allegations, 222
Alternate causation, 116–118
American Journal of Nursing, 35
American Law Institute, 190
American Medical Association (AMA),
  87, 179

American Nurse's Association (ANA),
  28, 29, 32–34, 36, 68–69, 74, 80,
  186–187
Anderson v. Hooker, 141
Anesthetics, 145
Appeals, 9
Appellant, 14
Appellate courts, 17–18, 222
Appellee, 14
"Approved Medical-Nurse Proce-
  dures" (Canada), 71
Arkansas State Board of Pharmacy v.
  S. W. Patrick, 25–26
Arrest, 194–195
  false, 147, 149
Assault, 180, 182–183
  and battery, 137–147, 215
  consent and, 139–143
  defined, 137–138
  justifiable, 138, 182
  tort laws and, 137–147
Assignable contracts, 163
Assignor, 163
Assistants, nursing, 30
Associations (see Nursing Associa-
  tions)
Attempted crimes, 183
Attractive nuisance, doctrine of
  115
Auxiliary personnel, 33

"Auxiliary Personnel in Nursing Service," 33–34
Availability in a will, 211

Bail, 195
Battery:
  assault and, 137–147, 215
  consent and, 139–143
  defined, 137–138
  tort laws and, 137–147
Bedside Nurse, The, 30, 240
Bilateral contracts, 165
Blackmail, 183
Black's Law Dictionary, 124, 149
Blood, 176
Board of nursing, 21
Borgia v. City of New York, 206
Borrowed-servant theory, 58–59, 61–63
Brandeis, Louis, 154
Breach-of-contract actions, 214–215
Breach of warranty, 174, 176, 225
British Columbia Association of Social Workers, 248
British Columbia Dietetic Association, 245
British Columbia Hospital's Association, 72, 73, 241–248
British Columbia Hospital's Association/Registered Nurses' Association of British Columbia (BCHA/RNABC) Committee, 241–248
British Columbia Pharmaceutical Association, 246
British North America Act, 19
Bureau of Drug Abuse Control, 197
Bureau of Narcotic Control (New York), 200, 202
Buyer, rights and obligations of, 174

California Board of Medical Examiners, 75, 93–94
California Nurses' Association, 74, 75
California Supreme Court, 190–191

Canada:
  delegation in, 67, 71–80
  drug laws in, 78
  English law and, 18
  language problem in, 45–46
  legal development in, 18–19
  nursing in, 22, 35–36
  test results in, 81
Canadian Society of Laboratory Technologists, 247
Captain-of-the-ship theory, 58, 59, 61
Care:
  standards of, 76, 109–115, 249–250
  terminal, 212–213
Case citations, 19, 37–38, 63–64, 100, 133–135, 150, 161, 173, 179, 195–196, 203, 207–208, 213, 225–226
Cause:
  intervening, 115
  proximate, 115–116, 222
  reasonable, 149
Charitable immunity, 61–63, 98–100
Charts, record-keeping, 127–129, 217–218
Circuit Court of Appeals for the District of Columbia, 111
City Court of New York, 16
Civil Code of the Philippines, 155
Civil Code of the Province of Quebec, 104
Civil law, 2–3, 8–11, 17, 189
Civil liability, 162, 214
Civil litigation, 216
Civil rights, 42–44, 156
Civil Rights Act of 1964, 42, 43
Civil suit, 10, 215
Claims, 53–54, 121–123
Code, French Civil, 126
Code of Ethics of the National Federation of Licensed Practical Nurses, 33, 239–240
Code of Hammurabi, 10
Code for Professional Nurses, ANA, 28, 33
Codefendant, 215
Collateral source doctrine, 224

College of Nurse-Midwifery, 89
College of Nurses of Ontario, 36
College of Physicians and Surgeons
    of British Columbia, 72
College of Physicians and Surgeons
    of Ontario, 92
Committee on Nursing, AMA, 29
Committee on Nursing Practice, ANA,
    68–69, 80
Common law, 2–5, 8, 103, 127, 166,
    189, 215
Communication, 157–160
Communism, 157
Comparative negligence, 123–124
Compensation laws, 50–54
Compensatory damages, 124, 168, 225
Competence, 60–62
Complainant, 13–14
Complaint, 216
Concealment, 137
Consent:
    anesthetics and, 145
    assault and battery and, 139–143
    drugs and, 144–145
    emergencies and, 143
    equipment and, 145
    forms for, 141–142
    grafts and, 146
    informed, 140–141
    minors and, 143–144
    transplants and, 146
    unorthodox procedures, 145–146
    withdrawal of, 146–147
Consequential damages, 168
Conservatorship laws, 210
Conspiracy, 180
Constitutional law, 5–7
Consumer goods, 215
Contract:
    abandonment of, 171–173
    acceptance of, 163–164
    agreement in, 164
    assignable, 163
    bilateral, 165
    breach of, 174, 176, 214–215, 225
    consideration of, 164

Contract:
    definition of, 163
    elements of, 163–164
    implied, 170
    intent and, 164
    invalid, 165
    law and, 11
    nonassignable, 163
    offer of, 163–164
    oral, 168–169
    problems of, 168–171
    responsibility and, 162
    termination of, 165, 167–168
    terms used in, 163
    types of, 165
    unilateral, 165
    void *ab initio,* 169
    warranty and, 174, 176, 225
    written, 165–166
Contractors, independent, 39–64
Contributory negligence, 121–123
Conversion, 147, 150
*Cornish v. Sterling Drug Company,
    Inc.,* 179
Courts, 4, 11, 222
    appellate, 17–18
    federal, 14–16
    local, 16–17
    state, 16
    trial, 17–18
Crime:
    abortion, 185–186
    alcohol and, 189
    assault and battery, 182–183
    attempted, 183
    blackmail, 183
    definition of, 102–103, 180–181
    drugs and, 189
    under duress, 189
    extortion, 183
    homicide, 180–182
    illegal adoption, 186
    and irresistible impulse, 189–190
    kidnapping, 186
    larceny, 183–184
    and Medical Practice Act, 187–188

Crime:
  mens rea, 189
  mishandling of valuables, 184
  and Nursing Practice Act, 186–187
  and temporary insanity, 189
  under threat, 189
  tort and, 102–103
Criminal codes, 214
Criminal law, 9–11
  and the nurse, 180–196
Criminal negligence, 181
Criminal offense, 180
Criminal statutes, 214
Croce v. Myers, 139
Cross examination, 222–223

Damages, 106
  compensatory, 124, 168, 225
  consequential, 168
  exemplary, 124–125, 225
  Good Samaritan Law, 126
  mental health and, 125–126
  for negligence, 224–225
  nominal, 124
  payment of, 214
  punitive, 124–125, 225
  special, 124
  tort law and, 124–133
De novo, trial, 17
Death sentence, 10
Deceit, 136–137
Decisional law, 7–8
Defamatory statements, 151
Defamatory torts, 151–161
Defendant, 14
Defense:
  contributory negligence and, 122–
    123
  libel and, 154
  slander and, 154
Delagee, nurse, 68
Delegation, 65–101
  drugs and, 77–79
  external cardiac massage and, 80
  formalizing, 71–80

Delegation:
  immunities, 94–100
  importance of, 69–71
  joint statements and, 73–79
  laboratory tests, 80–89
  litigation, 91–94
  of medical functions, 89–91
  nurse and, 65–101
  nursing team and, 69–71
  and the physician, 67
  problems of, 66–69
Democratic process, 11
Dependent nursing, 27, 73–76, 85
  function, 27–29
  joint statements and, 73–76
Depositions, 222
Depressant drugs, 197–203
Dereliction, 106
Detention, 148, 193–194
Diagnose, 188
Diagnosis, 80, 85, 188
  emergency, 88–89
  litigation and, 91
  by the nurse, 87
Dietary duties, 245–246
Digests, 2
Direct causal effect, 115–116
Direct causation, 106
  (See also Proximate cause)
Discipline, professional, 24–26
Discovery rule, 137
Discrimination, 9, 43
Disease, occupational, 51
Dispensing drugs, 201
"Dispensing of Drugs and Prevention
  of Medication Errors," 249
Dixon, Dr. B., 89
Doctrines, 54–61
Documents:
  invasion of privacy and, 156
  signing of, 157
Domestic Relations Law (New York),
  186
Douglas, William O., 188–189
Drains, 241–242
Dressing, 242

Drug Abuse Control Amendment of 1965, 197, 199
Drug Directorate of Canada, 103
Drugs, 77–79, 189, 215
  administration, 247
  in Canada, 78
  consent and, 144–145
  and crime, 189
  delegation and, 77–79
  depressant, 197–203
  dispensing, 201, 246
  federal law and, 197–198
  handling of, 129–130
  joint statements and, 77–79
  laws on, 77–79, 197–203
  nurse and, 77–79
  prescribing, 201
  state law and, 198–203
  stimulant, 197–203
  violations and, 197–203
Due process, 190
Duress, 189
Durham Rule, 190
Duty, 106
  dietary, 245–246
  housekeeping, 242
  medical, 129
  of the nurse, 129
  paramedical, 129

Eavesdropping, 156
Edelman v. Ziegler, 121
Education, 69
Educational hospitals, 98
Electrical Council of Underwriters' Laboratories, 178
Electrocardiography, 82–83
Eleventh Amendment, 96
Embezzlement, 183
Emergency, 143
  diagnosis, 88–89
Employee:
  assumption of risk by, 44–46
  civil rights of, 42
  definition of, 41–42

Employee:
  employer and, 42
  federal, 59
  nurse as, 39–64
  personal rights of, 44
  responsibilities of, 46–50
  statutory rights of, 44
Employer, 42
English common law, 2–5, 8, 103, 127, 166, 189, 215
Entrapment, 26
Equipment:
  consent and use of, 145
  labeling of, 177–179
  operating, 113–115
  x-ray, 145
Erickson, Andre, 132–133
Errors in laboratory tests, 80–81
Escobedo v. Illinois, 190
Ethnic discrimination, 43
Europe, laws of, 50–54
Evaluations, 76
Evidence, 222
Evolution of law, 1–19
Excusable homicide, 181
Executive Committee of the Registered Nurses' Association, 71
Exemplary damages, 124–125, 225
Expenditures, 225
Experience, 69
Expert status, 218–222
Expert testimony, 116, 220–221
Exposure of person, 154–155
Express warranty, 175
External cardiac massage, 80
Extortion, 183

Facts, 18
  recording of, 76
Failures, nurse liable for, 40
False arrest, 147, 149
False imprisonment, 147–149
Federal Bureau of Narcotics, 197
Federal court system, 14–16
Federal employees, 59

Federal Employees' Compensation Act, 45
Federal Internal Revenue Code, 225
Federal law, 5–7
  drug and, 197–198
Federal Rules of Civil Practice, 16
Federal Rules of Criminal Procedure, 190
Federal Tort Claims Act, 45, 95–96, 159
Federal Trade Commission, 175
Felonies, 181
Felonious homicide, 181
Ferrara v. Galluchio, 125
Fiduciary responsibility, 209–213
Fifth Amendment, 7, 42–43, 188
Fines, 10, 214
First amendment, 154, 156
Fish, Dr., 133
Flannery v. Estate of Mengel, 206
Florida Supreme Court, 179
Food, 215
Food and Drug Administration (U.S.), 197
Foreseeability, concept of, 107
Formalizing delegation, 71–80
  Canadian practice, 71–73
  drugs, 77–79
  external cardiac massage, 80
  joint statements, 73–79
  nursing and, 71–80
  tests and, 80
  U.S. practice, 67, 71–80
Foster, Professor Henry H., Jr., 127
Fourteenth Amendment, 43
Fourth Amendment, 191–192
Fowler, Campbell, 132
Fowler v. Norways Sanitarium, 187
Fraud, 136–137, 225
  statute of, 166
Fraudulent concealment, 137
French Civil Code, 126
Function, 88–89
  delegation of, 89–91
  dependent, 27, 73–76, 85
  independent, 27–29, 76–80

Function:
  joint statements and, 73–80
  medical, 89–91
  of the nurse, 27–29, 88–89
  of nursing, 27–29, 73–80, 85

General licensure, 20–21
Good Samaritan Laws, 126–127
Government hospitals, 98
Government immunity, 94–95
Grafts, 146
Grand larceny, 183
Great Britain, law of, 2, 18
Gross negligence, 105
Guaranty, agreements of, 174–179
Guidelines, 36–37

Harlem Hospital, New York, 90
Harrison Narcotic Act, 197
Harvey, Cyril, 133
Health sciences, 10–11
Henry, Mrs. Nancy, 25
Hill-Burton laws, 42
Hippocrates, 10
Homicide, 180–182
Honingmann, Paul, 132
Hospital Association of New York State, 75
Hospital Code and Regulations of the Board of Directors of Hospitals of the City of New York, 23
Hospitals, types of, 98
Hostile witness, 216
Housekeeping duties, 246

Illegal abortion, 185
Illegal adoption, 186
Illegal detention, 148
Immunity:
  charitable, 61–63, 98–100
  Federal Tort Claims Act, 95–96
  government, 94–95
  municipalities, 96–98

Immunity:
  nursing, 94–100
  respondeat superior, 98–100
  whole-citizen, 193
Implied contracts, 170
Implied negligence, 118
Implied warranty, 175, 215
Imprisonment, 10
  false, 147–149
Impulse, acting under, 189–190
In pari delicto, 168
Independent contractor:
  definition of, 40–41
  nurse as, 39–64
  status of, 50–51
Independent nursing:
  function, 27–29
  and joint statements, 76–80
Informed consent, 140–141
Insanity:
  law and, 204
  temporary, 189
Instruction for the jury, 223–224
Intentional torts, 136–150, 225
Internal Revenue Code, 197
Interpretation, 76
Interprofessional Agreement Concerning Administration and Dispensing of Drugs, 248–250
Intervening cause, 115
Intestate, 213
Intravenous therapy, 242–243
Invasion of privacy:
  documents and, 157
  eavesdropping, 156
  exposure of person, 154–155
  posthumous, 155–156
  publicity, 156–157
Invitees, 47
Irresistible impulse, acting under, 189–190

John of England, King, 5
John Hopkins University, 89

"Joint Recommendations on Medical-Nursing Procedures" (Canada), 72
Joint statements:
  delegation and, 73–79
  dependent functions, 73–76
  drugs, 77–79
  external cardiac massage, 80
  independent functions, 76–80
  medical practice and, 77–80
  nursing and, 73–80
  purposes of, 76
  tests, 80
Joint tort-feasors, 61, 108–109
Judge, 11, 17, 18
Judgment, 17, 61, 222
Jurisdiction, 13–18
  of appellate courts, 17–18
  of federal courts, 14–16
  of judge, 18
  of jury, 18
  of local courts, 16–17
  of state courts, 16
  of trial courts, 17–18
Jury, 11, 17, 18, 222–224
Justifiable assault, 138, 182
Justifiable homicide, 181
Justinian, Emperor, 2

Kerr-Mills law, 42
Kidnapping, 186

Labeling:
  of equipment, 177–179
  manufacturer's, 178
  of medical products, 177–179
Laboratory, 247–248
  tests in, 80–89
Language problem, 45–46
Larceny, 180, 183–184
Law:
  administrative, 8–9, 11
  agency, 8–9
  civil, 2–3, 8–11, 17, 189

Law:
  civil rights, 156
  common, 2–5, 8, 103, 127, 166,
    189, 215
  conservatorship, 210
  constitutional, 5–7
  contract, 11
  criminal, 9–11, 180–196
  decisional, 7–8
  drugs and, 77–79, 197–198
  English common, 2–5, 8, 103,
    127, 166, 189, 215
  evolution of, 1–19
  at federal level, 5–7, 197–198
  Good Samaritan, 126
  and the health sciences, 10–
    11
  Hill-Burton, 42
  insanity and, 204
  Kerr-Mills, 42
  liability, 214
  New York State Education, 43
  and nursing, 11
  political development and, 5
  private, 7, 214
  public, 7
  Roman, 2–3, 8–11
  at state level, 6–7, 198–203
  statutes of limitations and, 204–
    207
  statutory, 7
  tort, 104–124
  workmen's compensation, 50–54
Lawmen, Medicine Men and Good
  Samaritans (Foster), 127
Lawsuit, 13
Lawyer, role of, 11–13
Lay people, 69–70
Legal status, nurse and, 20–38
Liability, 225
  civil, 162, 214
  law and, 214
  physician and, 177
  third-party, 51–52
  warranty, 177
Libel, 151–161, 225

Licensed practical nurses (LPN), 30–
  33
Licensee, 46–47
Licensure:
  general, 20–21
  of nurse, 30–33, 69
  and nursing, 21–24
Limitations, statute of, 14, 206–207
Litigant, 13
Litigation, 91–94
  civil, 216
  delegation and, 91–94
  diagnosis and, 91
  and medical acts, 91
  and the nurse, 91–94
  and nursing, 91–94
Local court system, 16–17
Local regulations, 22–23

M'Naghten Rule, 189–190
McPherson v. Buick, 114, 175
Magistrate, 17
Magna Carta (1215), 5
Malicious prosecution, 147, 149–150
Malpractice, 104–124
  negligence and, 104–105
  and statutes of limitation, 205–206
  tort law and, 104–105
Manslaughter, 180, 182
Manufacturer's labeling, 178
Master-of-the-ship theory, 58, 59, 61–
  63
Material misrepresentations, 136
Mechanotherapist, 84
Medical acts, litigation and, 91
Medical diagnosis, emergency, 88–89
Medical Disciplinary Committee,
  132–133
Medical duties, 129
Medical examiner, 83
Medical functions, delegation of, 89–
  91
Medical practice:
  defined, 83–89
  joint statements and, 77–80

Medical practice:
  and the nurse, 83–84
  qualifications for, 84
  standards of, 112–113
Medical Practice Act, 187–188
Medical products, labeling of, 177–179
Medical record, 127–129, 217–218
Medical schools, 83
Medical Society of Nova Scotia, 71
Medical supervision, 85
Medical testimony, 214–226
Medicare, 42
Mens rea, 103, 189
Mental health, damages and, 124–126
Midwifery, 89
Minnesota Supreme Court, 117
Minors, legal position of, 143–144
Miranda v. Arizona, 190
Miscellaneous procedures, 243–244
Misdemeanors, 84, 181
Misrepresentation, 136
  negligence and, 137
Municipalities, immunity of, 96–98

Napoleonic code, 8
Narcotics (see Drugs)
National Communicable Disease
  Center, 80
National Federation of Licensed Practical Nurses, 30, 32, 33, 36, 239
National League for Nursing, 35, 36
Needs, interpretation of, 76
Negligence:
  action in, 106–107
  comparative, 123–124
  contributory, 121–123
  criminal, 181
  damages for, 224–225
  gross, 105
  implied, 118
  malpractice and, 104–105
  misrepresentation, 137
  per se, 109–116

Negligence:
  and statutes of limitations, 205–206
  tort laws and, 104–124
New York City Department of Hospitals, 109
New York City Hospital Code, 109
New York v. Goldwater, 158
New York State Board of Medical Examiners, 83, 86
New York State Board of Regents, 43
New York State Court of Appeals, 98–99, 109
New York State Department of
  Health, 200
New York State Education Department, 83
New York State Education Law, 43
New York State Fair Employment
  Practice Laws, 43
New York State Medical Society, 75
New York State Nursing Association,
  75
New York State Supreme Court, 109,
  125, 145
New York Wrongful Death Act, 16
Nominal damages, 124
Nonassignable contracts, 163
Non-nursing activities, 244–248
Nova Scotia Hospital Association,
  71
Nuisance, attractive, doctrine of, 115
Nurse:
  as agent, 39–64
  charts, 127–129, 217–218
  code of ethics for, 33, 239–241
  competence of, 60–62
  complaint, 216
  criminal law and, 180–196
  as delagee, 68
  delegation and, 65–101
  diagnosis and, 87–89
  and drugs, 77–79
  education of, 69
  emergency and, 88–89
  as employee, 39–64
  experience, 69

Nurse:
    fiduciary responsibility of, 209–213
    functions of, 88–89
    as independent contractor, 39–64
    laboratory tests and, 81–82
    lay people and, 69–70
    legal status of, 20–38
    licensure, 30–33, 69
    litigation, 91–94
    medical duties, 129
    medical practice and, 83–84
    medical records and, 127–129, 217–
        218
    paramedical duties, 129
    practical, 30–33
    professional, 20–38
    protection for, 91–92
    public status of, 20–38
    responsibilities of, 81–82, 130–133,
        162, 209–213
    role of, 20
    status of, 20–38
    summons and, 216
    the trial and, 214–226
    vocational, 30
    wills and, 209–213
    as witness, 216–221
    (See also Nursing)
Nurses Act 1961–1962, 36
Nursing:
    activities, non-, 244–248
    in Canada, 22, 35–36
    code of ethics, 33
    dependent, 27, 73–76, 85
    diagnosis in, 80, 85, 188
    doctrines of, 54–61
    evaluation in, 76
    function, 27–29, 73–80, 85
    immunities, 94–100
    independent, 27–29
    interpretation in, 76
    joint statements, 73–80
    laboratory tests, 80–83
    law and, 11
    other professions and, 130
    practical, 11, 20, 31–32

Nursing:
    procedures, 76, 241–244
    professional, 11, 20, 29
    regulations, 22–23
    state boards of, 21
    supervision and, 76
    team, 69–71
    techniques, 76
    ten golden rules of, 238–239
    (See also Nurse)
Nursing associations, 34–37
    guidelines for, 36–37
    objective, 35–37
    professionalism, 34–35
    standards of care, 76
Nursing Outlook, 35
Nursing practice:
    assistants, 30
    definition of, 68–69, 85–87
    delegation and, 65–101
    formalizing in, 71–80
    licensure, 21–24
    private-duty, 35
    public health, 35
    qualifications for, 86
Nursing Practice Act, 85, 86, 186–187
Nursing practice acts, 21, 22, 83–91
Nursing Research, 35
Nursing School of the University of
        Colorado, 90
Nursing team, 69–71

Objectives, 35–36
Obligee, definition of, 163
Obligor, definition of, 163
Observation, 76
Obstetrics, 243
Occupational disease, 51
Ohio Court of Appeals, 220
Ontario Hospital Association, 92
Operating equipment, 113–115
Opinion, 220–221
Oral contracts, 168–169
Orders, 88, 201, 244
Ordinary skill, 107

Organ transplants, 146
Orthopaedics, 243

Packing, 241–242
Paine, William Albert, 132–133
Paramedical duties, 129
Patients:
  responsibilities of, 46–50
  terminal care, 212–213
Patrick, S. W., 25–26
Payment of damages, 214
Penal Law of the State of New York,
    181, 185
Penalties, 84
Pennsylvania Occupational Disease
    Act, 51
Pennsylvania Supreme Court, 98
People v. Kane, 125
Person, exposure of, 154–155
Personal rights, 44
Personnel:
  auxiliary, 33
  selecting qualified, 70–71
Petty larceny, 183
Pharmacy, 246–247
Physical therapy, 84
Physician, 72, 84
  delegation and, 67
  laboratory tests, 81–82
  responsibility of, 67, 81–82
  warranty liability of, 177
  as witnesses, 218–222
Physiotherapy, 84
Plaintiff, 13
Police power, 21, 23–24, 35
Political development, evolution of
    law and, 5
Possibilities, 117
Posthumous invasion of privacy, 155–
    156
Practical nurse:
  code of ethics for, 239–240
  status, 30–33
Practical nursing, 11, 20
  statutory limits on, 31–32

Practice (*see* Medical practice)
  drugs, 201
Prescribing, 85
Pretrial proceedings, 194–195
Principal relationship to agent of, 40
Prison term, 215
Privacy, invasion of, 154–157
Private-duty nursing practice, 35
Private law, 7, 214
Privileged communication, 157–160
Privity, defined, 215
Probabilities, 117
Probate, 209–210
Procedures, 76, 243–244
Process, 150
Professional discipline, 24–26
Professional nursing, 11, 20
  statutory limits on, 29
Professional status, 20–38
Professionalism, growth of, 34–35
Promisee, 163
Protection, 91–92
Provide whenever necessary (PRN)
    orders, 201
Provincial Liaison Committee on
    Nursing, 71
Proximate cause, 115–116, 222
Public health nursing, 35
Public law, 7
Public need, 157–160
Public offense, 180
Public status, nurse and, 20–38
Publicity, 156–157
Pulse, 133
Punishment, 10, 11, 84
Punitive damages, 124–125, 225

Qualifications, 86
Qualified personnel, 70–71
Qualified privilege, 152–154
Quantum meruit, 168, 212
Quasicrimes, 180–181

Racial discrimination, 9, 43

Rape, 215
Raymond Rich Associates, 35
Real consideration, 170
Reasonable cause, 149
"Recommendations on Medical-Nursing Procedures," 244
Records, 76, 127–129, 217–218
Red Cross, 24
Registered nurse (RN), 27
Registered Nurses' Association of British Columbia, 72, 73, 241–248
Registered Nurses' Association of Nova Scotia, 71
Registered Nurses' Association of Ontario, 35–36, 92
Regulations, 22–23
Religious discrimination, 43
Religious hospitals, 98
Res ipsa loquitur, 118–121
Res judicata, 5
Respondeat superior, 54–58, 61–63, 98–100, 104, 127
Respondent, 14
Responsibility, 103–104
  contractual, 162
  of employee, 46–50
  fiduciary, 209–213
  of the Good Samaritan, 126–127
  in laboratory tests, 81–82
  limitations on, 58–59
  of nurse, 81–82, 130–133, 162, 209–213
  of patients, 46–50
  for tort, 103–104
Rich Report, 35
Rights, personal, 44
Risk, 44–46
Roman law, 2–3, 8–11, 189
Royal Alexandra Hospital (Edmonton, Alberta), 133
Rules of nursing, 238–239
Runnerstrom, Dr. Lillian, 89
Sacred Heart Hospital (McLennan, Alberta), 132–133

Safety, 44–46
Sanitary Code of the City of New York, 23
Saskatchewan Registered Nurses' Association Act, 30
Schempp v. City of New York, 113
Schloendorff Rule, 98
Schulz v. Feigal, 117
Schwartz v. Thiele, 160
Search, 193–194
Seizure, 192
Seller, rights and obligations of, 174
Sencer, Dr. D. J., 80–81
Sex discrimination, 43
Sixth Amendment, 191, 192
Skill, ordinary, 107
Skin grafts, 146
Slander, 151–161
Smith v. Hampton Training School for Nurses, 43
Social Security, 46
Social service, 248
South America, law of, 2
Special damages, 124
Special performance, 174–179
Standards of care:
  nursing associations and, 76
  purposes of, 110–111
  sources of, 109
Standards of medical practice, 112–113
Standing orders, 88
Stare decisis, 4, 8
State boards of nursing, 21
State court system, 16
State law, 6–7
  drugs and, 198–203
State Nurses' Association, 248–250
State Pharmacy Act, 248
"Statement of Functions of the Licensed Practical Nurse," 32
Statements (see Joint statements)
Status:
  expert, 218–222

Status:
  of independent contractor, 50–51
  legal, 20–38
  of practical nurse, 30–33
  of professional nurse, 20–38
  public, 20–38
Statutes:
  criminal, 214
  of frauds, 166
  of limitations, 14, 206–207
  of survival, 103
Statutory law, 7
Statutory limitations:
  on practical nursing, 31–32
  on professional nursing, 29
Statutory rights, 44
Stimulant drugs, 197–203
Subagent, 55–56
Subpoena, 216
Suit, 16, 225
Summary judgment, 22
Summons, 216
Supervision, 76
  medical, 85
Supreme Court of New Hampshire, 156
Supreme Court of West Virginia, 105
Survival statutes, 103
Sutures, 242

Team, nursing, 69–71
Technicians, 81–82, 222
Techniques, 76
Temporary insanity, 189
Terminal-care patients, 212–213
Testamentary capacity, 211
Testator, 209, 211, 212
Testimony, 220–221
  expert, 116
Tests (see Laboratory tests)
Texas Court of Civil Appeals, 99
Therapy:
  intravenous, 242–243
  physical, 84
Third-party liability, 51–52

Threat, 189
Tort, 95–96, 214, 225
  assault and battery, 137–147
  crime and, 102–103
  defamatory, 151–161
  defined, 102
  -feasors, 61, 108–109
  intentional, 136–150, 225
  law and, 102–161, 215
  respondeat superior and, 104
  responsibility for, 103–104
  types of, 103
  unintentional, 102–135
Transplants, 146
Trespasser, 46
Trial:
  admission against interest, 221–222
  civil law, 17
  complaint, 216
  court, 17–18
  expenditures, 225
  jury and, 17, 223–224
  medical records and, 217–218
  medical testimony and, 214–226
  nurse and, 214–226
  physician and, 218–221
  summary judgment, 222–223
  summons, 216
  witness, 216–221

Uberrima fides, 48
Uniform Commercial Code, 175
Uniform Narcotic Drug Act, 198
Unilateral contracts, 165
Unintentional tort, 102–135
United States:
  civil law in, 9–10
  court system of, 4
  delegation in, 67, 71–80
  drug laws in, 78
  English law and, 18
  language problem in, 45–46
  law of, 2, 9–18, 50–54
  legal growth of, 15
  test results in, 81

United States:
   workmen's compensation laws, 50–54
United States Bill of Rights, 99, 102
U.S. Bureau of Narcotics and Dangerous Drugs, 197
United States Congress, 6, 7
United States Constitution, 5–8, 14, 19
   Eleventh Amendment, 96
   Fifth Amendment, 7, 42–43, 188
   First Amendment, 154, 156
   Fourteenth Amendment, 43, 191–192
   Fourth Amendment, 191–192
   police power and, 21, 35
   Sixth Amendment, 191–192
U.S. Department of Health, Education, and Welfare, 43, 197
U.S. Department of Justice, 197
U.S. Food, Drug, and Cosmetic Act, 103
United States House of Representatives, 6
U.S. Information and Educational Exchange Act, 94
United States Senate, 6, 80
United States Supreme Court, 6, 14, 16, 154, 190–192
U.S. Treasury Department, 197
University of Colorado, 90
Unorthodox procedures, 145–146
Unreasonable search, 192
Unreasonable seizure, 192

Valuables, mishandling of, 184
Vendee, 163
Vendor, 163
Veterans Administration Career Residency Training Contract, 170
Vietnam War, 211
Violations:
   drug, 180, 197–203
   of the Medical Practice Act, 187–188
   of the Nursing Practice Act, 186

Visitors, responsibilities of, 46–50
Vocational nurse, 30
Void *ab initio,* 169
Voidance, 169

Warner v. State of New York, 148–149
Warrant, search, 194
Warranty:
   agreements of, 174–179
   breach of, 174, 176, 225
   express, 175
   implied, 175, 215
   liability, 177
Whole-citizen immunity, 193
Willig, Sidney, 65–69, 83–84
Wills:
   administration of, 210
   availability in, 211
   form, 211–212
   importance of, 209–210
   nurse and, 209–213
   oral, 211
   responsibility in, 210–211
   terminal-care patients and, 212–213
   written, 211
Withdrawal of consent, 146–147
Witness, 215
   hostile, 216
   nurse as, 216–221
   physician as, 218–222
   reimbursing, 221
Workmen's compensation, 46
   laws, 50–54
Written contracts, 165–166
Wrongful death action, 121

X-ray, 248
   equipment, 145
X-ray Advisory Council, 248

Zophy v. New York, 93